RETOOLING THE HUMANITIES

Retooling the Humanities

**THE CULTURE OF RESEARCH
IN CANADIAN UNIVERSITIES**

Edited by
Daniel Coleman & Smaro Kamboureli

THE UNIVERSITY OF ALBERTA PRESS

Published by
The University of Alberta Press
Ring House 2
Edmonton, Alberta, Canada T6G 2E1

LIBRARY AND ARCHIVES CANADA CATALOGUING IN PUBLICATION

Retooling the humanities : the culture of research in
Canadian universities / edited by Daniel Coleman and
Smaro Kamboureli.

Includes bibliographical references and index.
ISBN 978-0-88864-541-8

1. Humanities—Research—Canada. 2. Humanities—Economic
aspects—Canada. 3. Universities and colleges—Economic aspects—
Canada. 4. Academic-industrial collaboration—Canada.
5. Entrepreneurship—Canada. 6. Corporate culture—Canada.
I. Coleman, Daniel, 1961- II. Kamboureli, Smaro
LC1085.4.C3R48 2010   378.1'030971   C2010-907798-9

All rights reserved.
First edition, first printing, 2011.
Printed and bound in Canada by Friesens, Altona, Manitoba.
Copyediting and Proofreading by Brendan Wild.
Indexing by Adrian Mather.

The University of Alberta Press is committed to protecting our natural environment. As part of our
efforts, this book is printed on Enviro Paper: it contains 100% post-consumer recycled fibres and is
acid- and chlorine-free.

The University of Alberta Press gratefully acknowledges the support received for its publishing program from The Canada Council for the Arts. The University of Alberta Press also gratefully
acknowledges the financial support of the Government of Canada through the Book Publishing
Industry Development Program (BPIDP) and from the Alberta Foundation for the Arts for its
publishing activities.

Canada

trañsCanâða
—INSTITUTE—

CONTENTS

ABBREVIATIONS

AUCC	Association of Universities and Colleges of Canada
BNA	*British North America Act*
CAUT	Canadian Association of University Teachers
C-CHEF	Canadian Corporate Higher Education Forum
CFHSS	Canadian Federation for the Humanities and Social Sciences
CFI	Canada Foundation for Innovation
CIHR	Canadian Institutes of Health Research
CRC	Canada Research Chair
CURA	Community-University Research Alliances
INE	Initiative on the New Economy
LCC	Law Commission of Canada
MCRI	Major Collaborative Research Initiatives
NGO	Non-governmental organization
NSERC	Natural Sciences and Engineering Research Council of Canada
RTS	Research Time Stipend
SRG	Standard Research Grant
SSHRC	Social Sciences and Humanities Research Council of Canada
UNESCO	United Nations Educational, Scientific and Cultural Organization

ACKNOWLEDGEMENTS

THIS PROJECT OWES EVERYTHING to the colleagues and students with whom we have been working and dialoguing across the intricately woven community of academic life in Canada. If there is a single thing that marks academia, at least in our experience, it is the virtually seamless, albeit arduous, way in which our profession not only becomes an integral part of our lives but, more often than not, also seals who we become as subjects. To use the verb that frames Bruce Robbins's discussion in his book *Intellectuals: Aesthetics, Politics, Academics*, we are "grounded" in (and through) the complex realities of the institutions with which we work. As Robbins argues, "the grounding of intellectuals is no longer in question. It provides the new common basis for debate and analysis" (xi). And so we are indebted to a large number of colleagues and students—too numerous to list here—for the discussions that have shaped the directions this project has taken, but especially to the contributors to this volume. Their deep care for the profession has been instrumental in "grounding" this project in ways that reflect the concerns about our profession not only among Canadianists, our immediate scholarly group, but also among the academic community at large. We are also indebted to the generous support we have received from the institutions with which we are affiliated. It is precisely because we acknowledge their importance and are concerned about their future that we have produced this volume.

A direct outcome of the TransCanada project and the three conferences that have animated it (Vancouver 2005, Guelph 2007, and Sackville 2009), *Retooling the Humanities* would not have been conceived and materialized without the three conference grants the project received from SSHRC; they helped create the fora for formal and informal discussions about the issues with which this collection of essays engages. Smaro's CRC Tier I in Critical Studies of Canadian Literature and Daniel's CRC Tier 2 in Critical Ethnicity and Race Studies have provided both time and resources without which this project would not have been possible. Our respective institutions have been similarly generous, especially with regard to the panel discussion and public forum that took place at the University of Guelph in October 2006, as well as the workshop that followed on the same weekend and where most of these essays were first presented and workshopped. At the University of Guelph, Alan Wildeman, the Vice-President (Research) at the time, helped co-finance the panel discussion and workshop and participated in the forum; the Office of the Dean, College of Arts, offered support through Jacqueline Murray, the outgoing Dean, and Donald Bruce, the Dean that took office that fall; David Murray, Acting Director at the School of English and Theatre Studies at the time, offered financial support and valuable organizational advice, while the Dean of the Ontario Agricultural College made available its comfortable and elegant boardroom to the workshop participants gratis. At McMaster University, Allison Sekuler, then Associate Vice-President, Research, co-financed the above-mentioned panel discussion and participated in the forum; Mary O'Connor, Chair of the Department of English and Cultural Studies, and Antoinette Somo, Administrative Officer in the same department, enthusiastically supported our work on this project and ironed out wrinkles in transferring funds between universities.

We also wish to thank Wendy Robbins who participated in the public forum, as well as Patricia Clements and Cheryl Suzack who participated in the workshop discussions. Their contributions were invaluable in shaping our arguments. We must give particular thanks to Ben Authers and Rob Zacharias, doctoral students at the School of English and Theatre Studies at the University of Guelph, who helped with various organizational matters and attended the workshop, as well as Smaro's research assistants, Paul Danyluk, also a contributor to this volume, who was instrumental in organizing the public forum and the workshop, and Rob Zacharias and Derek Murray, who worked diligently and with great dedication on the preparation of the manuscript at different stages. Elizabeth Jackson, who completed her doctorate at McMaster during the course of this project, helped collate the final manuscript and assisted with various editorial matters before it was submitted to the press.

We also wish to acknowledge the careful commentary we received from the publisher's two anonymous readers. In addition, Les Monkman and Will Coleman, who agreed to read our preface and introduction, raised many questions that helped us refine our argument. Needless to say, we claim full responsibility for any errors in fact or judgement.

We are very grateful to the publishing and editorial team at the University of Alberta Press, who greeted the proposal for this project with enthusiasm. Michael Luski, who has since moved on to other work, gave the proposal its initial welcome in his role as acquisitions editor, and we are grateful to Peter Midgley who stepped into that role. We appreciated his support for the project and his editorial advice.

PREFACE

THE WESTERN UNIVERSITY HAS LONG been a player integral to the cultural, social, and economic well-being of society. Whether universities in the West were founded in order to advance the development of a particular nation-state, or to benefit the needs and aspirations of individuals, or to implement some form of social engineering, or to enable the pursuit of disinterested inquiry—or for all of the above reasons—their institutional role has been defined by the perceived social contract that binds them to the state *and* the community at large. Because how this social contract is professed depends on the conditions and socio-economic politics at any particular time and space, the ways in which the university services the community have been under constant negotiation and revision throughout its history. For those who do not work at a university, the post-secondary academic institution may not look that different from the way it did in the first part of the twentieth century, but its goals, systems of governance, organizational structures, sponsors of research, demographics of faculty and students, and priorities for learning and discovery have been subjected to major changes. This process of negotiation and change has intensified at the beginning of the twenty-first century, and its impact has been felt most acutely by the humanities, the particular area of post-secondary education with which this book engages. Far from suggesting that these recent changes signal a departure from the university's history in general and that of the humanities in particular, we see them as belonging to the continuum of transformations and pressures that Frank Donoghue, in *The Last Professors: The Corporate University and the Fate of the Humanities*, says extend back through more than a century of America's industrialization.[1] Taken together, the essays collected in this book assess the current situation of university culture in Canada, particularly in relation to the humanities and the emergence in the past thirty years of what we call the culture of research. They do so from the vantage point of literary scholars who have a vested interest in the study of Canadian literature and culture in general, and thus focus, by design and by necessity, on the implications of carrying out their humanistic work within this research climate. We have deliberately designed our collection to reflect the diverse perspectives of a group of scholars working within the terrain of Canadian literary and cultural studies because this is an area most familiar, and therefore of utmost concern, to us. In addition, most existing studies of the place of the arts in the contemporary university focus on the United States, while studies that engage with the Canadian university tend to do so primarily from the perspective of the social sciences.[2]

The *culture of research*, as we employ the term here, refers to the intensification within Canadian universities of the pressure to attract external research funding from governments and corporations to balance their budgets, but also to produce knowledge that is directly applicable to the needs and priorities of the community at large as identified (chiefly) by the private and government sectors. This pressure has compelled universities to adopt an entrepreneurial approach to the production of knowledge, most evident in the rhetoric of commercialization and the ethos of managerialism. By *managerialism*, we refer to the instrumentalist approach to research that considers knowledge a commodity that can be processed, audited for efficiencies, and moved out to its consumers. The managerial ethos at Canadian universities can be witnessed in the rise over the past three decades in offices of research services usually staffed by a team of managers, accountants, and public relations officers rather than scholars, whose mandate is to co-ordinate and prioritize university research, to cultivate external donors and markets, to manage research funding, and to maintain close interaction between the university and the three federal research granting councils (CIHR, NSERC, and SSHRC). Far from being a neutral change that simply exchanges one set of revenues or one form of rhetoric for another, the intensification of the culture of research not only signals a recasting of the social contract, it also involves a "radical reconceptualization" of higher education (Gilman, *Fortunes* x). This reconceptualization, though often naturalized in the current culture of research as inevitable, can be traced and brought to light in the rhetoric of late-capitalist logic that marks most research policy documents—be they generated inside or outside the university. The contributors to this volume, interdisciplinary literary scholars who study Canadian culture in relation to the nation-state, the politics of representation, and the language employed to articulate cultural practices, are particularly attuned to the fact that the economic discourse that predominates in this culture of research does not reflect a disinterested approach to university affairs; rather, they hear this discourse as one that defines in advance what can be said, who can say it and have their statements carry weight, who it is addressed to, and who is expected to benefit from it.

Thus university culture in Canada has been changing ideologically because the role the governments have assigned to universities has shifted over the past thirty years to one designed to fulfill a specific part of the nation-state's social contract with the public[3]—that of economic vitalization and viability in these global times—and it has been changing structurally because the universities' avenues of funding have altered radically over the same period. In their study of the entrepreneurial university, Sheila Slaughter and Larry L. Leslie argue that universities in Australia, the United States, and the United Kingdom "developed [between 1970 and 1995] national higher education and R&D [Research and Development] policies that promoted academic capitalism. The exception was Canada....Canadian higher education did not undergo the same degree of change as the other countries" (214).[4] If only this were true. The shifts that have occurred within universities, largely in response to how their function is perceived by government, business corporations, and funding agencies, testify to the way Canadian universities are not exceptions from this international trend. The changes we are concerned with here, and which are the impetus behind this volume of essays, may have occurred at a different pace and, in some instances, for different reasons than in other countries, but their impact has been similarly far reaching.

In essence, the contributors to this volume share a concern over the ways in which the intensification of the culture of research is homogenizing universities' priorities and procedures. The emphasis on research as fund-generating and on the immediate perceptibility of its social relevance runs the risk of flattening out or restricting the kinds of scholarly activities that universities recognize, promote, and reward.[5] This emphasis urges universities to give most of their time and attention to pure research, or what Ernest Boyer calls discovery, and applied forms of scholarship, and is thus a model that affords less energy or fewer resources to other kinds of scholarly contribution. Teaching and learning, for example, are increasingly seen as tangential spinoffs from discovery or applied research, which many universities now purvey as their signal contribution to society. Of course, Canadian parents still want their children to receive a university degree, since they believe that such a degree guarantees its recipient a respectable income, but given their quiescence about higher tuition fees and larger class sizes across the country, they seem less concerned about the content or quality of this degree than they are that their children simply get one.[6] In this climate, Canadian universities operate less and less as institutions of higher learning and more and more as complex research conglomerates, still largely organized around the traditional disciplines, although they are now often administered not by experts in these disciplines' curricula but by non-academic managers of research funds and portfolios, who bring to post-secondary education expertise from the corporate and government sectors. As Slaughter and Leslie have observed, universities now function under the dictates of "academic capitalism," starved of public funding and therefore more and more beholden to the market economy to secure external funds (46). In Canada, the focus of post-secondary institutions' search for external funds has fallen squarely on research, narrowing that focus from a broader academic capitalism to what we are calling *research capitalism*.

The development of the culture of research capitalism is having significant impact on the structure of internal and external university relations. In a recent *Higher Education* article assessing Canadian universities' increasing reliance on external research grants, Claire Polster indicates some of the structural changes that result from this emphasis on external research sources:

> The new importance of research grants is also helping to spur universities' investment in research centres and institutes, which are generally less expensive to support than departments and faculties and also more successful in generating and managing research grants. This reallocation of university resources based on grant generating ability has the potential to restructure the university's core and its periphery as well as the relations between them, and to significantly reorganize relations between administrators and academic workers. ("Nature" 605)

As university administrators see the importance of educating their faculty about the programs of research granting councils so they can attract more grants, she writes, "administrations are arguably acting more as agents of the granting councils with respect to faculty than as agents of their faculty who represent the latter's interests to external parties" (607).

Some disciplines within the university system can adapt readily to the culture of research capitalism, especially those primarily focussed on what we might call discovery-for-application. But others, especially those such as the humanities, where the outcomes of discovery are not perceived to have immediate practical results or where work often takes the form of critical reflection, do not. The reasons for this adaptability are not simply matters of inclination or progressiveness: in fields where discovery-for-application produces knowledge that can be made into patentable, commodifiable products, research findings can be sold for profit in the public market. In addition, the empirical nature of the knowledge produced in these fields favours large classes with low professor-to-student ratios, since the delivery of instruction can be conveyed expeditiously in large lecture halls and learning can be assessed readily by means of computer-graded exams. Also in these fields, graduate student training fits smoothly into the protocols of the corporate laboratory. Here, apprentice researchers make use of a faculty member's or research team's technology to produce data that can lead to quantifiable knowledge that can then be sold on the public market. There are ready partners in the pharmaceutical, agricultural, manufacturing, or technological industries to sponsor many of the costs of establishing these expensive laboratories, and they in turn can capitalize on research results without carrying the total bill, since many of the costs of facilities and personnel are provided by the university infrastructure. This ostensibly efficient and self-capitalizing system of exchange between universities and government or business clients is a welcome relief for university administrators in a period of shrinking public funding. Its responsiveness to immediate public needs—for medical technologies, agricultural improvements, technical designs, or consumer products—has made research capitalism the primary model of what the twenty-first-century university is all about. The double need to maintain and update existing infrastructures as Canadian universities are coming of age, and to establish new ones as these become necessary, has increased the financial stress on universities. While the federal government has responded by establishing, for example, the Centres of Excellence in 1989, the CFI in 1997, and the CRC program in 2000, these programs' terms of reference have further complicated the culture of research capitalism. Increasingly, universities' financial situation means that faculty are under constant pressure to apply for research grants. Indeed, the old publish or perish paradigm has now found a twin in the fundraise or perish paradigm. But grant applications for collaborative projects that involve researchers and other partners from different universities and sectors are elaborate and time-consuming and, once awarded, they require an equally elaborate management and public accountability process. While accountability and management are necessary in safeguarding the role and function of universities, they are implemented, more often than not, in ways that have modified substantially the administrative aspects of a professor's job. In the view of Marc Renaud, President of SSHRC from September 1997 to August 2005, this managerialism is part and parcel of the "visionary and pragmatic"

("Personal" 3) goals of SSHRC's reconfiguration into "a knowledge agency" (SSHRC, *From Granting*, vol. I). As the *Consultation Framework on SSHRC's Transformation* recognizes, "A new collective culture of 'research entrepreneurship' [has] emerg[ed] as an important dimension of research activity in Canada" (SSHRC, *From Granting*, vol. I, 9), a culture that demands that humanists and social scientists "become far more proficient at moving the knowledge from research to action and...linking up with... stakeholder-partners across the country" (3).

Of course, for the disciplines and sub-disciplines that do not readily fit the discovery-for-application model, for the areas of inquiry that do not produce quantifiable knowledge, that do not invent new technologies and may in fact produce cautionary findings about them, that do not process large numbers of students in massive lecture halls, or that do not have ready links to industry and investment income—for these disciplines, the culture of research means prohibitive competition that forces them to compete for funding and support in a climate that clearly disadvantages them. Although the privileged fields struggle with the pressures that come from sponsorship—for example, faculties of medicine are pressed by pharmaceutical companies,[7] faculties of engineering by industry—fields that do not primarily operate within the discovery-for-application model face a different set of problems. For example, the increasing emphasis on generating "impact"—understood in terms of a funded research project's relevance to or influence on government, health, or business sectors—as the benchmark for appraising the value of research results across the board applies pressure on researchers whose work does not fit the discovery-for-application model; they are compelled to tailor their research programs accordingly or run the risk of having their research perceived as immaterial. In addition, the desire of research sponsors to achieve readily marketable results can short-circuit the scientific method's disinterested testing of a hypothesis and willingness to report the positive and negative results. Adopting this kind of knowledge production as the gold standard for research has an adverse impact on the intellectual, cultural, ethical, and practical pursuits that are at the core of research in such fields as the humanities.

Suffice it to say, the funds allocated to research in the humanities are miniscule compared to those available to the so-called hard and soft sciences, with the result that faculties of arts or humanities often stand cap in hand, hoping that a philanthropist will bypass market demands and give them a donation. These, too, usually have strings attached, though more often tied to the donor's sentiments than to the needs of the researchers or of society at large. Humanities disciplines are primary among the fields that are disadvantaged in the culture created by research capitalism, though the effects of disqualification and disempowerment can be seen in any field where knowledge cannot be readily patented and corporate sponsors see adverse rather than positive effects on their markets. Disqualification in this instance does not merely refer to lack of access to adequate funds; in the context of research capitalism, it also speaks, for example, to the increased pressure on humanists to adopt science and social science models and thus diversify and modify their research so that it produces knowledge that is presumed to be of greater relevance to the community at large than that conventionally attributed to humanistic research. While such pressures are often categorized as "innovative" and rationalized as being readily applied to meet societal needs, they also exhibit a misconstruction of the distinctiveness of the humanistic object of research. Implicit in this attempt to refashion the humanities is the assumption that humanistic knowledge production as such is irrelevant to the well-being of the polity. In this climate of fiscal responsibility and public accountability, humanistic research is often configured as a frivolous, self-indulgent pursuit at best, or redundant at worst. The methodological, ideological, ethical, and practical concerns that emerge from this research capitalism are precisely what the essays in this volume are concerned with.

Nothing of what we have said here is startlingly new or previously unheard. Indeed, there is a large international literature reflecting on the precarious future of the humanities in the "corporate university," and some of the concerns we voice were raised in Canada over twenty years ago, during the period of severe cutbacks to universities in the late 1970s and early 1980s. We address several of these discussions in more detail in our introductory chapter. For the present, however, what is striking from our perspective a quarter of a century later is how the language of research knowledge as a solution to economic crisis, language prevalent during the recessions of the 1980s, seems to have become normalized as *the* rationale for the culture of research ever since. It is our contention that the culture of research in its current formation in Canada assumes a discourse of research capitalism that tends to delegitimize the contributions of humanities researchers.

Our goal, then, in gathering these essays together, is not only to offer a collective critical analysis of the current situation, but to explore, also, the possibilities for "retooling" the humanities—in both senses of "re-equipping" and "re-organizing" them—for survival and re-invigoration.[8] In preparation for this project, we invited a diverse group of literary and cultural studies scholars from across Canada to meet on the weekend of 20–22 October 2006 at the University of Guelph to confer about the present challenges and to discuss how the humanities might effectively retool themselves to respond to the culture of research without necessarily capitulating to every aspect of it. We were conscious that the challenges we face in the humanities call for critique as well as adaptability, and, although we did not want to sidestep a vigorous analysis of the adverse conditions we face, we were determined not to spend our entire time elaborating a victimhood for the humanities.

We selected the participants for our workshop for the diversity of their experience, the solidity of their commitment to discussion and debate about humanistic research in relation to the state as well as to the community and the body politic at large, and the strength of their vision for the future. We wanted scholars from various positions within the university-research institution across the country: from PHD students and post-doctoral fellows to academics who are also cultural practitioners, to senior tenured faculty who have served on the boards of, among other national organizations, SSHRC and CFHSS. We also included people who have been the recipients of different kinds of research grants, ranging from SRGs and post-doctoral fellowships to MCRIS, CRCS, and CFIS, thus bringing different perspectives to bear on research capitalism and the funding agencies that support it. And while we kept the size of the group small because we wanted the discussions to be coherent and intensive, we selected participants who would help us engage with a wide range of perspectives, from different social constituencies to various fields of expertise to diverse ideological viewpoints. Thanks to the resourcefulness and vision of these participants, plus a few others we have been able to include since the October workshop, this volume puts forth a debate that addresses crucial aspects of research culture today and that, we hope, will generate further discussion. As editors, we have not attempted to force or craft a single vision among our contributors; the views presented in some of the essays differ sharply from those argued in others, as well as from our own views as editors. We believe that this diversity constitutes productive and vital dialogue, and we trust that our readers will perceive in it a plenitude of routes forward rather than one prescribed path that should apply for all.

There is no doubt that the culture of research capitalism is in the ascendant at the beginning of the twenty-first century. Although universities in Canada have always negotiated their revenues with outside sources such as governments and various community and corporate stakeholders, they have not always accorded such power to the market place and its values to determine their own goals and priorities. This fact suggests that there is no reason to think that the current situation is inevitable. As we point out in our introduction, there is a specific trajectory that has led to the present situation. It is our hope that by gathering these essays together and discussing the conditions that shape the range and dynamism of the Canadian research community—especially those that affect the participation of humanities researchers—we can draw attention to the implications of research capitalism while generating new perspectives that can point towards a more inclusive, diversified, and ethical culture for scholarly research.

Daniel Coleman & Smaro Kamboureli
Hamilton/Guelph, August 2008

1. We wish to thank Les Monkman for drawing our attention to Donoghue's book.

2. For American authors in the field see Ohmann, Graff, and Nelson. For recent examples of Canadian publications, see Adrienne Chan and Donald Fisher's *The Exchange University* and Paul Axelrod's *Values in Conflict*. The recently released Canadian title, *Academic Callings: The University We Have Had, Now Have, and Could Have*, edited by Janice Newson and Claire Polster appeared while our book was in production.

3. Though John Aubrey Douglass focusses on how American universities execute or manage their social contract with society, his study is pertinent to the point we are making here, especially Part IV, "Whither the Social Contract? The Postmodern World and the Primacy of Higher Education," 235–92.

4. See also Slaughter's *The Higher Learning and High Technology: Dynamics of Higher Education Policy Formation*, as well as Slaughter and Leslie's *Academic Capitalism: Politics, Policies, and the Entrepreneurial University*.

5. Concerned about a similar flattening in the United States, the Carnegie Foundation for the Advancement of Teaching commissioned the late Ernest Boyer in 1987 to investigate and report on the meanings of scholarship. In the resulting volume, *Scholarship Reconsidered* (1990), Boyer offered an influential (and much debated) model that recalibrated the relationship between research and teaching and allowed for a more varied understanding of the kinds of work academics do. He identified four interrelated modes of scholarship: (i) discovery, which refers to the creation of new knowledge, "the commitment to knowledge for its own sake" (17)—what many think of as pure, basic, or frontier research; (ii) integration, which involves "making connections" between existing forms of knowledge, contextualizing, interpreting, and "educating nonspecialists" (18); (iii) application, which examines how existing knowledge can address problems in the social and natural world as well as how this process generates new theories and understanding, a form of scholarship whose agenda today is often set by institutions and government; and (iv) teaching, which involves not only transmitting knowledge but also transforming and extending it. His study may have radically questioned and realigned the conventional binary relationship of research and teaching, as well as that of disinterested and interested inquiry, as many scholars have noted, but it remains inscribed by an implicit hierarchy as is evident in his ranking system and the ways in which he attempts to justify the scholarships of integration and application in relation to that of discovery. Still, Boyer's paradigm is valuable, for it invites reassessment and recognition of the various tasks the professoriate performs.

6. In *Values in Conflict: The University, the Marketplace, and the Trials of Liberal Education*, York University professor of education Paul Axelrod reports that

provincial expenditures on higher education fell 12% between 1992–1993 and 1999–2000. University revenues from government sources dropped from 74.5% in 1978 to 55.6% in 1998, while tuition fees rose 224% between 1981 and 1998. Sponsored research rose from 9% in 1972 to 17% in 1997–1998 (93–94). Compare these statistics to the 2007 CAUT Almanac of Post-Secondary Education in Canada, which reports that federal cash transfers for post-secondary education fell by approximately one-third from 0.56% of the gross domestic product in 1983–1984 to 0.19% in 2004–2005 (2). Government funding covered 81.3% of university operating revenues in 1975; this share dropped to 56.7% by 2005, with the result that tuition during the period doubled from 14.7% to 30.4% (4). Average tuition fee increases for students in the arts (social sciences and humanities) rose 154.7% across Canada between 1991–1992 and 2006–2007, with Alberta (at 213%), Nova Scotia (at 194%), and Ontario (at 184%) topping the charts (37). Between 1992–1993 and 2004–2005, the Canadian university student population (part-time and full-time together) increased by 32.9% (20), while the number of full-time faculty increased by less than 1%, from 32,400 to 34,002 (6). Sources of funding for Canadian universities reached a ratio of 50.6% public funding as compared with 44% private funding by 2003. The only countries in the world with more private funding than Canadian post-secondary institutions are Australia at 52%, Japan at 60%, Korea at 74%, and the United States at 56% (53). Interestingly, the 2009 version of the CAUT Almanac does not separate out statistics on various disciplines, and thus it is not possible to isolate statistics specific to the social sciences and humanities. Under the remaining categories, listed above, the differences are marginal.

7. For an example of the ways sponsorship can skew certain kinds of research in the medical sciences, consider the case of physician and medical researcher Dr. Nancy Olivieri, the head of the haemoglobinopathy program at the Hospital for Sick Children at the University of Toronto. Olivieri had signed a research contract with Apotex Inc., for her investigation of the company's drug deferiprone in the treatment of blood disorders. Her initial enthusiasm for the drug's potential soured as she came to question its long-term effects, and she eventually felt compelled to break the "confidentiality clause" she had signed with Apotex to publicize her concerns about these long-term effects. She subsequently lost her position as head of the haemoglobinopathy program, which in turn prevented her from continuing her clinical trials. It was not until the case was widely publicized that she was reinstated in her position at the hospital in January 1999. See Axelrod, *Values* 105–06; Jon Thompson, Patricia Baird, and Jocelyn Downie's *The Olivieri Report*, and Daniel Schugurensky, "The Political Economy of Higher Education in the Time of Global Markets: Whither the Social Responsibility of the University?" in *The University, State, and Market*, eds. Robert A. Rhoads and Carlos Alberto Torres, 301–20.

8. The term *retool* was given prominence by SSHRC during the Transformation process (see for example *Knowledge Council* 14 ff.).

Introduction

CANADIAN RESEARCH CAPITALISM:
A GENEALOGY OF CRITICAL MOMENTS

Daniel Coleman &
Smaro Kamboureli

THE "PUBLIC" FACE OF THE UNIVERSITY

IN MAY 2008 A HIGH-GLOSS, FOUR-COLOUR bilingual insert appeared in *The Globe and Mail* entitled *Cultivating Excellence: A Special Report Celebrating the 30th Anniversary of the Social Sciences and Humanities Research Council.* The first of the insert's twenty pages consists of a message from SSHRC President Chad Gaffield inviting readers to join him in celebrating, "with profound pride, the significant role that SSHRC has played in helping Canada become one of the world's most successful societies" (1). In the subsequent paragraphs of his letter, he takes the reader back to the 1970s, when most Canadian schools imported curriculum content, business and policymakers relied on studies from other countries, and "we were just beginning to 'know ourselves.'" Thirty years later, he notes, through a "rigorous selection process that ensures excellence and accountability," SSHRC supports ten thousand researchers and graduate students across the country, helping to "build a broad, strong foundation of Canadian knowledge and expertise." He credits SSHRC with supporting professors who "inspire and mentor the next generation of Canadian leaders, thinkers and visionaries" by helping social sciences and humanities students—60 per cent of all full-time university students—become "culturally informed and politically knowledgeable individuals now sought worldwide."

Gaffield's pride is justified. Faculty and students whose research and scholarship have benefitted from SSHRC support would readily acknowledge the invaluable role SSHRC has played in supporting research excellence in the humanities and the social sciences. Established by an act of Parliament in 1977,[1] SSHRC has been instrumental in cultivating and bolstering through its various programs research by both faculty and graduate students. It would be hard, if not downright impossible, to imagine a vibrant humanities culture in Canada without SSHRC figuring prominently in the academic landscape. Precisely because its mandate as the only funding agency designed to meet the research needs of humanists and social scientists is so crucial, SSHRC's response to the social and political economy of the times operates as a barometer of the larger culture of research across Canada.

As is the case with universities and other institutions, SSHRC has had to keep abreast with the increasingly volatile economic and social climate to remain an agency that is at once responsive to the new directions of research in academe and is accountable to both the public and the government. More specifically, as a body that dispenses public monies and directly reports to the federal Ministry of Industry, but whose raison d'être as an arm's-length granting council is to serve the research interests of humanists and social scientists, SSHRC occupies a hugely important yet awkward position—awkward because of the double status of its mandate: to translate and validate the importance and relevance of research in the humanities and the social sciences to the Ministry of Industry in order to appeal for funds and, at the same time, to justify to its community of researchers the budgetary decisions and program changes it often makes in response to government pressures. In the institutional frameworks within which it operates, then, SSHRC must fulfill its mandate by executing, gingerly, a process of constant mediation and negotiation. While one would certainly expect the choreography of such political negotiations to differ considerably depending on the priorities of the government in power, the structural and institutional contexts in which SSHRC's activities take place draw attention to the complexity and ambiguity inscribed in its role as a government-funded agency. Thus the adroitness required of the SSHRC president is, to state the obvious, of utmost consequence. What's more, it is virtually impossible for the president of SSHRC to see eye to eye with all the diverse constituencies he or she represents, let alone meet their respective expectations, while at the same time acting as the chief liaison between the federal government and the Canadian research community. The fact that the SSHRC president is appointed by the federal government and not elected by a membership further points out the political complexity that accompanies the immense challenges this position already entails.[2]

Indubitably, the double directive that governs SSHRC's mission is behind the emphasis in the current president's letter on a SSHRC vigorously engaging the future. When he writes that "we are now embracing new approaches to research and intensifying our commitment to making Canada a leader in international research excellence"—examples he provides include "programs that enable innovative partnerships with community organizations, businesses and government agencies," and "international research networks"—he celebrates the paradigm of research ushered in under the auspices of his predecessor, Marc Renaud; at the same time, his rhetoric of newness also performs an exercise in public accountability in terms that bring into relief the culture of research capitalism.

The SSHRC flyer contains congratulatory notices from nineteen universities that double as advertisements, all of them furnishing self-branding mottos that posit research and innovation as the twofold pledge of a successful future. While they affirm the universities' social contract, these advertisements, together with the examples of SSHRC-funded research projects, leave no doubt about the research priorities and values SSHRC is "embracing" today. *Embracing* is the operative word here, for it is a metaphor Gaffield employed in a public lecture he delivered early in his appointment as SSHRC president. Serving as his acceptance speech on the occasion of receiving the Distinguished Academic Award from CAUT in 2007, the lecture also provided him with the occasion, as president, to announce his position about SSHRC policy. Titled *Embracing the New*

Metaphor for 21st Century Universities, the speech adopts the same millenarian rhetoric that characterized Renaud's Transformation project that refashioned SSHRC from "Granting Council" to "Knowledge Council" in 2003–2005. Symptomatic of the intimate affiliations that Gaffield suggests SSHRC ought to forge between itself and diversified partners— partners to be found in places beyond post-secondary institutions—in order to execute its mandate effectively, "embracing" identifies SSHRC as an agency that must significantly configure its mission in the name of accountability.

Applied to university culture and the principles that have historically informed how post-secondary institutions evaluate faculty members' distribution of effort, the changes Gaffield calls for in this lecture, and which he celebrates in the SSHRC flyer, have ideological and ethical implications for the long debate over how the academy's traditional three pillars of research, teaching, and service interrelate. As he acknowledges in the conclusion of his speech,

> what to keep, what to change and how to support our cultures, policies,
> and structures to embrace the new metaphor of "interacting, intertwining,
> helical-like strands of teaching, research and service" to the community is,
> I think, the key question for universities. How we respond will play a major
> role in determining Canada's prospects in the 21st century. (12)[3]

Gaffield here employs a metaphor that the recipient of the same award in 2006, Bernard Robaire, articulated in his own acceptance speech, wherein the "helical-like strands" model is intended to "dismantle[] the metaphor of distinct pillars" (2) and to emphasize the organic rapport that exists between research, teaching, and service. Nevertheless, Gaffield "embraces" this DNA-like model because, in his view, it promises "a fundamental rethinking of university life" as we have known it "until quite recently" (3). But this metaphor is not as "new" as Gaffield suggests; Canadian universities have gone through various changes in the second half of the twentieth century that, though not always following cohesive or universally accepted policies, have attempted to address the tensions in the interrelationship of research, teaching, and service. Instead, what is "new" in this metaphor is that it announces a strategy already in place, a strategy that incorporates into SSHRC's policy the material economies produced when the humanities and social sciences are recast as knowledge industries.

This strategy is evident in the research projects that the SSHRC anniversary insert showcases. Grouped in pairs under a common theme, they demonstrate the emphasis Gaffield placed in his 2007 speech on "advanc[ing] knowledge" through "both specialization (the discipline of the discipline) and contextualization (discipline-based interdisciplinarity, campus-community collaboration, and Canadian-global connections)" (7). The first pair, for example, lists the theme "Aging Populations" and profiles an international network involving forty-six researchers headed by an economist and a research centre established by a sociologist. Subsequent pairings include: "Building Business, Managing Life," which highlights a political science and geography team that studies clustering between business, university, and other entrepreneurial industries and a business professor whose research examines workplace stress; "Environment and Sustainability," which showcases international research teams, one of them facilitated by a professor of environmental studies who investigates the impact of international corporations on agriculture; and "Where Art and History Meet the Digital World," which involves a historian who has linked up with fifteen community organizations to collect oral life stories of Montreal immigrants in a digital archive, as well as two professors of dance who are producing multimedia performances that abstract dancers' movements into flows of colour and particles on screen. These, supplemented by a final, single-project profile entitled "Cultural Wellness," about a linguist who works on revitalizing the endangered Dene language, constitute the insert's presentation of the kinds of research that are going on in the social sciences and humanities in Canada today.

Collectively, the research projects celebrated in the insert highlight social problems that are crucial for our times. They underscore work done by collaborative, inter-university, and international research groups, and they assert the usefulness of these projects by noting their uptake by policymakers, government ministries and commissions, public and private corporations, community partners, and NGOs. Clearly the evidence of these projects' success lies in their *impact*, a key term employed by SSHRC since 2006, in response to government pressures "to demonstrate the value for money from public investment in research": the researchers involved in these projects are now "in demand with governments and corporations"; one of them has "travelled to Australia... to launch a new study" (6); their work has been "cited in a report to the United Nations Economic and Social Council" (14); and a project is anticipated to produce seventy-five graduate degrees (16).

But isn't something missing here? Where are the kinds of scholarship conducted in what most people would think of as the humanities? Isn't anybody studying classical Sanskrit? the history of the slave trade? the writings of Michael Ondaatje or Goethe, not to mention Shakespeare? Do they still debate and dissent at university? Do they discuss the philosophies of Marx and Adam Smith, Gandhi and the Fraser Institute? Does nobody at Canadian universities study German? or piano? or community theatre? The only recognizably humanities-style research projects highlighted here are focussed on digital technology. Are all researchers busy flying around the world consulting with international research groups, writing policy papers, meeting with government departments, building multimedia databases, and launching multi-million-dollar, multi-year collaborative research institutes? Do any of them read books and scholarly articles or go to the library? Do any of them engage in the quiet, solitary acts of note-taking, study, analysis, synthesis, and—especially—*writing*?[4] Do they still carry out the sustained, patient, long-suffering work that produces substantively researched scholarly books? Do any of them still teach?

Yes, they do, but these activities don't exactly fit either the "new" metaphor of the helical-like strands of research, teaching, and service or the rhetoric of the anniversary insert, which is aimed at explaining to *The Globe and Mail* reading public why they should be proud to support SSHRC and its researchers through their tax dollars. The rhetoric of a document like this is emblematic of the desire to affirm that the humanities, commonly understood in some circles to be inimical to material progress, can share in the entrepreneurial spirit and commercial relevance of disciplines better equipped to contribute to "problem-driven research" (SSHRC, *From Granting*, vol. I, 9). Celebrating this image of the humanities is tantamount to espousing a research strategy that decidedly privileges the culture of research capitalism. This is made abundantly clear in the president's letter, which notes that, in May 2007, "the federal government announced a science and technology strategy to make Canada a global economic leader through world-class research, a highly skilled workforce and strong partnerships across business, academic and public sectors." "At SSHRC," the letter goes on to say, "we welcomed this strategy as it builds upon our work over the past 30 years: generating new ideas and cultivating research excellence, increasing and retaining the highly skilled individuals that Canada needs to thrive in the global economy, and connecting knowledge to practical applications for the benefit of society."

If SSHRC is representing the humanities' collective mandate in this way, it is because the arm's-length principle that is supposed to determine its transactions with the federal government is acutely compromised by the government's interventions into how research priorities are established and by whom. Clearly, SSHRC is expected to harmonize its research agenda with the research areas targeted in the federal budget, or it runs the risk of seeing no budget increase. Increasingly of late, the federal government has targeted areas for research development and provided funds to SSHRC (and the other research councils) for new grant programs. Although funds were allocated in the early 2000s for areas such as Aboriginal and Northern Communities research, more recently we have seen a consistent pattern according to which federal government allocations to SSHRC and the other granting councils target areas such as science, technology, business, and management as particular priorities. Chapter 5, "A Stronger Canada Through a Stronger Economy: Knowledge Advantage," of the federal government's Budget 2007 directly links its increases of SSHRC's budget to these targeted research areas. As the section "Targeting Research to Priorities" states, the government promises to "increase its support for post-secondary research" but, as it makes abundantly clear, "this requires that the [three granting] councils adopt a more strategic approach and increasingly support multi-disciplinary collaborative research to address complex issues and create a real advantage for Canada." Under this proviso, Budget 2007 allocates "11 million for SSHRC, targeted to research in management, business and finance."[5] Thus it is not because the majority of social scientists and humanists are engaged with the business and finance sectors that a Research Communication Grant (without a dollar ceiling) was especially designed, for example, in 2008 to "mobilize...research results in the areas of management, business and finance to a range of audiences beyond academia."[6] Rather, SSHRC's strategy here is responsive to the contingency factor that links federal funding to designated research areas, hence its allocation of a large portion of its 2008 budget to projects designed to "stimulate... research and training in management, business and finance" (without a dollar ceiling), or its new mandate to develop "policy-relevant research about participation in sport in Canada" ($250,000 for up to three years per project). Similarly, the 2009 budget, in its section on "Granting Councils," states that these granting agencies "are streamlining operations and aligning programs with the objectives of the Government's Science and Technology Strategy and national research priorities." As the federal document goes on to say, "Through closer coordination, these agencies are improving the effectiveness of existing programs, aligning their programs with their core roles and fostering the development of innovative new programs."[7]

One does not need a research grant in management to figure out that "streamlining" and "coordination" in this instance signal not only a concerted attempt to administer and control research interests and funds, they also articulate interventionist policy that compromises the arm's-length principle that presumably characterizes the relationship of university research and state fiscal policies. While it would be naive to assume that there is no correlation between the two, and while we recognize the importance of co-ordination, as well as the need for SSHRC to develop strategies that will allow it to withstand the pressures that come from difficult fiscal times, we remain concerned that what we assume to be a survival strategy on SSHRC's part goes so far in its 30th-anniversary flyer as to celebrate this drastic diversification of its core research mandate. The funds for targeted areas, above and beyond SSHRC's regular budget and for activities outside the scope of the core disciplines in the humanities and social sciences, reflect the intensification of economic and commercial priorities in the Canadian culture of research.

If the SSHRC Council finds that government initiatives in science, technology, and management fit smoothly into its mandate, we are seeing an instance of what L.M. Findlay in his chapter in this volume refers to as "extraordinary rendition." That is, SSHRC's recent initiatives reflect the discourse of research capitalism. Though such SSHRC core programs as the SRGS remain intact, SSHRC has refashioned itself in ways that allow it to get a slice of the research pie as delineated by the federal government while, at the same time, as we suggest above, rendering invisible what still constitutes, to a considerable extent, its core research priorities. Our response to the SSHRC flyer, then, reflects the concerns raised in the AUCC *Momentum 2008* report. As this report states,

> Funding research requires...[different] forms of balance...such as the balance between providing appropriate support for existing research activities and for pursuing new avenues of research. It may be both necessary and desirable to engage in new priorities, but when funding, personnel or equipment are limited, this can mean pulling resources away from existing activities and thereby undermining current domestic and international research partnerships and [*sic*] consequently, Canada's reputation as a country committed to research collaboration and excellence. Likewise, there may be a pressing demand for targeted research in a particular field, but this demand may draw resources from the basic research that can lead to the serendipitous discoveries that drive all research disciplines.
>
> Basic research...also serves an important function as a national strategic reserve. When unexpected events occur, such as a terrorist attack, severe economic or financial dislocations, or the outbreak of a new illness such as SARS, Canadians rely on experts to interpret and explain what has happened and to help find solutions for the issues at hand. A healthy strategic reserve of basic research across disciplines ensures that, no matter what the political, social, cultural or economic challenge, Canada will have the expertise it needs to address the unexpected. (26)[8]

Understood in this light, the privileging of the kinds of SSHRC-funded research projects the SSHRC flyer celebrates is not only another instance of the harmonization of government research policy and SSHRC's mandate but also a capitulation to a logic of research that reflects a desire to gain persuasive purchase on an imagined public. Accountability in this discourse usually means accounting: this means that knowledge is a "product" freighted, as Kit Dobson notes in his essay, with exchange value that must be moved expeditiously out to its consumers. Knowledge in this discourse is a technology or a technique that can be applied to and solve social problems, a process that must produce "deliverables" that can be counted. In turn, the public imagined in this "new" narrative of accounting is a client preoccupied with getting a return on its tax investment: a public indifferent to the life of the mind or to a nuanced understanding of the past; that does not care for the development of intellectual discipline or self-knowledge, or about the making of responsible citizens; a public unconcerned if, as Donna Palmateer Pennee argues in her essay, "curriculum deficits" compromise intellectual and pedagogical rigour. It is dangerous to assume that this public is the only one that exists, or the only one that matters.

What has made it possible to reconfigure the Canadian public in these terms? What has been happening in post-secondary education in Canada that compels universities to adopt the self-branding and entrepreneurial strategies of the corporate world? Why do we feel more comfortable celebrating only the kind of humanities research culture that lends itself to commercialization or policy making? Why do we hide away, as the SSHRC insert does, the kinds of intellectual pursuit that do not readily yield to easy consumption? Why do we slip into the mode of apologia when we try to account for intellectual work that, chances are, won't gain a popular audience?

Our goal here is not to offer a portrait of the culture of research in Canada today, let alone do so in an exhaustive fashion. Rather than presenting a comprehensive historical narrative in the pages that follow, we focus on selected critical moments in the second half of the twentieth-century history of Canadian higher education that are paradigmatic of the conditions that have led to the current ascendancy of the culture of research capitalism. In the twenty-first century this culture has been institutionalized by such initiatives as SSHRC's Transformation, and, most recently, the federal government's interventions to promote science, technology, and business. Raymond Williams observed that "you cannot understand an intellectual or artistic project without also considering its formation...the relation between a project and a formation is always decisive" ("Future" 151). The contributors to this volume provide careful analyses of what the various elements of the broad project of research entails. Our task in this introduction, then, is to provide a context for its formation. As Derek Bok, former President of Harvard University and Dean of the Harvard Law School, acknowledges in his book *Universities in the Marketplace*, "Almost everyone concedes that competitive markets are effective in mobilizing the energies of participants to satisfy common desires. And yet the apprehension remains. However hard it is to explain these fears, they persist as a mute reminder that something of irreplaceable value may get lost in the relentless growth of commercialization" (17). A second purpose, therefore, is to give voice to some of these muted fears and conditions.

REFASHIONING THE UNIVERSITY /
MANAGING KNOWLEDGE

The culture of research capitalism this volume responds to did not emerge overnight. It has a complex but identifiable genealogy. A brief critical look at the ramifications, however contentious those might be, of some of the policies that have shaped Canadian universities in the second part of the twentieth century is, it seems to us, in order here. So, too, is the imperative to remind ourselves of the central role the humanities has played historically in society and the nation-state at large, and of the fact that we cannot properly understand, let alone negotiate, the intricate network of global and local relations without engaging with the broad spectrum of humanistic study. The widespread impact of Edward Said's *Orientalism* (1978) exemplifies the potential of humanistic study to influence in major ways the course of affairs as much within university culture as society at large. *Orientalism*, as Masao Miyoshi aptly remarks,

> radically challenged the orthodoxy in disciplines like history, anthropology, geography, and sociology, as well as literary criticism. Many branches of the humanities and social sciences had been formed during the colonial period with unexamined assumptions about the centrality of European and North American civilization, and intellectuals emerging in the just liberated former colonized world found in Said's criticism something both revolutionary and fundamental in mapping the history and geography of the future. The term "Orientalism" was added to the vocabulary of many languages as a name for the hegemonic ideology of domination. This was to be the beginning of a new paradigm of equality and the open mind. ("Turn to the Planet" 20)

Closer to home, Marshall McLuhan's work provides another notable example of a humanities scholar whose work has truly revolutionized our collective understanding of print and popular culture as well as the role of media technologies. While many members of the public may not recognize his name, his coinages "global village" and "the medium is the message" have become part of a general vocabulary across the globe. If McLuhan introduced us to the paradigm shifts of our information age, he did so through knowledge and skills he developed as a scholar of the classical trivium and Elizabethan literature, as a student of such literary scholars as I.A. Richards and F.R. Leavis. While not every scholarly book exerts as wide an influence as Said's *Orientalism* or McLuhan's *The Gutenberg Galaxy*, the cumulative impact of humanistic study is part and parcel of the acts of literacy and citizenship that individual communities rely on to envision and materialize a just and viable world community.

The organic role humanities research plays in society doesn't mean that humanists have ready-made answers; nor does it mean that the humanities can engage with the world community and the nation-state by holding onto inherited paradigms of knowledge production without retooling themselves. As David Leiwei Li asks, "If the humanities are social technologies that engineer autonomous individuals in modernity and sovereign subjects of the nation-state, what is [*sic*] its raison d'être in today's world where finance capital and televisual media crisscross national borders in the inculcation of global consumers?" ("Introduction" 3). It is important to remember, as Chickasaw legal theorist James Youngblood (Sákéj) Henderson stated in a talk on "The Indigenous Humanities," that the humanities historically were deadly "ammunition" in the colonial arsenal aimed against Indigenous peoples worldwide. Insisting that Eurocentric notions of civilization—education in phonetic literacy, Western religion, arts and letters—universally defined the human, colonial powers excluded Aboriginal groups from peoplehood, rationalizing literal and cultural genocide. Despite this horrific history—or, more accurately, because of it—Henderson and others at the University of Saskatchewan participating in the articulation of an Indigenous humanities insist that their oxymoronic neologism enables a decolonizing reinvention of the humanities. This reinvention borrows from and inhabits the traditional authority enjoyed by humanistic study, but it reroutes that authority with reference to the Indigenous knowledges that were long excluded from Western epistemologies. As Isobel Findlay, a member of this group, writes, "The Indigenous humanities lay claim to the rigour and authority of the traditional humanities, while their collaborative, cross-cultural, and cross-disciplinary practices act as a necessary corrective to past paternalism and resurgent neo-colonialism." Borrowing Audre Lorde's famous phrase, Findlay explains that "in this project we remain students, using, as it were, the master's tools to dismantle the master's house." The checkered history of the humanities, then, makes it necessary to ask: how can we continue to diversify the contents and methods of humanities inquiry despite the homogenizing pressures of an instrumentalist culture of research? Following the lead of Diana Brydon's essay in this volume, how can we reinvent the humanities in a way that animates the "human" in the humanities without reaffirming its elitist and Eurocentric roots? As is the case with other disciplines, the evolution of the humanities reflects, in part, the ways humanistic study has been interpellated by political and institutional structures. The answers to these questions, then, must unfold by bringing some historical understanding of university culture to bear on how to retool the Canadian humanities.

In the 1960s and early 1970s, the expansion period of Canadian post-secondary education, universities were largely trumpeted as institutions of higher learning with a corresponding focus on teaching and research. While that expansion was in keeping with population growth, it was also directly related to Canada's Cold War policy and the impact of the *Royal Commission on National Development in the Arts, Letters and Sciences 1949–1951*, commonly known as the Massey Report. Post-secondary education was beyond the purview of the Commission's Terms of Reference; still, Massey and his team "found it impossible to ignore the role which Canadian universities play[ed] in" the task they had been assigned (132), namely, to develop a defence policy against what the Report identified as the "American invasion." Universities were—and continue to be—an integral element of Canada's domestic and international cultural reputation. The changes the university culture went through in the first part of the Cold War period followed a broad strategic plan that belonged to the "regulatory interventions" of the federal defence policy (Cavell 86)—before strategic plans devised by university institutions became de rigueur in establishing their identity and goals. The Massey Commission's proposed master plan, much of the legacy of which still prevails, was to reinforce already existing institutions (e.g., the National Film Board, the Canadian Broadcasting Corporation, and the Canada Council for the Arts) and to establish new ones (e.g., the National Library) that would forge, in Jody Berland's words, "an explicit connection between autonomous culture and national defence" (517). The Commission recognized, indeed praised, the diverse and important functions of the university in Canadian society but placed its primary emphasis on the "national role" (Canada, *Royal* 134) of Canadian universities (133–34). Given the Cold War climate of the period, and the Report's mandate to marshal a "national security" (135) plan, stressing the university's "national services" (134) was not a fortuitous or unforeseen move. We find the instrumentality and instrumentalization of the university emerging from the Massey Report significant and historically relevant to our discussion here.

Because "Knowledge [is] valued as power" (161), the university as a place where received knowledge is studied and new knowledge is produced becomes, in the Massey Report, a site of special national importance. Thus while the university is understood to enjoy an arm's-length relationship with government operations, its autonomy is contingent on how it services the needs of the nation. In this context, nation and society become synonymous, or, more accurately, society understood as a diverse body that is often at odds with the nation is subsumed by the nation's putative homogeneity. If one way of understanding the anxieties that shaped the Cold War period is as fear of encountering, and being digested by, the foreign, then part of the legitimacy and strategic importance of the university resides in its ability to produce subjects trained to be good citizens. This instructive function of the university underlies the Report's equal emphasis on "pure or fundamental" as well as "applied" research (175–76) *and* teaching. As the Commissioners stated, "we found a remarkable degree of unanimity on the importance of associating fundamental research with teaching" (176). What's more, they acknowledged the essential role the humanities perform in society. They underscored "the profound importance of the humanities in the training of [both] young minds" (150) and that of doctors, engineers, and lawyers; a "professional school without the humanities," they wrote, "is little more than a technical institute." Thus they concluded that the humanities "should permeate the entire university" (137), a recommendation that has, sadly, gone unheeded.

"Teaching" and "training," employed interchangeably in the Report (though we would want to distinguish them),[9] along with privileging "high culture," help reinforce humanistic values but also operate as instruments of national pedagogy. The simultaneous emphasis in the period that immediately followed the release of the Massey Report on both fundamental and applied research *as well as* teaching legitimized not only the need to support universities but also the vital role the university plays in the *Bildung* of the nation. The old adage that the nation is structured like the family, and vice versa, is analogous to the function of the university as a national institution. Canada has never fit smoothly the paradigm of a homogenous nation, as is obvious in the Report. In its very first section, the Commissioners made an apparently benign distinction between "formal" education and "general" education (7), and they said they were supported in making this distinction by submissions they received from the Canadian Catholic Conference and *Comité Permanent de la Survivance Française en Amérique*. The distinction here is vital to the Commission's desire to finesse Section 93 of the 1867 *British North America Act* (BNA), which placed education under provincial rather than federal jurisdiction. Section 93's placement of education under the provinces was crucial to the BNA's attempt to appease French Catholic Canadians' anxieties about Confederation in the first place, and it also explains why Canada does not have a national university system to this day. So the Commissioners' distinction between general education and formal schooling was central to their desire to open elements of the former—basically, cultural institutions such as galleries, museums, and theatres, as well as university-based archives, libraries, and research—to federal jurisdiction. According to this logic, cultural institutions such as the Canada Council for the Arts (and, later, SSHRC) could be established by the federal government—especially if they remained arm's length from government—without contravening the BNA.

Canadian research culture is shaped by the Commissioners' distinction to this day, where, for example, SSHRC, as an arm's-length federal institution, can fund research but not undercut provincial authority in education. Educational funding in Canada flows from the government in Ottawa to provincial legislatures through federal transfers, but, in accordance with the BNA, provinces decide on education budgets, curricula, and so on. There are several important consequences of this jurisdictional division that shape the culture of research in Canada. First, research funding becomes the federal government's most direct way to influence the priorities and directions of Canadian post-secondary education. Second, this influence skews university priorities, since federal funds are always tied to research and its "indirect costs"[10] and not to teaching. On the other side of this division, provincial funds for teaching are tied to numbers of students in programs. This makes research funding much more flexible and adaptable for university budget managers than student funding, which is one reason why university administrators increasingly emphasize research as an area of growth. Third, provinces, concerned for various reasons about a federal monopoly on Canadian research, have launched their own research-funding agencies and corporations that make another layer of research funding available to researchers, including those at universities.[11]

As the federal-provincial division of mandates shows, how the university is structured, managed, and funded mirrors, on the one hand, the tensions underlying the national imaginary and, on the other hand, the state's desire to establish a certain self-image within its borders while projecting it beyond them for economic and strategic reasons. As an institution, the university performs its mission at once within the domestic and international spheres, a double mission that has typified the role of the university for the greater part of its history but which became more prominent in the modern university. The increased funding that helped build new universities and strengthen the infrastructure of existing ones, paired with the establishment of generous research grants for faculty and fellowships for students in the 1960s and 1970s in Canada, speak to the ideological and strategic roles of the university within the provincial, national, and international contexts. There is, therefore, no "golden age" when the university purveyed neutral and universally beneficial knowledge to an undifferentiated world of learners.

Indeed, the nation-state has always employed culture as an ideological and material instrument of education and instruction. As Peggy Kamuf writes, public education and instruction take place "on the stage of what might be called a politics of memory" (57). This politics of memory shapes what kind of history the nation-state wants the public to remember or the kind of past it seeks to repress, but also how to move toward a future by memorializing or avoiding certain aspects of the past. The symbiotic relationship between the nation-state and cultural institutions demands that the nation-state collaborate with as well as influence the directions of cultural production and humanistic study; at the same time, cultural institutions contribute to building the image of the nation-state but often do so by exercising their own agency, memorializing but also questioning and rethinking its past. So the covenant that binds the nation-state and cultural institutions, such as the university, is fraught with problems but is also full of possibilities.

It is precisely because of the fundamental role the university plays in the articulation of politics and government policies that, in the period following the expansion of the Canadian university system, the tight alliance between research and teaching was recalibrated, this time reflecting the ethos of the Thatcher-Reagan-Mulroney era of the 1980s and early 1990s. The pressures of the economic ideology of the time, added to the already existing pressures in favour of research as described above, had the result that teaching was demoted to a by-product of research and research was increasingly put in the service of the knowledge economy. This shift, of course, did not come out of nowhere. In *The Age of Discontinuity: Guidelines to Our Changing Society* (1968), economist Peter F. Drucker wrote that by the time of World War II, America's economy had changed from "an economy of goods...into a knowledge economy" (263); knowledge had become "the economy's central resource" (152). His new term *knowledge economy* registered that the "productivity of knowledge ha[d] already become the key to productivity" itself, that "knowledge ha[d] actually become the 'primary' industry" (264). This paradigm shift was supported by a shift in American occupations. The "largest single occupation" in the United States, Drucker noted, was "teaching, that is, the systematic supply of knowledge and systematic training in applying it" (264). Here teaching-as-training is not so much concerned with instructing students about, say, cultural memory and social values—an important tenet in the Massey Report's national agenda—but with producing the next generation of technologically advanced labour. Implied in the changeover to the kind of training needed in a knowledge economy, then, was an ideology of forgetting, the production of knowledge workers evacuated of the cautions and complications of cultural memory and therefore free to invest themselves fully in a new, technology-guaranteed future. At this stage of academic capitalism, research and teaching continued to complement each other, but the particular "generation of knowledge" required to feed the marketplace was becoming increasingly inflected by its commercial target (Gilman, *Fortunes* 7). From that point onwards, the knowledge economy has involved a pedagogy that has a similarly clear-cut goal: to fashion citizens capable of servicing and advancing capitalism. It was this intensification of academic capitalism, noted already by Drucker in the 1960s, that began to solidify the entrepreneurial university and set in motion the decentring of humanistic study.

This "new" order of things was not immediately felt in or summarily embraced by universities in the heady days of the 1960s and early 1970s. "New" in quotations marks because, as we register in our choice of the word *intensification*, there was little about the relationship of academe to the private sector that was truly novel at this time. Canadian university boards of governors or trustees already consisted, as Michael B. Katz notes, "largely of businessmen or other non-academic professionals, who often stressed the importance of athletics, businesslike management, and a conservative faculty" (8). There was no doubt, as Margaret E. Fulton states, that the generous support universities received in that period was a clear instance of "contribution as an *investment*" with the patent goal "of 'honing' a competitive edge to Canadian postsecondary education" (233). No matter how covert or subtle its interventions might have been, a strategy of incorporation into the knowledge marketplace was already at work.

Katz, writing in 1986, observes the fundamental changes that leading American universities had gone through by the end of the nineteenth century and, in doing so, further asserts that the pressure to establish a more widely adopted alliance between capital and post-secondary education was unavoidable, an eventuality to be reckoned with. As he points out, the

> transformation of the leading universities signified a new era in the history of capital....By managing to capture the process through which they were produced and to transfer the actual production of much new knowledge from outside their walls to within them, universities staged one of the great coups in the history of capitalism. Moreover, they met only minimal resistance because the imperial interests of universities and the self-protective instincts of professionals reinforced each other nicely. Together,

they made credentials dispensed by universities the hallmark of professional expertise. Universities, thereby, became the gatekeepers of the
advanced technical-managerial society. (9)[12]

His abridged account of how capitalism entered the academic world,
and vice versa, a century and a half ago illustrates not only the advent of
a new phenomenon at the time—an instance of "innovation" in the academic idiom of today—but also intimates the conditions of the gradual
adaptation post-secondary education was about to undergo.

Katz exposes the complicity between universities and industry in
the nineteenth century, but this scenario of conversion cannot be applied fully or as easily to the late-twentieth-century university. His
choice of diction—"staged" and "great coups"—assumes a willingness, if
not wilfulness, on the part of universities to go beyond accommodating
themselves to the corporate world so that they would eventually be able
to compete within it. While there is no doubt that in certain respects the
university is an "imperial" institution (one of the implications of the so-
briquet "ivory tower"), we don't think that the conversion Katz is talking
about occurred as effortlessly in the university world at large as he seems
to suggest. For one thing, the kind of agency he assigns to the university as an institution depends on what Robert Hassan, in an overview of
"The University in Western Society," has called the "fiction of autonomy"
under which universities were perceived to operate in the mid-twentieth century (73).[13] Nor can we assume that the faculties of the humanities
and the social sciences have been implicated in the university's capitalist
ambitions to the same degree as other disciplines. That Katz does not find
it necessary to differentiate between the humanities and the discovery
and applied sciences or the professional schools is symptomatic of the peripheral role the humanities has been customarily relegated to and of its
presumed inconsequential participation in the knowledge economy. It is
crucial at this point to note that we should not understand the university as a homogeneous or cohesive institution, not simply because of the
diverse, if not contradictory, interests of its various faculties but because
of the divide that often separates its administration from its faculty and
students. An example of this division appears in the strongly pronounced

views of J.A. Corry, President of Queen's University, in his book *Farewell the Ivory Tower: Universities in Transition* (1970). At a time before academic capitalism predominated university discourses, he advocated a notion of "the Canadian university as a public utility in the employ of a political-economic system, which it *persisted* in thinking it was still free to criticize" (qtd. in Fulton 233, our emphasis).

This persistence to criticize—a healthy sign still, we hope, of life in the academy—has continued unabated. Indeed, from the mid- to late 1980s there was no shortage of dialogue and research that debated the place of the university in the changing global economy;[14] there was, too, a noticeable swing in how and in what contexts research was being discussed. For example, in 1983 Concordia University sponsored the launch of C-CHEF, "a sister organization of the Business-Higher Education Forum in the USA." C-CHEF's founding meeting put "major Canadian public and private corporations in contact with the presidents, principals, and rectors of Canadian universities," with the expressed goal "to promot[e] better mutual understanding" between the university and industry that could be developed out of the limelight. As Douglas T. Wright, President of Waterloo at that time and a member of C-CHEF, put it, "the Forum is perhaps not as widely known as it should be, but this has been partly by design" (128). This Canadian initiative to meld university research and industry felt it could better advance its goal by working in camera. We can see the same covert strategy operating in the way Geraldine A. Kenney-Wallace, Chair of the Science Council of Canada at that time, talked about research:

Research is a way of exploring, it is a state of mind, forever curious, rigorous, enquiring, imaginative,...and, yes, [it is] curiosity. But curiosity, alas, has got us into trouble. I certainly have learned in the last eight months at the Science Council not to use the phrase 'curiosity-based research' unless in really private company, because people immediately have an image of an economist or writer, dealing with unreality, or a scientist in white lab coat, fuzzy gray hair, slightly shortsighted, who is wandering around aimlessly being curious all day. Even people who should know better do not believe that curiosity-based research activity can be real. Nor does a wider public believe that curiosity-based research is accompanied by intellectual

rigour, that there is a business plan—except it is an intellectual-moti-
vated strategy....While I think that curiosity-based research is a wonderful
phrase, please use it within a *specific* context. (25–26)

Concealment—in this instance a form of containment—was a recurring
trope in those days; it was emblematic of the response to the recession in
that period but also of the ambivalence that characterized the university's adoption of the corporate model. Moreover, it signalled the distrust
in which university officials held the "public," whose perceptions of
research would henceforth need to be managed carefully. It is revealing
that Kenney-Wallace equates "rigour" with a "business plan" in her view
of what an uninformed public would expect from "real" research. Significantly, she can construct this image of a public only by excluding herself
from it and by suppressing the exercise of curiosity that she articulates in
private as an accurate model of the research endeavour.

The new wave of changes whose implementation would radically
alter university culture was still to come. Nevertheless, the apprehension
about what was just around the corner was palpable. That apprehension
was the result, on the one hand, of concern about the Canadian deficit and the recession in the early and the late 1980s; on the other hand,
it was prompted by the growing uncertainty about how to respond to
the demands of globalization. In both cases the apprehension was fully
justified.[15] It should be said, though, that those sectors of the university
world that had long waited to see the university play an entrepreneurial
role saw their chance to make a move. Writing at the time of that crisis, William A. Cochrane, Dean of Medicine at the University of Toronto
and President of Connaught Laboratories, sums up what was a common
sentiment, especially among upper-level university administrators.
Concerned with convincing the public of the value of university research
activities, he stresses the importance of the university "assess[ing] society's expectations" of it: "To this end," he goes on to say, "one of the most
important statements I have heard from business professionals and particularly from senior executives and marketing managers is, 'Stay near
the customer.' This short and simple prerequisite of a successful business should be at the forefront of any activity of universities" (29). This

statement exemplifies the extent to which business in this context operates as a synecdoche for the public at large.

A tad subtler in his approach than Cochrane, Wright offers his own recommendation about how to bridge the gaps between business and universities: "Universities," he states, "do not usually identify the marketing of their research and research capability as an important responsibility. But it is important for universities to have a single office from which researchers can be identified in response to inquiries from industry to government" (130). This practical recommendation echoed the report *Spending Smarter: Corporate-University Cooperation in Research and Development*, which had been sponsored by c-CHEF and produced, as Wright notes, by "a small committee chaired by Raymond Cyr of Bell Canada" (128).[16] But Wright does not pause to consider the impact this co-operation would have on the university's mission or what its collateral damage might be on the kind of research that does not lend itself to immediate transfer into the commodity market. Thus, while these developments gave the professoriate, especially humanists, cause for alarm, for university administrators it gave reason for excitement about untapped opportunities and new alliances, precisely what Cyr's report was aimed to identify. Either way, the anxious and challenging economic conditions at that time provided universities with the impetus to seek ways to both protect and reinvent themselves.

The publications that resulted from two important conferences in that period, "The University into the Twenty-first Century" and the "National Conference on University Research and the Future of Canada," which took place at the University of Victoria in 1984 and the University of Alberta in 1988, respectively, and from which we have drawn several of our examples above, epitomize that climate of anxiety and divided opinion. *Universities in Crisis: A Mediaeval Institution in the Twenty-first Century*, the result of the Victoria conference, co-edited by William A.W. Neilson and Chad Gaffield, and *University Research and the Future of Canada*, the revised papers of the Alberta conference, edited by Baha Abu-Laban, are different in some respects yet similar in others, because they respond to a shared concern: how the university can remain relevant as a cultural institution and contribute to a diversified culture and economy. While the title of the former frames the situation universities confronted in the language of crisis and the possibility that they may have outlived their relevance, it adopts the same anticipatory stance announced by the latter—the future orientation that we drew attention to earlier. Additionally, as their contents amply demonstrate, the tenor of their common concern with the future role of universities is at once reactive and proactive: reactive in that they both respond to the "cutbacks in financing" (Neilson and Gaffield xiii) in the hope of curtailing further fiscal restraint in the allocation of grants to universities; proactive in that they address the challenge they face and offer specific solutions to these problems.[17]

Though, technically, we're still in the Cold War period, these volumes indicate that it is no longer the nation, which figured so prominently in the Massey Report, that universities must protect (or protect themselves from). They are not even primarily engaged in dialogue with the nation—or its citizens; rather, it is the state and its entire apparatus, along with the public and private sectors, the marketplace, and globalization, that the university is now called upon to serve and collaborate with. The sovereignty of the nation is replaced by the dominance of market logic. Far from diminishing the value and instrumentality of the university, this turn of events signals a far-reaching realignment of the university's terms of engagement with the polity, producing what William V. Spanos calls, in his book *The End of Education*, a *"diversified loyalty"* (125): loyalty to the state's newly articulated neo-conservative agenda and loyalty to the public. But as we indicated earlier, this public is not to be understood exclusively in terms of the general population. It is not the public inscribed in the notion of the common good as assumed, for example, in the Massey Report. Rather than signifying the community at large, the public is now co-opted by the interests of the private and corporate sectors, a shift that inevitably redirects the ends of university education, research, and teaching.

A dramatic example of the way in which the new concept of the public restricted what research leaders allowed themselves to say can be seen in Interim SSHRC President John Leyerle's speech, in Abu-Laban's volume, when he tells his conference listeners that this is not the place to argue at length the inherent value of the humanities and social sciences, great though those values are. We must foster and protect our humanities and social sciences because they are basic to individual freedom, to social order, to good government, to justice under law, indeed, to the whole dignity of man and woman. If these values are weakened, science and technology become instruments of oppression and destruction, as has happened all too often in this century. Although the argument here is utilitarian, the argument on the inherent value of the humanities and social sciences is the fundamental one. I emphasize that reality, even though I do not dwell on it now. (526)[18]

He could not dwell on it because the forum to which he had been invited was utilitarian; that is to say, its economy of possible topics was restricted to the urgent necessity of addressing the financial shortfall in research funding. The discourse of knowledge *as economy* caused him to refrain from what he considered to be the fundamental argument for the humanities and social sciences.

This shift in versions of the public is noticeable in both essay collections, and it is problematized and heralded at the same time. Also apparent is that post-secondary institutions have already begun to advance their agenda and to redefine the roles of research and teaching—this time openly—in collaboration with non-university agents and in dialogue with international associates. Both conferences involved not only presidents of the three major research councils, university presidents, and other upper-level university administrators and professors from Canada and overseas, but they included high-level representatives of the provincial and federal governments, as well as executives from the corporate sector. But it would be naive to see these gatherings only as defensive measures against the defunding of universities. As Fulton put it at the Victoria conference,

Whether the knife, when it cuts, will be wielded in the name of "Corporate R&D," "Skills Training," "Fiscal Restraint," or "Strategic Planning" by bureaucrats or business leaders or colleagues—who can say? But it is true that both twins [research and teaching], even before the knife has touched them, *are* dying. Something vital has already been taken from them, without which their death is as sure as if they had already been parted.... And when death comes, we shall be culpable because while recognizing the outward signs of their illness, we ignored the root cause of the disease. (231)

The diagnosis she offers alerts us to the illness plaguing the university at the time—an illness, it should be said, that can be traced not only to the university's fiscal plight but to the way in which that plight simultaneously contributed to and distracted attention from ethical concerns in the university and beyond. Fulton refers to the glass ceilings and difficulties in hiring, achieving tenure, and entrance into university administration that were encountered by women—and, we would add, so-called minorities—a situation that still needs to be addressed today, as Ashok Mathur and Rita Wong argue in their essay.[19]

The narrowed focus of a strictly economic evaluation regarding the health of university life excluded attention, in both of the volumes we are discussing here, to the debates in the public sphere about identity politics and cultural appropriation that were on the rise during this period. From our vantage point a decade after these debates, it is striking that the central and vigorous public role played by humanities scholars at the time has since been recuperated by the rhetoric of irrelevance that figures prominently in the discursive economy of research capitalism. Consider, for example, Marjorie Stone's essay in this book that discusses the Metropolis Project (of which she is a member) and its multilateral approach to its investigative agenda on immigration. As she elaborates, Metropolis has evolved primarily into a series of research clusters of social scientists; the result is that humanists who played such key roles in these public debates have had a very low profile in the Metropolis Project. Along the same lines, Diana Brydon's contribution to this volume decries the government's recent cancellation of funding for the LCC as a way of noting how humanities scholarship—especially interdisciplinary and collaborative work—can address not only questions of political and ethical relevance but also usher in what she calls a "new humanism."

As we have noted, political and ethical concerns, and culture in general, were not central concerns in the debates of the mid- to late 1980s that addressed the ill health of post-secondary institutions; the overwhelming concern—that is, how to facilitate the production of knowledge that the state and the corporate world required—obscured other considerations. The fiscal cure sought and eventually implemented during that period would change the future course of university institutions in fundamental ways. It was as though the anxiety over university research funding in the 1980s cemented research capitalism as the *only* discourse available to address and understand the role of the university in public life. The refashioning of the university that originated under those conditions of duress would bring about fundamental changes in how we conceptualize and are expected to practice research and teaching. The university hierarchy displayed leadership, but the direction it took reflected, in many ways, its capitulation to a rhetoric of commerce.

This does not mean that research and teaching in the humanities relinquished their particular ethical and educational imperatives and spontaneously consented to this state of affairs. In part because of its vulnerable position within the university, and in part because of its growing attention to issues concerning race, ethnicity, multiculturalism, citizenship, gender, and sexuality, humanistic research in Canada since the 1980s has sustained an intellectually rigorous offensive against the inherited regimes of "truth"—including traditional curricula and methodologies. Paul Danyluk's focus in this volume on artist, poet, and professor Roy K. Kiyooka details the kinds of cultural, pedagogical, and professional praxes humanists were able to develop in response to and against the rise of knowledge economies. What's more, the differential knowledges that humanists began producing in this "new university landscape" had already initiated a transformation of the humanities *and* humanism as much by "link[ing] scholarship with human needs," which SSHRC would announce as an imperative in its Transformation project twenty years later (SSHRC, *From Granting*, vol. 1, 8), as by questioning the foundational assumptions of their discipline. Melissa Stephens' essay in this volume on how humanists' first-person scholarship can operate as testimony to the politics and ethics of accountability within the university offers one example of how the humanities are capable of recognizing and thematizing their own genealogical origins in the colonialist and hegemonic discourse of humanism.

The results of the university's reformulation in the mid-1980s affected the overall ethos of university life. At an immediate level, fiscal restraint led to, among other things, lack of jobs and the elimination or forced amalgamation of programs.[20] But while these measures were of the kind that could be reversed relatively easily, the changes that occurred at the policy level were to have an enduring impact because of the incentives, and their respective ideologies, that triggered them. Research maintained or even increased its paramount value, but it attained a particular instrumentality because it was at the core of the movement that would add to universities the moniker *knowledge industries*.[21] Like the term *knowledge economy*, *knowledge industries*, too, was a product of the heady 1960s. These two concepts together signalled a new stage of modernity for university culture, one in which knowledge was not only to be produced by university researchers but also programmatically harnessed as a resource both inside and outside the university. It was in this context that interdisciplinarity and collaboration emerged as instruments of strategic importance as they were deemed necessary to produce the knowledge that industry could not generate single-handedly. The university's autonomous status may have always been a fiction, but the arm's-length relationship that universities had long maintained with institutions outside their perimeters was now abandoned in favour of full incorporation.[22] Pure research, which maintained its importance, evolved into what we have called discovery-for-application because of its anticipated uses in the corporate and industry worlds; the result was that the differences in function and value between pure and applied research became even less distinct than they had been.

A direct side effect of these changes was that the worth of the humanities was thrown into perennial doubt. Here was a patient that proved to be too resistant to cure! While most of those actively engaged in refashioning the university from within and applying pressure on it to change from without paid homage to the role of the humanities, they did not go so far as to factor the humanities into their research and development plans. The Massey Report's caveat that the humanities should permeate the entire university was forgotten. Nevertheless, as we have already noted, the humanities would refashion themselves as well: partly because deans of humanities and SSHRC were under immense pressure to prove the relevance of their faculty members' research, and partly because humanities faculty would take it upon themselves to analyze and contextualize the situation confronting them. The ongoing morphing of the university into a site intended to play a utilitarian role was achieved through careful management of the knowledge economies. As Andreea M. Serban and Jing Luan show, the concept of knowledge management would be created and turned into a movement by corporations in the early 1990s (5)[23] to systematize knowledge production between research funding agencies and corporate, state, and university partners. This development meant, among other things, that universities had to work on public image and media relations mechanisms that would shape and amend public opinion, often by reference to statistics on how they fared in securing research grants.

As Anne L. Jefferson says, "Accountability in terms of public interest... involves issues of equity, efficiency, quality, relevance, responsiveness, and intellectual freedom," but because accountability is a form of "public interest" and thus "encapsulate[s] not only the preferences of the giver but [also those of] the receiver," its "character...must be carefully considered." Jefferson goes on to point out that the "current tendency to endorse value-for-money accounting can potentially place the social contract between society and universities in greater disarray than it is now perceived to be. The judgment on whether the programs on which the money is spent represent value-for-money becomes a political judgment" (349). Accountability, then, is at the heart of the matters we are concerned with here. But while it figures prominently in today's discourse of research capitalism, it is typically restricted in two ways: first, as we have already suggested, accountability is often taken to be synonymous with accounting, and, second, the onus for accountability falls squarely on universities and their faculty members (and very rarely on government or larger society) to ensure that they are adequately resourced to offer essential critical perspective and genuinely new knowledge.

Because the rise of research capitalism posited itself as an accountability act designed to respond to what SSHRC calls "New world, new needs" (*From Granting*, vol. 1, 7), teaching was given lip service, but only insofar as it provided training; the widely perceived need to sustain and augment the knowledge economy through a resource-oriented approach to research meant that teaching fell increasingly to secondary importance. Nevertheless, while it may appear that teaching was marginalized by the overwhelming focus on research in this period, the Smith Report of 1991 is intriguing for the way it appears to show otherwise. This report of the *Commission of Inquiry on Canadian University Education*, launched by the AUCC in 1990, was undertaken by Stuart Smith, President of Rock-Cliffe Research & Technology Inc. and formerly a professor of psychology.

Anxious to affirm the importance of teaching in the university mandate, Smith resists the dominance of research; nevertheless, his consistent use of a rhetoric of currency reveals how the instrumentalist approach of research capitalism has already become naturalized in university discourse. The fundamental premise of the Smith Report is the following: "If university professors are being paid to improve their own knowledge and to engage in scholarly activities, it is primarily so that the teaching they offer to successive generations of students will be enriched, and only secondarily because society perceives a need for the research findings themselves" (31). Thus the Report practises one of the strategies developed at the time of the rise of academic capitalism—managing the university's public image—while it simultaneously restores in the term *public* some of the meaning and power it lost when it was used, as we saw earlier, in a truncated fashion that privileged primarily the corporate sector.

There is no doubt, however, that the mandate of this Report is not only an instance of "money talks" but also a matter of producing a disciplined professoriate. Though it barely engages in any sustained fashion with pedagogy (despite its advocacy of teaching), its genre is that of a teaching lesson, and a harsh one at that. The Smith Report, then, is as much interested in putting the public's money to work as it is in paying attention to restoring the, allegedly lost, value of teaching. For example, it is against the use of performance indicators (124), but it neverthe-less introduces detailed recommendations about maintaining teaching dossiers, participating in workshops offered by learning and teaching centres, rewarding (via tenure and salary increments) the development of technological and other tools for use in the classroom, minimum num-bers of teaching hours for all professors, and the dismissal of tenured faculty who do not practice effective teaching (47–65, 134–46). Through recommendations such as these, the Smith Report multiplied the col-umns on the university professor's accounting sheets. In some respects, its impact was more intrusive than many other such interventions on university life. Since the Smith Report, the discourse of account-ability-as-accounting, in its different guises, has become pervasive, especially in the ways research and teaching are now managed, moni-tored, and evaluated.

The 1990s Smith Report brings us to the brink of the twenty-first cen-tury. From the Massey Report and the period of Cold War–era university expansion, when the emphasis was on the university as producer of ed-ucated national citizens, to the period of economic decline in the early and mid-1980s when universities and the research councils worked to compensate for the defunding of universities, and onwards to the Smith Report with its economic rhetoric of accounting and efficiency, we have, by addressing these, attempted to sketch some of the major develop-ments that set the context for the culture of research at the beginning of the twenty-first century.

RETOOLING THE HUMANITIES

We have lingered this long over the period of the mid- to late 1980s because what transpired at that time is key to the developments that have led to what we are concerned with here, namely that the university has transfigured the resilience it has always displayed into a widespread accommodation of the ideologies and practices of capitalist logic. In so doing it has surrendered its responsibility to generate knowledge that produces critically aware and informed national and global citizens by submitting to the pressure to generate knowledge that meets the needs of the marketplace—a marketplace shaped as much by the demands of the present economic climate as the desire to meet the challenges of the twenty-first century. For it was in the lead up to the millennium that a whole host of initiatives were launched to bring together the various stakeholders within this university culture. For example, to existing funding programs that supported individual research projects, as well as journals, workshops, and book publishing, SSHRC added the MCRI in 1993, collaborated with UNESCO on the Metropolis Project (1995), established CURA in 2000, and became the administrative home for the CRC program established by the federal government in 2000. At the same time, SSHRC began a process of revisionary consultation in 2001 that resulted in the report *Alternative Wor(l)ds: The Humanities in 2010*, which, even before it could be implemented, was replaced in 2005 by another initiative, *Transformation: From Granting Council to Knowledge Council*. Each of these initiatives had the effect of "retooling" humanities research in the double sense of redesigning and re-equipping: redesigning humanities research to fit the protocols of research capitalism, and re-equipping it to produce knowledge relevant to the citizens of today.[24] This retooling, then, was a remedial response to the long-held assumption that humanities research is not easily transferable to the global knowledge economy and thus does not warrant public investment.

In this context, the CRC program was introduced as a strategy designed to acknowledge and further foster—to use its own lexicon—a nationally and internationally recognized "star" culture (*Canada Research Chairs Program Guide* 4); it also enabled the federal government to address the anxieties at the time over Canadian researchers leaving the country for positions elsewhere. Nevertheless, because it required universities to develop strategic plans and provide matching funds, and because of its allocation system,[25] the CRC program, as Claire Polster argues, has intensified the speed of the shift in the Canadian university system from the priorities of teaching and learning to those of research capitalism ("Break" 281). It may have created unique opportunities for individual researchers to pursue their research in a manner that

helped develop collaborative clusters involving other faculty and graduate students, and it has certainly enabled faculty members to enter into
meaningful mentoring relationships with junior scholars of the kind
advocated by Jessica Schagerl in her essay, but it has also increased the infrastructure required to manage such elaborate research programs.

The ambivalence that characterizes the rationale and effects of the
CRC program is also evident in SSHRC's quick transition from the recommendations included in *Alternative Wor(l)ds* to its transformation
"From Granting Council to Knowledge Council." First, the Council
commissioned an eight-member Working Group on the Future of the
Humanities[26] to write a report based on four workshops organized across
the country and a workshop-style conference that took place in Toronto. The resulting report, *Alternative Wor(l)ds*, contained detailed and
practical recommendations about how the Council and humanities researchers could meet the challenges of the new century. The proactive
spirit of the report can be summed up in one of the guiding principles:
"We must re-emphasize—and promulgate widely—the fact that humanities research and education are vitally important to developing and
maintaining a knowledgeable and productive workforce and that they
are central to the viability of national cultures, civil society, and to the
health of democratic institutions" (23). With its repeated emphasis on
the role of humanists as public intellectuals, the Report thus epitomized
an act of citizenship, for it manifested the accountability of the humanities at once to the university and a truly broad public. The shift, however,
from *Alternative Wor(l)ds* to the Transformation initiative four years later
signals how SSHRC's eventual reconfiguration, in effect, aligned itself with the forces of research capitalism and its attendant managerial
ethos. This alignment can be seen in the prescriptive, cautionary, and
visionary terms with which President Renaud launched the consultation process in his open letter circulated among more than ten thousand
SSHRC-funded researchers across the country in October 2003: "because
SSHRC, as it is currently structured, cannot foster a culture of collaboration within and across academic disciplines or among researchers and
users of research; and because the SSHRC agency and community are not
organized in a way to provide and deliver the knowledge that Canadians

need to build a better society," transformation was a necessity. It can also be seen in the subsequent implementation of Transformation with the addition of large amounts to SSHRC's budget for SRGS, dissemination and cluster grants, MCRIs, and other such programs whose targeted themes and overall methodological directions were determined in advance.[27]

It has not been our purpose here to analyze each of these twenty-first-century developments in detail, for many of their specific elements and implications are taken up by the contributors to this volume. We have drawn attention to them here to emphasize that the evolving culture of research capitalism we have been tracing through the twentieth century has produced a volatile climate, one in which, as our contributors demonstrate, there are many hazards and many possibilities. There is no blueprint to indicate how the humanities are to negotiate this volatile research climate. However, such a climate behooves everyone involved—from researchers themselves to universities and research agencies—to do what humanities scholars have long held as their ideal: to envision a just and lively future out of a self-aware and informed understanding of the antecedents that have shaped the present context. It is our hope that by tracing significant moments in the intensification of research capitalism as the currently ascendant paradigm of higher education, this introduction provides a schematic outline of the formation that shapes the project of academe in Canada. Perhaps by naming that formation, by scrutinizing its linkages, strategies, and presumptions, we can find ways to retool some of its constitutive elements: its restricted view of the public, for instance, or of accountability, or of what constitutes social relevance, and what it means to transfer knowledge. Ultimately, such retoolings may invigorate a more holistic and variegated approach to knowledge itself.

NOTES

1.   Until then, humanists and social scientists' research needs were handled by the Canada Council for the Arts.

2.   It is worth noting, though, that the SSHRC president need not be an academic, according to the act of Parliament that established SSHRC.

3. That Gaffield here refers to teaching, a part of post-secondary education that does not fall under the jurisdiction of the federal government and is thus not of direct concern to SSHRC, reinforces the point we have already made, namely, that the SSHRC president, especially when this office is held by an academic, as is the case with Gaffield, inhabits a hybrid position that demands she or he engage in a challenging choreography that creates meeting points, albeit often contentious ones, between the research community and the federal government.

4. Marc Renaud's 2004 message offers a reply to our last question here. As he writes, "In the academic world of the 1970s, the role of a university professor working in the human sciences was to teach and write books. Nobody observed, or foresaw, that a huge part of the job would be to get grants, find money for graduate students, stimulate discussions with external audiences, participate in national research teams or to work with other disciplines....By contrast, in the academic world of the 21st century, the responsibilities of university faculty extend well beyond students and postsecondary institutions" ("Message" 2). Though Renaud's statement would appear to render the point we raise anachronistic, we are here concerned with questioning the inevitability that marks SSHRC's approach to "research entrepreneurship," as well as its "pragmatic" implications regarding knowledge production and labour conditions.

5. See Budget 2007: Aspire to a Stronger, Safer, Better Canada, <http://www.budget.gc.ca/2007/pdf/bp2007e.pdf>. The same strategy of targeted research themes is also present in Budget 2008 (this time targeting the environment and the North).

6. For details of these SSHRC programs, see <http://www.sshrc-crsh.gc.ca/site/apply-demande/program_index-index_programmes-eng.aspx>. Site visited 25 August 2009.

7. See the 2008 Budget Speech <http://www.budget.gc.ca/2008/pdf/speech-discours-eng.pdf> and the 2009 Budget Plan <http://www.budget.gc.ca/2009/pdf/budget-planbugetaire-eng.pdf >.

8. What further reinforces the argument made here for basic research, and which is also implied in the inability of our present research system to distinguish between research funded by the granting councils and research pursued independently in universities, are the statistical figures mentioned in this report: "Statistics Canada currently [2008] estimates that 20 percent of research performed by universities is in the social sciences and humanities, 40 percent is in health and 40 percent in sciences and engineering other than health" (AUCC 27). Needless to say, these figures reflect the federal government's distribution of its total research budget among the granting councils rather than the actual number of scholars in each of these fields, where researchers in the social sciences and humanities constitute approximately 40 per cent of all university researchers in Canada (CAUT Almanac 2008–2009, 11).

9. As explained below, one of the differences of the two terms echoes the fact that the BNA designates education, and thus "teaching," as the responsibility of the provincial governments; this explains why SSHRC, a federal-level agency, is not concerned with "teaching" or students but, instead, with the research and professional "training" of "highly qualified personnel."

10. What the federal government introduced as a one-time program in 2000–2001, "the indirect costs" program became institutionalized as a permanent program in 2003. Distributed to universities in proportion to the funding they receive from the granting councils, indirect costs help universities deal with expenses incurred from such things as administering research grants and intellectual property.

11. Consider, for example, that Québec established Fonds de la recherche en santé du Québec in 1964 and, subsequently, Fonds de la recherche sur la nature et les technologies as well as Fonds de la recherche sur la société et la culture; other provinces have followed suit, establishing research councils of their own, including the Alberta Research Council, Saskatchewan Research Council, the British Columbia Innovation Council, etc.

12. While Katz is correct in his assessment of universities' success in becoming the gatekeepers of knowledge and its credentialization, his focus on the nineteenth century misses subsequent developments such as the large segment of academic capitalism controlled by the research and development wings of what Dwight D. Eisenhower called the "industrial-military complex." In his farewell address to the nation, delivered on 17 January 1961, Eisenhower noted that since the end of the Second World War, the United States had developed an unprecedentedly massive, government-funded, permanent arms industry, which by that time employed three and a half million workers. The implications for how knowledge is produced, he predicted, would be enormous: "Today, the solitary inventor, tinkering in his shop, has been overshadowed by task forces of scientists in laboratories and testing fields. In the same fashion, the free university, historically the fountainhead of free ideas and scientific discovery, has experienced a revolution in the conduct of research. Partly because of the huge costs involved, a government contract becomes virtually a substitute for intellectual curiosity....The prospect of domination of the nation's scholars by Federal employment, project allocations, and the power of money is ever present and is gravely to be regarded. Yet, in holding scientific research and discovery in respect, as we should, we must also be alert to the equal and opposite danger that public policy could itself become the captive of a scientific-technological elite."

13. Writing in Australia, where the Howard government of the late 1990s and early 2000s intervened directly and unabashedly in university governance, Hassan argues that, considered historically, Western universities had little-to-no autonomy before the mid-twentieth century when their numbers and enrolments grew exponentially and they received considerable public funds. He

insists that this period was a brief bubble, but that any university autonomy that remains is on the wane with the shrinking of public funding, the corresponding need for universities to seek corporate money, and the increased intervention of governments and corporations that privilege the priorities of business (72–73).

14. Studies published during this period include: A.W. Johnson's report to the Secretary of State, *Giving Greater Point and Purpose to the Federal Financing of Postsecondary Education and Research in Canada* (1985), the Commission on the Future Development of the Universities of Ontario's *Ontario Universities: Options and Futures* (1984), the Ontario Council of University Affairs' two reports, *System on the Brink* (1979) and *Once More, with Feeling* (1982), and the report of the *Parliamentary Task Force on Federal/Provincial Fiscal Arrangement* (1981).

15. Canada went through a deep recession in 1981–1983, during which "aggregate unemployment rates jumped to double-digit levels and peaked at 11.8 percent in 1983" (Marshall and McPherson 102), and in the late 1980s, this time as a result of an unprecedented 22.6 per cent collapse of the Dow Jones Industrial Average stock on Black Monday, 19 October 1987. Another reason, of course, for the dire mood in universities at the time was the persistently high unemployment rate in the academic market, a direct consequence of the cutbacks.

16. Wright's endorsement of Cyr's report (see 128–30) was far from being universal. For example, David M. Cameron's review of the report calls it "suggestive, superficial and slick" and laments the fact that "not one quote appears to have been included which disagrees with the committee's analysis" (530). As he writes, "*Spending Smarter* is probably more important as a public statement of intent than as an assessment" (531).

17. For example, the Abu-Laban volume closes with an appendix containing a list of resolutions, with particular emphasis on the Centres of Excellence the federal government had just announced, agreed to unanimously by all the delegates at the conference.

18. While Leyerle at least gestures toward the "inherent value" argument that he cannot make, Harry Hillman Chartrand, then research director for the Canada Council for the Arts, quickly dispenses with the notion that the arts give us access to people's inner lives on his way to his main argument for the value of the arts, where he observes that arts are central to engineering design, advertising, and a host of other cultural economies. "Compared to the twenty-two main Canadian manufacturing industries in 1983," he writes, "the arts industry was the largest with more than 234,000 employees, the fifth largest with salaries and wages of $3.1 billion, and the tenth largest with revenue of $9.2 billion....[T]he Canadian arts industry was $19.3 billion in 1983 or five per cent GNE [Gross National Expenditure]" (188).

19. For recent expressions of concern on these matters, see CFHSS, "Feminist & Equity Audits 2006: Selected Indicators for Canadian Universities"; CFHSS, "Postsecondary Pyramid: Equity Audit 2007"; and Pennee and Smith, "Statement from a Coalition of Academics of Colour" (2007).

20. From the high point of 31 per cent of university revenues spent on academic salaries in 1977, the downward trend began in the 1980s and has continued to fall, to the low point of 19 per cent in 2005 (see CAUT, "Changes in Spending..."). Between 1976 and 2006, government contributions to overall university budgets fell from 83.6 per cent to 56.8 per cent (CAUT, "Government Funding...").

21. The term *knowledge industries* was first introduced in 1962 by Fritz Machlup, a Princeton economist, in his book *Production and Distribution of Knowledge in the United States*. Though it caught on fast, originally in the area of information knowledge industries, Machlup has been criticized for his broad definition of knowledge, which ranges from intellectual, spiritual, and accidental knowledge to the knowledge entailed in manufacturing and secretarial work. See also Michael Rogers Rubin and Mary Taylor Huber with Elizabeth Lloyd Taylor.

22. It is ironic that at the same time that universities reconfigured themselves to build more intimate relations with industrial and corporate partners, the 1982 report of the *Federal Cultural Policy Review Committee* (better known as the Applebaum-Hébert Report), the first major report on Canadian culture since the Massey-Lévesque Commission, reinforced the emphasis Massey-Lévesque had placed on the importance of the arm's-length relationship between artists and the institutions supporting them. Commissioned by the Trudeau government in 1980, and led by composer Louis Applebaum and publisher and writer Jacques Hébert, it resulted in three volumes: *Speaking of Our Culture* (1981), *Summary of Briefs and Hearings* (1982), and *Report of the Federal Cultural Policy Review Committee* (1982), all government publications.

23. According to Serban and Luan, there are different definitions of *knowledge management,* but the following two are "widely recognized as best capturing the concept: according to the first one, 'Knowledge management is about connecting people to people and people to information to create competitive advantage' (*Knowledge Management News*); according to the second one, 'Knowledge management is the systematic process of identifying, capturing, and transferring information and knowledge people can use to create, compete, and improve' (American Productivity and Quality Center)" (1).

24. See the 2002 Killam lecture Martha Piper, then-President of the University of British Columbia, delivered, which caused a great buzz and played a major catalytic role in how things unfolded regarding SSHRC's Transformation.

25. Two thousand of these chairs would be established at universities across Canada, with $200,000 annual grants for senior Tier I research chairs and $100,000 for junior Tier II chairs. These chairs were distributed across universities based on

how much external funding—not numbers of grants, but actual dollar totals—
each institution had previously received, and the same allocation formula
was applied within each university to apportion the chairs internally. Thus,
universities and disciplines with a record of attracting large sums of research
funds received the lion's share of the CRCs, while those with just as many grants
but smaller totals received fewer. Because the federal funding envelopes varied
between the CIHR at approximately 40 per cent, NSERC at another 40 per cent,
and SSHRC at the remaining 20 per cent, despite science and humanities faculty
constituting approximately 60 per cent of all university faculty, inequity was built
into the allocation system from the start.

26. This Working Group included the following participants: Benjamin Berger,
Faculty of Law, University of Victoria, the only student member; Daniel Costello,
Executive Assistant to the Minister, Citizenship and Immigration Canada;
Patricia Demers, Vice-President of SSHRC, a professor of English at the University
of Alberta; Linda Hutcheon, President of the Modern Language Association,
a professor of English and the Centre for Comparative Literature, University
of Toronto; Stephen McClatchie, Department of Music, University of Regina;
Doug Owram, Vice-President (Academic), Department of History and Classics,
University of Alberta; and Louise Possant, École des arts visuels et médiatiques,
Université de Montréal.

27. SSHRC has just announced yet another attempt to retool the humanities and
the social sciences. *Briefing on SSHRC's Renewed Program Architecture*, released
in March 2010, proposes to introduce structural changes intended to "reduce
complexity, eliminate overlaps in program objectives, and minimize logistical
barriers for applicants." This new initiative reinforces SSHRC's emphasis
on collaborative research through various "Development," "Partnership,"
and "Outreach" grants. Under its "new program architecture," "all funding
opportunities will fit within three umbrella programs" labelled "Talent,"
designed for graduate students and post-doctoral scholars; "Insight," open to a
wide range of potential applicants, including those from the private and not-for-
profit sectors and the public; and "Connection," intended to support "specific
activities and tools that facilitate the multidirectional flow of knowledge." This
document appeared in the middle of our volume's production, so we are not in
a position to respond to it here. See <http://www.sshrc.ca/site/whatsnew-quoi_
neuf/renewal-renouvellement-eng.aspx>.

ONE

Extraordinary Renditions

TRANSLATING
THE HUMANITIES NOW

L.M. Findlay

WITHIN THE LARGER CONFIGURATION of the human sciences, the humanities remain emphatically text-based and contingently multilingual, offering disciplined access to dead, living, and endangered languages as invaluable cultural archives and communicative tools for groups and individuals. Despite, or perhaps because of, their complex understanding of textuality and orality, the humanities are under constant pressure from the dominant instrumentalities of our time, inside and outside the academy, and inside and outside Canada, to make languages function more simply and economically, both in themselves and in relation to each other. Yet whether they succumb to instrumentalist demands or resist them, the humanities seem too often apologetic or obscurantist in the ways they represent themselves. Their commitment to the processes and products of linguistic communication has not "translated" as readily or as fully as one might expect into understanding of and support for what they do, and this despite more than a decade of concerted pressure and resistance (see L.M. Findlay, "A Way Ahead"). Indeed the humanities remain, it might be said, surprisingly opaque to themselves—both as purveyors of useful knowledge and as pursuers of knowledge for its own sake—and worse than opaque to many of their possible or actual external constituencies (see, e.g., Daniel Tseghay's coverage of the 2007 Congress of the CFHSS in Saskatoon). The humanities need, therefore, to be translated both inside and outside their ever-shrinking or self-instrumentalizing academic domain, and rendered in terms that challenge their own predominantly Eurocentric values and presumptions to engage with those who critique them on the basis of insufficient understanding or ideological antipathy.

THE HUMANITIES AND HUMAN RIGHTS

Here I respond to the question of humanities translatability by attempting a conceptual and communicative "retooling" of this multidisciplinary formation to improve its accessibility, assertiveness, and capacity for critique, but also to defend more effectively its necessary and productive links to indeterminacy. Such retooling presumes that the humanities have already been tooled, and that, to change the metaphor, we have a more or less sound base on which to build new structures and renovate or refurbish those that remain important to our community, our institutions, and our publics. Retooling in this essay will be explored through connecting linguistic or translinguistic renderings to a notion that has emerged during the so-called War on Terror, namely, the outsourcing of interrogation to intelligence-gathering contexts where testimony can be extorted and its validity probed beyond the porous but indispensable safeguards of the Geneva Conventions. This form of gathering and decoding information, already associated with "educational" establishments like the School of the Americas, where some of the most brutal torturers have been trained by United States experts (Gill), is now known by the new euphemism *extraordinary rendition*.[1] It is justified, when admitted to at all, as a necessary operation to safeguard the American homeland. It is an exceptional practice in a time when the power of the dominant to define the state of exception (see Giorgio Agamben on Carl Schmitt) produces a sovereignty eager to eliminate or circumvent all threats to its own authority, including those posed by domestic and international law, but ultimately incapable of doing so—at least not without detection, contestation, and even denunciation (see Grey). Extraordinary rendition expresses authoritarian desire while marking its discursive, legal, and ethical limits. It marks a radical departure from (ordinary) rendition in that it does *not* bring enemies of the state *home* to justice and due process by a process of internationally agreed extradition supplemented by occasional snatches of notorious fugitives like Carlos the Jackal (Grey 221). Instead, outsourcing fuses in extraordinary rendition with the ultraviral. It safeguards the nation only by performing the nation's instabilities and aporias and by contradicting its own identification with and commitment to human rights and the rule of law.

Looking for weak spots in abusive power formations includes, but is not restricted to, scrutinizing the language in which they clad themselves. The detection of such weakness and its vigorous exposure allow humanities disciplines to do what they do best and ought to do more often, namely, reading justly and reading for justice. (If this sounds embarrassingly utopian, you might recall hard-headed legal theorist James Boyd White's work on "Justice as Translation." If you want support for the view that such ethical aspiration is typically Canadian, see Byers.) In pursuing just rendering and just outcomes, the humanities refuse to the powerful the luxury of an unquestionable alibi. In demanding that accountability be at the very least a two-way street, the humanities also confirm their own distinctive role in anything remotely resembling what Pierre Eliot Trudeau (in)famously called "a just society," where difference features as enrichment rather than as contamination or disfigurement. Trudeau's aspirational phrase ought to pester and challenge Canadians still, and Canadian humanists should be busy translating that notion into terms appropriate for a Canada both the same as, and very different from, the country whose mettle Trudeau tested four decades ago.

Alas, today notions of justice are too often reduced to considerations of law and order, to justice as a system for allaying the concerns of the national-security state rather than addressing the needs and concerns of its most vulnerable citizens. For a scholar-activist like Michel Foucault it was all about keeping alive in ever-changing circumstances the capacity for "parrhesia," or fearless speech. For Edward Said, Manning Marable, and others (see L.M. Findlay, "Speaking"), it was about "speaking truth to power" and refusing the tainted privileges of the embedded intellectual or political insider. (For a reaction against some of the self-intoxicating, bourgeois academic vanguardism that sometimes impels those who use such phrases, see Stefan Collini.) For humanist activists in Canada it is a matter of using the tools and topics of our disciplines, especially "culture" and "language" (as in Dorland and Charland), while modifying or exchanging them for others, constantly retooling for critique and challenge. And there is a strong incentive to do this, in that the humanities have already been appropriated by dominant governmental and corporate power formations, and in ways that ought to tell us, if we ever doubted it, that the humanities retain a powerful legitimizing force as well as tremendous capacity for critique. If others think it worthwhile to "snatch" the humanities and then render them extraordinarily in contexts like "military humanism" (Bartholomew and Breakspear 126), for example, or to appropriate cultural or civilizational discourse by recruiting and embedding humanities scholars in government bureaucracies and corporate think tanks, then we ought to return the favour, but in a more critical register.

And there is a second major incentive to retool the humanities; namely, to speak from disciplinary authority under the venerable but fragile aegis of freedom. But how exactly can this be done? The dominant (but by no means universal) ideology of the twenty-first century hitherto has expressed itself through notions that include freedom, pre-emption, terror, and civilization. Much of this is strongly associated with Bush doctrine first codified in September 2002 and vigorously debated ever since.[2] However, the dominant ideology of our times is also inscribed in social and economic relations. The corporatization of political policy, like the corporatization of education policy, shows the derivation of extraordinary rendition from corporate secrecy, corporate espionage, and corporate bribing of officials domestically and transnationally: in other words, extraordinary rendition is a known (or knowable) associate of market rationality, market muscularity or clout, and executive privilege, appurtenances, and outcomes (see Grey 4, 30, 132; and Klein). The allegedly necessary practice of extraordinary rendition derives also from the practice of concealing transactions via the creation of shell companies, in this case airlines working out of a mailbox, rather than transporting suspects via the CIA's Air America and its successors. Extraordinary rendition derives also from the creation of "black sites" that are as elusive and impenetrable as tax havens and actuarial black holes so often secreted both in-house and offshore. This illegal abductive practice tracked so damningly by Stephen Grey, Michael Byers, and Kerry Pither (as well as by the Council of Europe, the legal representatives of those rendered, and human rights activists around the world) derives from the location of production in friendly (i.e., discreet and permissive) jurisdictions, and from the outsourcing that makes dependents and converts of the beneficiaries, serfs and prisoners of the exploited. The militarization of economic production is reflected in the militarization of knowledge through "enhanced interrogation techniques" (Grey 261), while the whole intelligence operation proceeds on the basis of an alarmist imaginary (the War on Terror) whose ability to deceive and conscript owes much to mantras like "Global Competition." In sum, extraordinary rendition is embedded within, yet not fully captured by, First World capital's agenda of deregulation, and Guantanamo Bay now stands as a model maquiladora or free intelligence-enterprise zone. Both the economic and the political agendas require that the rules be followed by others, but not by oneself. "We" ought to be free to do as "we" wish; others ought to be "freed" so as to serve more efficiently the interests of the dominant "we."

But domination always admits or incurs dependencies too. Scripting freedom entails various forms of proscription but also continuous translation, lest it be understood for what it truly is and lose influence on the original of the Other as less dependent on or inferior to its own myth of origins. Extraordinary rendition exploits the hegemony of English but also lives its limitations—and the limitations of Anglocentric technologies such as the portable translation machine known as the "phraseolator" (Price 2). Subjects may be interrogated in the language of ancient liberties and modern economics (i.e., English), but interrogation is also outsourced to those who know the native language and culture of terror suspects. The Other's knowledge is a threat, unless speaking the language of the Other yields the comprador or quisling results desired by the dominant (graphically illustrated in Pither 71). But of course, language acquisition and use, like education more generally, cannot be fully controlled without making its results inadequate or seriously misleading. The unilateral declarative force of a state of exception renders all declarations made by those subject to it suspect at best, the provision of intelligence whose necessary corroboration is, literally, infinitely difficult. Linguistic and humanist indeterminacies can never be made fully subject to American (or similarly imperious) inevitabilities. This irreducible resistance to manipulation is the burden of the humanities and their direct link to human rights today.

T-T-T-T-T-TRANSLATIONS

All translation involves a stammering of sorts, whether as a socially acquired mannerism or as the consequence of an involuntarily embodied impediment to enunciation. Stammering is depleted or deferred yet effortful iteration. And so is translation. Translation is hard work, and even then it can be "good" or "bad." Walter Benjamin uses these judgemental terms in his famous essay of 1923, "The Task of the Translator." There, translation is classified as either a repetition of what we already know, or a replay of what we cannot fully know, or a return to the "mode" (*Form*) of "translatability" as such (the option Benjamin prefers: 70). In Benjamin's account there are cautions and rebuffs aplenty for authoritarian desire, as when he insists that "translations do not so much serve [*dienen*] the [original] work as owe their existence to it" (72). Translation is haunted by the possibilities of purity and totality but remains the record of encounter of two contingent linguistic histories. Its intrinsic incompleteness is an affront to such anti-Terror projects as Total Information Awareness (promoted by Admiral John Poindexter et al. to "counter asymmetric threats" to U.S. security after 9/11, see "Information Awareness Office"), but serves as a trigger for "philosophical genius that is characterized by a yearning for that language which manifests itself in translation" (77). Following Mallarmé, Benjamin suggests languages lack a "supreme one" (*manque la suprême*) while tantalizing would-be supremacists with that very possibility. Consequently, "translation, with its rudiments of such a language, is midway between poetry and doctrine" (77), even, or especially, if the doctrine in question is the binarist and pre-emptive Bush Doctrine.

And if one follows Benjamin's argument, matters get worse for interrogators and propagandists: "it is the task of the translator to *release* in his own language that pure language which is under the *spell* of another, to *liberate* the language *imprisoned* in a work in his recreation of that work" (80; emphasis added). Material and mental control experience limits and frustrations as they attempt to render the language of the Other in their own terms. They may employ the most brutal of tortures in the most sequestered of places, where concentration can be virtually complete and uninterrupted, and either directly or by means of proxies of whom such things are expected, but still "a translation touches the original lightly and only at the infinitely small point of sense, thereupon pursuing its own course according to the laws of fidelity in the freedom of linguistic flux [*nach dem Gesetze der Treue in der Freiheit der Sprachbewegung*]" (80; German 67). The more intense the pursuit of firm and faithful equivalence via translation, the more likely the violation of international law, and the increased appeal of other laws and another fidelity, the fidelity of the Other, "in the freedom of linguistic flux." Extraordinary rendition can accordingly be seen through the prism of Rudolf Pannwitz's *Die Krisis der europäischen Kultur* as cited by Benjamin: "Our translations, even the best ones, proceed from a wrong premise. They want to turn Hindi, Greek, English into German instead of turning German into Hindi, Greek, English" (80). The attempted unidirectionality of dominance is a major mistake, self-impoverishing and ultimately futile.

Benjamin is reflecting on cognitive, linguistic, and political imperialism after a century and more of inquiry and debate in German about how one forms and sustains the linguistic nation. It is a fascinating and pertinent story that might begin with an edgy multiculturalist like Herder sounding just like George W. Bush at his most emphatically paranoid: "*Wer nicht mit mir ist, ist gegen mich.* Barbar und Gehässiger! Fremdling,

Feind!" (Kristmannson 2.115, emphasis in text: *Whoever is not with me is against me*. Barbarian and spiteful one! Foreigner, enemy! See also Kamboureli, *Scandalous* 122–24 on "Herder's Trojan Horse"). The interplay of openness and xenophobia is there too in Herder's admiration of (Ossianic) "translation without an original" (Kristmannson 1.261) as an essential tool of nation-building, and the nationalist contradiction is solved neither by the rise of Humboldtian receptivity nor by the emergence of the modern research university with which Humboldt's name is so closely associated. Here is Schleiermacher writing in the Humboldtian register soon to be ridiculed by Marx and Engels in *The German Ideology* and *The Communist Manifesto*: "Our language can thrive in all its freshness and completely develop its own power only by means of the most many-sided contacts with what is foreign" (qtd. in Bermann and Wood 174). By the time Pannwitz and Benjamin are writing, the political implications of encounter-through-translation have become much more sombre, and they will of course get much worse in the 1930s as German intellectuals work "in the shadow of catastrophe...between apocalypse and enlightenment" (as Rabinbach entitles his book). To be sure, many of the European states involved in nation-building via translation were also, virtually simultaneously, involved in acquiring colonies and empires. It comes as no surprise, then, that humanities disciplines would play a prominent role in justifying a civilizing mission and that they would play an increasing role in decolonizing too. More particularly, just as translation was central to the acquisition of foreign possessions by European states, so it became a crucial instrument of decolonizing projects and of post-colonial scholarship (Brydon, "Canada and Postcolonialism" 54, 76n6; Granqvist).

Therefore, when I speak of translating the humanities now, I am thinking like a decolonizing humanist about the humanities and *their* others, masters, accomplices, and native informants. I am thinking multilingually, historically, philosophically, believing that each of these disciplinary modes poses a special problem for the current hegemony because empathy, memory, and reflection, like education more broadly, can too easily get out of hand and refuse the recipes of alleged affordability and added value that keep so many injustices in place. I am thinking of the United States as a linguistic hyper-nation understood so very differently by Huntington or Boyd White, Rorty or bell hooks. I am thinking also of Canada as a middling linguistic nation realized through the mutual mistranslations and untranslatability of the common law and the civil code (see Dorland and Charland ch. 7), and the shared aversion of both these Euro-Canadian legal traditions to "First Nations jurisprudence" as a key component of the Indigenous humanities (Henderson *First*).

SSHRC'S FIVE-YEAR PLAN AS MISTRANSLATION
AND MILITANT TRANSLATION

So how do the humanities fare in the SSHRC Plan that the Council's new President, Chad Gaffield, is understandably eager to implement (Tamburri)? The Council's attempt to refashion itself into a "value-added knowledge council" by "leveraging opportunities" (*From Granting*, vol. 3, 11) is, at the very least, an attempt to preserve state support for academic work that is arguably as important to the future of Canada as work done under the aegis of the other granting councils. One may perhaps be able to ignore or forgive some of the protective rhetorical colouration in the planning document, especially if one has any experience making arguments for resources, inside or beyond one's home department, when others seem to have already made the more fashionable or practical case. It is only too easy to disparage efforts that do not fit exactly with one's inclinations, needs, or principles. Moreover, a hermeneutics of humanistic suspicion turns only too readily into a hermeneutics of futility or contempt that does little to help an already difficult situation. Having said that, one needs to work with as well as against the Council's efforts to resituate the humanities more centrally, positively, and accessibly in governmental and public understanding. One may feel the need to pursue critique vigorously but to circulate its findings only strategically. And so one may be willing most of the time to go along with the account of peer review as "the international gold standard for judging the quality of research proposals" (*From*

Granting, vol. 3, 7) and with the management-speak in which a good portion of the document is cast. The discourse of "change" is acceptable enough, even though one might wish to quibble with the versions of agency and outcome expressed in an adjacent claim: "Today, after months of campus consultations across the country, the research community is united as never before" (9). Was this true? Is it still the case? How do we know? And how can we tell if the basis of unity is an appropriate or an alarming one, something beyond a willingness to link inquiry to prosperity via a "deep and diverse knowledge base" (10)? The latter phrase sounds well-meaning but odd, a region of great unevenness rather than a natural site for take-offs and landings or the foundation on which new superstructures might be raised.

The desire to inform and persuade the Plan's different target audiences means that textual scholars may have to hold their sophisticated noses and accept awkward combinations of "retooling" and "fine-tuning," acceleration and scope (*From Granting*, vol. 3, 17), and the hyping of the Council relative to its three sister organizations (13). We may even be able with a little coaxing to align ourselves at least some of the time as researchers with the four "key new strategies: clustering research, mobilizing knowledge, connecting people and building tools" (16). However, attempts to recast our usefulness and relevance do occasionally go too far, as, for instance, with the allusion to "the spread of 'freelance' political violence" (16), phrasing whose unexamined individualism cannot be redeemed by the use of scare quotes. The document opens on a promisingly multilateralist note regarding the "religious, economic and political" sources of terrorism, but this comes immediately after a crass claim for "immigrants, Canada's sole source of population growth" (2). If you are a First Nations or Métis person reading this, what are you likely to think? Your growing population is ignored once again, or perhaps accorded only a tacit infantilizing and criminalizing of the growing Aboriginal population. Or maybe Aboriginal people are *not* supposed to be reading the Plan, far less developing the Indigenous humanities in ways I will propose later in this essay.

To keep a critical focus on ourselves as well as SSHRC, but in terms deliberately more provocative than those employed by Diana Brydon to similar ends elsewhere in this volume, I find it useful to think of the planning document as *both* an attempt to render the humanities (and the social sciences) extraordinarily *and* an effort to resist such attempts and the interests they represent. Despite all the talk about consultation, and the new president's determination to move forward "aggressively," the Council might be suggestively construed as a "black site" remote from the academic world, a place where representatives of humanities disciplines shorn of collegial and contractual protections are interrogated coercively in order to yield the message the powerful want to hear, namely that humanists can be broken and remade in the name and image of "the" market and the academy's "new managerialism" (Reed)— and that this is the transformation currently underway. Such a negative interpretation is supported by the fact that business is well represented in SSHRC's document but labour scarcely at all. Moreover, a recurrently apocalyptical tone licenses *dirigiste* translation of humanities values into a dietary supplement for disastrous greed: "to expand the idea of 'return on investment' to include benefits other than mere commercial ones" (*From Granting*, vol. 3, 16). We are presumed by authors of the Five-Year Plan to be entering the action late, as is clear in a section promisingly entitled "Bottom Lines" that rapidly lapses into weak pluralism, failing to mention, never mind embrace, the powerful new accounting practices that link economic to cultural, social, and environmental assessments in the quadruple bottom line. Into a narrowly utilitarian frame we humanists (and social scientists) intrude, armed with nuance and under the aegis of expansion rather than contestation or displacement. This is not the kind of shift from "a politics of representation toward a politics of accountability" for which Diana Brydon has argued compellingly ("Canada and Postcolonialism" 73). It is, rather, the retooling of academic mendicancy to meet the demands of the new usury. My words are harsh, but some of the writing in the Five-Year Plan alienates academics while doing little to placate avaricious instrumentalists eager to advance their own interests in the guise of the public interest. Lots of readers and re-readers of this document experience a sense of violation with which community groups and NGOs are only too familiar. We have to try to pass, but the terms in which we endeavour to do so are provided for us from opaque sources in repugnant mistranslation of our capacities and resolve. Thankfully, this is not the whole story; but it is an alarming part of a tendentious narrative we must not ignore.

SSHRC's Five-Year Plan yields opportunities and obligations as well as threats and challenges from the process of nominal consultation plus extraordinary rendition. In crucial and potentially inspiring respects the document insists not on a flight from accountability into an impenetrable ivory tower, but the doubling of that tower as necessary sanctuary and admonitory inukshuk. SSHRC wants more accountability in order to promote awareness of what the humanities can contribute to national and international problems besetting our species and the life forms and eco-systems with which we share the planet. This is a kind of counter-rendition or militant translation, rendering very public issues into the languages, methodologies, and values of academic disciplines not usually thought of as having research capacities relevant to "the real world." Like parliamentary privilege, academic privilege can and must be understood and exercised as interrogating the assumptions and actions of those who make decisions affecting us all. For too many people, the humanities are "black sites" where arcane texts and questions are tortured at length by largely nameless, faceless experts to yield interpretations of little or no consequence to non-academics. Such sites have to be shifted from obscurity to notoriety, their existence publicized not by reporters following the occasion scandal or controversy spawned by supporters or debunkers of so-called political correctness, but by humanists entering the public fray in ways beyond the narrow understanding of expertise and professional prudence. And the Plan can be read in part as advocating precisely such a plainly interventionist course.

RENDERING THE HUMANITIES EXTRAORDINARILY

Happily, we are not starting from scratch or playing catch-up in all areas of self-transformation. For instance, among the most important recent reflections by Canadian scholars on the future of the humanities is an essay by Imre Szeman in which he concludes as follows:

If the role of the humanities is to explore and to understand the circulation of forms of symbolic and cultural production, if its task is to bring to
the surface of social consciousness normally latent processes that take
place in these forms—and to do so in a critical fashion, rejecting the com-
monplaces of the day—it needs to direct itself to the ways in which the
profound transformation in circulation of culture that we have called globalization *has also been* accompanied by a profound transformation in
culture itself...this is not a demand for that most precious of commodities—a whole new theory of culture—but a suggestion that one way
forward is to reassert or reaffirm those theories that have long drawn
attention to the shape of our ideologies of culture, while also giving up on
the identity of the humanities as the guardian of the good against commodity culture and commodity aesthetics. (176)

This is very good advice for several reasons. First, it refuses to uncouple
the humanities from the present or to make them irretrievably ancillary to what is going on around them. Second, it connects education to
demystification of the dominant and to that unapologetically ambitious
abstraction, "social consciousness." Third, the notion of circulation links
both production and consumption to circuitry whose ownership and
control is a major impediment to humanists getting their versions of "the
word" out to the general public. Fourth, it requires us to act culturally
while we still lack a grand theory of culture itself. And it demands that we
activate the archive of ideological critique while, at the same time, refusing to align ourselves exclusively with the immutable or the unworldly.
Articulating cultural change in tandem with the globalizing reach of
contemporary capital is, for Szeman, a means of returning the humanities to a role that they have, sometimes willingly, sometimes reluctantly,
forsaken. His own practice continually underscores how much can be
learned by rigorous engagement with contemporary commodity culture.
A new generation of humanists like him, and including those working in
the Indigenous humanities and a wave of students anything but apoliti-
cal, could well shape a new humanities worthy of the name.

One of Szeman's more senior collaborators who has for some time
been keeping the long history of decolonizing alive, most prominently

through her indispensable five-volume collection, *Postcolonialism: Critical Concepts in Literary and Cultural Studies* (2000), is Diana Brydon. She is a scholar remarkable for her own willingness and ability to take on some of the most difficult questions she poses for others. Since registering concern that the kind of action I was recommending in my "Always Indigenize!" essay was in reality perhaps too "optimistic," Brydon has herself begun putting the kinds of infrastructure and collaborative capacities in place to move from inventory to transformation. In linking "address" to "redress," and both to culture, globalization, and individual and collective autonomy, she has created a research and pedagogical space where openness is never exhausted, difference is allowed to be difficult, and critique rarely constrained. Her discussion of the new humanities here gives us yet another example of self-critique and self-assertion essential to retooling for accountability. Meanwhile, the reclaiming of citizenship as a humanist site by Smaro Kamboureli, Roy Miki, Daniel Coleman, and the growing cohort attracted to the TransCanada initiative demonstrates that it is not only Alan Cairns and Will Kymlicka and their disciplinary fellows who are worth attending to for understanding of this foundational, formative, and deformative set of legal prescriptions and cultural actualizations. But this willingness to engage with notions like citizenship is about much more than academic market share of a topic both sexy and scary. Indeed, it goes to the heart of post-secondary education and the need to produce a double subject combining economic agency with critical citizenship. The humanities need to change in order to meet that double obligation, but in ways distinct from that "defensiveness or flippancy" (Brydon in this volume) that might well be in evidence every time humanists dare to speak of serious matters like war, or human rights, or justice. When we entitle our work like I have entitled this essay, we had better not be drawing a line in our sandbox but making an intervention that insists on the value of what we know or seek to know, and are eager to share and debate. That insistence can and should bring elements of risk along with the certainty of hostile scrutiny, but who would wish or expect it to be otherwise, given the values beneath values-talk of First World nations committed still to the development of underdevelopment at home and internationally?

As most humanists would probably concede, it is easier to criticize than to propose alternatives and work for their implementation. So, having done my share of criticizing here, I conclude with a schematic, provocative attempt at translation. I suggest that the medieval academic quadrivium of arithmetic, geometry, astronomy, and music have in their current iterations been rendered, more or less extraordinarily, as economics, computer modelling, the militarization of space, and the technologically determined domination of the culture industries. What this does is take traditional number-based disciplines and corporatize them as profit, growth, defence, and distraction. Since numbers are generally aligned with wealth and words with culture, re-inscribing a venerable disciplinary divide, this calls in turn for an anti-corporate update of the medieval academic trivium to give a modern counter to the hegemony of numbers and a reductively singular or weakly plural version of the bottom line. Given the outstripping (and asset stripping) of nations by corporations in many economic and other respects, the anti-corporate can be read as broadly supportive of nation-states. The claim to retool the humanities then becomes a claim to a place in rebuilding the nation and its internationalism within and beyond its bodies politic, and this leads to the socio-historic inflection of the linguistic, and to the Canadian alignment of the trivium's grammar, rhetoric, and logic, with the anti-Eurocentric Indigene,[3] the Anglo-French colonizers, and participants in the immigrant-diaspora, in one possible version of the new humanities.

To this end, I look to a new rendering of the traditional trivium that remains critically logocentric while becoming more robustly culturist and more publicly, continuously committed to the interface between translation and justice, informed not only by the insights of a Benjamin or a Boyd White, but also by the efforts of a young Canadian scholar to demonstrate that a foundational moment in the development of modern politics occurs in Thomas Hobbes's *De Cive* and is "the result of a double translation: on the one hand it is a barbaric appropriation of a foreign term [representation] and on the other, it is a translation of a term from one domain of thinking (aesthetics) to another (politics)" (Panagia 35). A comparably transcultural, transdisciplinary rendition of the humanities now would no doubt create great commotion among humanists, but self-induced turmoil seems preferable to the currently imposed combination of immiseration and complicity. The revitalized trivium I am propos-ing, expressed along the axes of ethnicity and demography, might, like a three-row wampum belt, feature three streams bearing distinctive his-tories, epistemologies, and forms of knowledge-keeping on a common ground. It would re-centre the humanities to meet some of the concerns Marjorie Stone raises in her chapter in this volume; and it would inscribe interdisciplinary collaborative practices at its triple origin and within the ongoing fluency of the three streams of the sustainable nation. It would Indigenize and historicize more plainly and concertedly than SSHRC's Plan does with its focus on immigration as solution and its inspiration by native-newcomer rather than invader-settler discourse. It would pro-ductively, if provocatively, situate the Indigenous humanities in relation to the Euro-Canadian humanities; it would refuse, or at least defuse, the Anglo-French difference in the name of European continuities both heartening and heart-breaking; and it would translate the trope of Can-ada as a nation of immigrants as an immigrant-diasporic component of this larger trivium. To map a trivium such as this onto Canadian in-stitutions might spring difference from the carceral grasp of academic managers and institutional branders who appeal to "diversity" in order too often to advantage wealth-generating activities at the expense of the human sciences in general and the humanities in particular. And that might then give us the old and new tools we need to do the job we would like to do.

NOTES

1. Stephen Grey (133–35) traces the expression back to the 1970s but emphasizes that it has enjoyed a new and more ominous currency since rendition has been uncoupled from abductive "repatriation."

2. The Bush administration's key analyses and remedies appeared in the *National Security Strategy of the United States* (2002). The historical antecedents and main

policies deriving from this doctrine were defended by Robert Kaufman and a host of neo-conservative peers, and ably countered by Chris Dolan and many others. The crucial shift from exemplifying democratic values to forcefully imposing them is well charted by Jonathan Monten. For the contamination of Canadian foreign and domestic policy by Bush doctrine, see the numerous examples in Kerry Pither.

3. The formation of the Indigenous Humanities movement at the University of Saskatchewan has roots in law, literary and cultural studies, education, and art history. The movement features a variety of collaborations across Indigenous/Euro-Canadian knowledge-keeping practices that involve Marie Battiste, Sákéj Henderson, Lynne Bell, Isobel and Len Findlay, and increasing numbers of students. For a sense of what this movement entails in particular disciplinary sites, see, e.g., Isobel Findlay's essay.

TWO

Taking it Personally and Politically

THE CULTURE OF RESEARCH IN CANADA AFTER CULTURAL NATIONALISM

Donna Palmateer Pennee

IN 2004–2005, SSHRC INITIATED consultation exercises with its primary constituency (academic researchers in social science and humanities disciplines in Canadian universities) to inform its "transformation" from a "granting" council to a "knowledge" council. This transformation exercise was initiated under then-President Marc Renaud, whose objective was to double SSHRC's budget to $500 million. During this period, Paul Martin's Liberal federal government, whose track record was generally sympathetic to intellectuals and academics, fell to Stephen Harper's Conservatives. The ambitious increases sought for SSHRC's budget met with a mere $6 million top-up in the first round of budgetary decisions made on an explicitly neo-liberal economic platform for governance ("New SSHRC president's").[1]

While we have no way of knowing whether the Liberals would have doubled the funding sought for SSHRC at that time, Renaud's departure from the Council coincided with an unmistakable chill in the political climate of the day, for though the transformation exercise was explicit in seeking funding to enable Canada's social scientists and humanists to fuel Canada's competitiveness in a globalizing "knowledge economy," the kind of knowledge studied and produced by workers in *les sciences humaines* was not of the sort in which this particular Conservative government was willing to invest. The transformational language of "knowledge council" signalled an explicit attempt to retool these "soft" disciplines for incorporation into Canada's research platform under a neo-liberal state, but, in the new federal order, humanist and social scientist research and knowledge were treated as a drain on the public purse. A transformation from granting council to knowledge council did not entrepreneurs and innovators make, but, on the ground, many academics in disciplines traditionally "other" to business as usual nevertheless felt compelled to be entrepreneurial and innovative: the alternative was to risk no SSHRC funding, demotion (on some campuses and in some departmental cultures) to a teaching stream, and diminished internal credibility in universities pushed toward the corporate turn by the state's retreat from investment in public goods. The transformation exercise, particularly the budget allocated, met with resistance not just from the governmental top down, but from the professoriate ground up, where resistance was significant.

The transformation exercise coincided with shifts in my own place in the academy, from primarily that of a teacher and scholar of Canadian literatures and a researcher studying the role of culture in Canadian foreign and economic policy under globalization, to an associate dean of Arts and Social Sciences, with responsibility for administering Bachelor of Arts curricula at a "comprehensive" mid-size university. At that time, I was also a member of the executive of the CFHSS, which is funded for the most part by, and lobbies on behalf of, both the SSHRC and some seventy scholarly associations representing more than fifty thousand humanists and social scientists in Canada. In these various roles, I heard the aspirations and concerns of faculty colleagues as teachers of curricula, supervisors of graduate students, and researchers in publicly funded universities. I also heard the aspirations and concerns of deans and more senior university administrators to whom I reported and among whom I worked as an associate dean. Faced with fixed tuition fee structures and cuts to operating budgets from public-sector funding, administrators looked to researchers to earn external dollars, and to leverage thereby other monies for operating expenses, infrastructure, and advancement.

Not surprisingly, the exercise at SSHRC was experienced by most colleagues as chillingly parallel to the mid-1990s "restructuring" exercises in universities across the country, where cuts to programs and widespread early-retirement incentives changed the working conditions in post-secondary education in ways not easily forgotten. As such, whether the transformation exercise was meant to achieve the objective of doubling federal investments in our research or not, it served to deepen the cynicism on those campuses where colleagues were already feeling frozen out by shifts in funding envelopes that flowed increasingly toward "entrepreneurial" and "innovative" disciplines, and by the greater (or at least more immediate) capacity for science, business, and technology to access corporate and other private monies. Humanities researchers particularly felt vulnerable, given that new programs at the SSHRC were already tending toward large-scale, collaborative or team-based research, and favouring social science disciplines that could claim more immediate relevance and applicability to solving social and economic problems than humanist disciplines could. Despite the fact that citizen-students vote with their feet in choosing humanities and social sciences (or arts degree programs) more so than the sciences, federal decision-makers budgeted against the aspirations of the sector's "customers."[2]

But I do not wish to get trapped by the too-easy binarism of humanities "loses to" science, or even of humanities "loses to" social science, because while recent and current circumstances *do* in various ways engineer fundable research opportunities towards the social sciences (e.g., cluster grants, university-community collaboration grants) and the natural and engineering sciences (e.g., CFI infrastructure grants and matching corporate and industry funds), "basic" or curiosity-driven research even in the "hard" sciences is at risk. As such, my concern is more directly with these changing governmental determinations of the fiscal and administrative culture for academic labour for everyone, with their re-engineering of the cultures in which university research, teaching, and service take place. I am concerned with the public defunding of the university as a sign of decreased state support for any component of Canada's "social safety net." In the context of the withdrawal of state accountability to a public sphere, and in a context where hospitals are as compelled to turn "corporate" as universities are, when budgets for "student services" on campuses rise while those for library acquisitions decline, and when even small increases to the SSHRC pot are targeted to research proposals in business, finance, and management, I might be forgiven for thinking that the funding for, and therefore the function of, public education and research is morphing towards welfare provision and corporate subsidies. Cynical, eh?

I think there is something specifically national, and felt at a deeply personal level, in the shock and disbelief of many Canadian academics that federal funding is flowing away from the humanities and social sciences. While officers at the SSHRC remain sensitive to calls for sustaining the most typical humanities and social sciences research envelope, the SRG, whose outcomes may not be immediately instrumental, quantifiable, or technology-transferable, the fact remains that re-engineering of relevance and capacity, not disciplinary representativeness, has come to direct governmental spending. Note, for example, the reallocation of funding for the Canada Graduate Scholarships away from the humanities and social sciences, despite the student demographics (cited above). I think there is also something specifically Canadian in the shock and disbelief that provincial funding for universities (from federal transfers) is similarly flowing away from the provision of a liberal education, from a well-rounded (i.e., diversified) academic mission and a replenished professoriate, toward fundraising, data collection, managerialism, and the production of increasingly instrumentalized and narrowed outcomes. I have heard the shock and disbelief pronounced along a continuum of response: angry cynicism, weary skepticism, wary acquiescence, self-protecting compliance, and even coercive advice to others to comply so as not to put the already-compliant at risk. At the more collective level, faculty unions or associations, concerned that profits from the corporate turn be distributed to faculty, may produce unintended consequences for those fellow citizens seeking access to the profession at the entry point of the pay scale, particularly PHDs who may also be racialized, Aboriginal, and/or contractually limited.

The shock and disbelief of which I speak, however they manifest themselves, represent how interpellated teachers and scholars have been by the particular national form of governmental "R&D" programs under which most universities in Canada were created in the 1960s and, until the 1990s, mainly flourished. While both the consultation process and the final report have had their critics, the Massey Commission (1949–1951) played an important role in securing the provision of public funding for universities and cultural production in Canada. In the same period (mid-twentieth century), the Canadian state committed to the provision of federal social security programs—an investment produced in the same spirit and climate as the Massey Commission, with its post–World War II holistic view of the role of the state to counter the re-emergence and acceleration of materialism in the mid-twentieth century. In the aftermath of the Great Depression and war as the stimulus to economic recovery, and in the context of Canada's colonial relation to other imperial powers at the time, the national project was also a *social* and *cultural* security project. This nationalist (or, in administrative terms, federalist) project represented terms for and investment in a social contract for which Canada is still (if erroneously) perceived to be unique; that is, an investment in the collection and redistribution of wealth and opportunity through the provision of accessible education and health care, employment and old age security, and other anchors for a social safety net against both the vagaries of the movement of capital and the resiliency of the principles of capital gain. Not surprisingly, some of the most vocal opponents of the SSHRC transformation exercise that I heard, symptomatic of global trends in relations between governments and academics, came from those colleagues who left U.S. and British Commonwealth academies to come to Canada, in flight from the anti-academic consequences of neo-liberal state engineering of post-secondary education elsewhere.

The retreat of the Canadian state from the provision of social security beyond that assumed necessary against threats to capital accumulation (to person, property, or point of view), is, I think, the source of Canada's professoriate's (and not only humanists') shock and disbelief. The national project under which I had the opportunity (the first in my family) to attend university, and in which I have invested my energies and earned my living as student, teacher, scholar, and administrator, is no longer a project in which the Canadian state seems prepared to invest. Given that the social safety net was a federalist project, this retreat of the state at the national level means that provincial governments and university administrations are increasingly unable (at best) or unwilling (at worst) to continue to invest in the national-and/as-local project. The university, along with the continuum of teaching-research of humanities through university programs and personnel, no longer has the role of contributing to, through benefitting from, social security. The cycle of investment in and profit from post-secondary education, understood as collective and diversified inputs and collective and diverse outcomes, has been broken. It is as if the university is expected to secure direct access to capital for its graduates, as if universities alone were responsible for the production of both the worker *and* the opportunity, a feat that is impossible for any one institution, and especially when the state's project has become the project of subsidizing global capital. Civil servants in education, health, and social agencies might be forgiven for feeling that the state is not with us but against us.

I take this state of affairs (or this monogamous affair of state with capital) personally and politically, just as I take personally and politically the related state actions (at the international level) of withdrawal from the Kyoto Protocol, from the 2009 United Nations World Conference Against Racism, and from other United Nations actions such as the declaration to enshrine rights for Aboriginal peoples. I take personally and politically such actions (at the national level) as the Harper Conservative government's cutting of funds to cultural and equity-seeking groups and the closing of the Law Commission, while extending the "mission" in Afghanistan and cutting corporate and personal taxes. Such actions strike at the heart of my identity (and my local and global identification) as a Canadian citizen; they also strike at the heart of my work as a teacher and scholar of Canadian literatures and cultural analysis, and an administrator of curriculum in a Canadian university. I also take it personally and politically that the position of Canada's Science Advisor has been cut by this same Harper Conservative government. In other words, my personal and political response is not about disciplinary turf, though my reaction, and the reaction of others in the humanities to the fiscal engineering of the culture of research in Canada, and the erosion of state-supported forms of critique and renewal, is, to be sure, explicitly informed by my disciplinary training and location (i.e., by the role of humanities and social sciences in the formation of cultures, of structures of feeling, specific to Canada). Disciplinary inequities do exist, but as academics we need to think and act with the intersectionalist and coalitionist methods developed by anti-racist and decolonizing teachers, scholars, artists, and activists. We need collectively to attend to those particulars that differentiate us while we work to change the conditions we share in post-secondary education at this time. The state's differentiation of us by disciplinary value, and as civil servants in the university sector, may be felt by us personally, but the politicizing of our differences as a consequence of state budgetary decisions and global actions means that the political project of making Canada a truly multiracial, multicultural, socially just, and globally cosmopolitan polity is far from over—even though people continue to come to Canada from elsewhere expecting just such a utopia. Why retreat to the lowest common denominator of global capital when we have this globally recognized but unfinished national project?

Under the cultural nationalism and judicious taxation that produced (relatively) accessible university education in Canada in the second half of the twentieth century, many of us acquired the cultural and social capital to contribute to necessary debates about the nature, value, practice, and artifacts of democracy in a social security state—including debates about the fissures of cultural nationalism in the Massey and subsequent models, whether they be Centennialism, official multiculturalism, or others since then. Through mass (though still not equal) education, we train another generation to carry out those specialized but generalist civic duties that underwrite and arise anew from a liberal arts education, wherever our students find themselves after their university education. But when the mission for higher education is no longer funded as a democratic or a broadly cultural one insofar as the state is concerned, our capacity is diminished to equip subsequent generations—many of whom still want to study and produce culture—with the repertoire and skills to contribute to necessary debates about democracy in a capital security state. Indeed, with federal scrutiny of the activities of "lobby" groups, both the CFHSS and the SSHRC may be at risk, just as the Law Commission proved to be.

Governmental scrutiny under the name of balancing the budget comes with the imperative to produce and behave in certain ways. I have lost count of the number of times I have heard executive heads say some version or other of how insufficiently grateful we are, or have been heard to be by government, for the funds we have received, however diminished. This kind of scrutiny can have its parallel in the university environment where faculty and students can be made to feel reduced to the lowest common denominator of "costs" when revenues for postsecondary education go into decline. In this environment, the culture of research is explicitly and implicitly driven by the twin engines of state-university relations and university-worker relations. In the pages that follow, I simply list some of the effects I have observed on academic labour of the retreat of the state from the public good of funding postsecondary education, effects that signal our collective need to intervene, even as it seems that no one is listening—or willing to hear.

THE 4A SYNDROME

The combined circumstances of new disciplinary targets for the SSHRC funds (e.g., to business-related projects), decreases in funding for operating costs of universities, and increased numbers of grant applications (from our own and other disciplines), have produced increased numbers of grant applications.[3] In the rigorous peer evaluation process, those proposals that score "4" and "4A" are deemed to have proposed research that is worthy of funding. However, a score of "4A" designates those projects that, though worthy, are not funded because the funding in the pot for that particular fiscal year has been used up by the number of applications ranked as "4" (this predicament explains the difference between the "success rate" and the "funding rate" in the SRG statistics). How many times do you need to be told that your proposed research is "good enough but not funded" before you become too demoralized to try again? New faculty are particularly vulnerable here. Deans and vice-presidents of research, compelled to search for alternative sources of revenue as provincial funds decrease or are targeted elsewhere, turn to faculty, especially new faculty, to apply for research funding before they may be ready, which can produce 4A rankings (or worse). (Indeed, money formerly spent on a faculty position or an academic counsellor for those increased numbers of undergraduate students may well be spent on a professional grants officer for the Faculty—usually someone who does not teach, does not sit on academic committees, does not him- or herself apply for grants or conduct research). Pressed too early (in many cases without a sufficient publication record) to apply + reduced or targeted monies in the SRG pot + increased nation-wide competition under the institutional imperative for individuals to alleviate the burden of reduced operating budgets = not surprisingly, many tenure-track faculty who learn cynicism and self-protection very early on, are vocal about not doing service, and either immerse themselves entirely in teaching (to feel useful and valued, but thus also imperil their prospects for tenure), or promise a later commitment to teaching and service—that is, after (if) they publish and secure external research funding. What is the message that we may inadvertently send to our graduate students in this environment? For what may we be "building capacity"?

THE CULT OF CELEBRITY

Faculty of an earlier generation who have secured serial research grants or the more recent large research grants, particularly of the kind that show multiple partners, quantifiable results, and immediate media opportunities, work under a halo of entitlement in the administrative firmament of reward. This is not an ad hominem or ad feminem remark: it is an observation of a relatively recent phenomenon in the workplace, one that demonstrates a hierarchy not unlike that determined by what used to be called class background or class status. The priority assigned to "track record" in grant competitions (i.e., the dissemination of funded research as the major criterion for continued investment) raises questions for those who enter the academy during recessionary times. Even with the provision of the New Scholar category, the 4A syndrome, or lack of (or targeted-to-elsewhere) funding for worthy projects disadvantages those whose projects would in richer and less fiscally-engineered times have ensured a strong foundation for access to continued funding for their career. To be sure, working conditions vary from campus to campus, from department to department, and across faculty ranks (e.g., in access to "start up" and internal travel/research funds, reduced course assignments, protection from service, and so forth for new faculty, all to help them become better competitors for external funding; or in protection from or expectation of service and teaching for those mega-dollar-figure research grant holders whose value lies in part in leveraging more dollars). CRCs also have extraordinary variability in their terms of appointment and working circumstances; that is, having access to research funding and research infrastructure does not necessarily guarantee "freedom" from teaching and service to do research. This perception, however, can contribute to the morale deficit in an already demoralized workplace, where people may also be labouring under a structural deficit (where expenditures exceed revenues in the base budget for fixed operating costs), a situation the implications of which they do not, and have never before had to, understand—but for which we may well (be made to) feel personally and politically accountable.

THE CULTIVATION OF DRONES

In the humanities, the historical and continued norm is unfunded research and the integration of research and teaching (and often service as well), the practices and results of which are not "measurable" in most performance indicator regimes, yet are evidenced in a population of trained professionals across a broad spectrum of employment and other pursuits beyond the academy. Many humanists, when confronted with the imperative to seek external research funding, note that their needs are minimal: time to read, reflect, conduct time-intensive research (more reading and reflecting), and write. Many of the sandwiched generation hired in the 1990s who apprenticed to the academic profession during the mid-90s "restructuring" had little to no access to course or service "relief" or start-up funds; this same generation was drafted into department- and university-wide service when a whole generation of faculty retired. Many people at mid-career are particularly disadvantaged in a research environment where a track record for funding, established early and uninterrupted, is ipso facto taken as a record of quality of proposed work. This same track record is imperative to secure funding for leave time (RTS) or research assistance to continue with teaching and service. Those faculty who do secure grants but whose research-funded record may be insufficient for their project to rank at the very top of the competition (where RTSs "relieve" researchers from prep, teaching, and marking time), are nevertheless subject to the same expectations of returns-on-investment as those grant holders *with* RTSs, even though their labour situation during the grant period is significantly different. (RTSs are funded jointly by the SSHRC and by deans of those faculties where research holders reside; interestingly, as of fall 2009, RTSs will no longer be funded by the Knowledge Council).

Details of variability in working circumstances signal that different university administrations respond differently to the underfunding of post-secondary education and the withdrawal of the social security state, but most of them, subject to reduced government monies and increased expectations, seem to require faculty to teach more students (in a false economy of attracting small guaranteed provincial funds at the huge cost of a morale deficit for students and faculty alike); to acquire more external funding (in a false economy of attracting what in the corporate world would be only modest sums, and in the university world is never enough to cover the losses in the classroom or in informed membership on supervisory and other committees); and to take on more internal service to administer working conditions under these reduced circumstances —all in a race to show preparedness for monies that *might* flow to post-secondary education. That hoped-for flow also depends now on meeting the terms of a "quality" agenda, one measure of which is faculty-student ratio....(Recent experience in Ontario shows that while the university must be accountable for the monies it receives, the government is not accountable for flowing even reduced monies to university budgets within an annual cycle.)[4]

THE EROSION OF CURRICULA AND HABITS OF MIND

More deleterious for the culture of research over time are the effects of underfunding on curricula, and thus the effects of underfunding on subsequent generations of academics, other professionals, and citizens in general who are trained in university environments, whatever their destination. (Often) well-meaning administrators faced with budget cuts have to figure out how to teach more students with fewer faculty and fewer resources of other sorts; rather than be shut down or told what to teach, we engage in curriculum restructuring and pretend that we are still somehow self-regulating, but at enormous cost. One cost takes the form of students who are less and less academically prepared to enter graduate programs, but who are nevertheless given offers to enrol in growing numbers, in a bid to bring in the most recent version of "guaranteed" (but in real overall terms, diminished) operating funds. These students require remedial teaching and increased supervision and generate other forms of make-work for faculty and staff, but these are also the same students who will be scrutinized, and departments penalized, if they do not race to complete a degree within the few semesters of funding allotted. Curriculum deficits (themselves produced by funding deficits) produce this preparedness deficit, which in turn leads to deficits in other areas of the academic workplace (e.g., in the quality and capacity for undergraduate teaching, service, scholarship, and morale). Curriculum deficits also produce longer-term intellectual and productivity deficits: in the narrowing of the kinds of questions that student-citizens will ask, in the diminishing of the capacity to recognize a problem in all its complexity, and in the wherewithal to eschew the expedient solution.

These are losses of habits of mind through which creative linkages can be made. These are losses of the socially-responsible motivation to raise informed objections; these are losses of the courage and faith it takes to expect challenges and pleasures from informed participation in collective decision-making; these are losses of the willingness to reap and reinvest the profits of creativity, pleasure, challenge, and informed participation within and across our various communities. These deficits, which are deficits of habits of mind, are already so engrained that unprepared (but deficit-trained) new faculty sometimes reproduce deficits in the academic workplace: "mentoring," for example, so easily fits an outcomes-based measurement that closely resembles the undergraduate's expectation that the payment of tuition will equal a particular outcome. In other words, the erosion of curricula as a consequence of defunding also erodes morale, competence, comprehension, and commitment in the academic workplace and in those workplaces and life-spaces outfitted in significant part by university-educated minds. Cumulatively, these become personal and political costs: the demise of community and a sense of purpose, of self-worth and disciplinary worth, of institutional relevance—these are real costs of prolonged budget cuts for students, faculty, and other citizens alike, real costs of the withdrawal of the social-security state.

"NEVER APOLOGIZE, NEVER EXPLAIN?"
"ALWAYS APOLOGIZE, NEVER COMPLAIN!"

Have you been told lately by your local department chair, dean, provost, or president, "Stop whining?" On some campuses, this is the only form of transparency on offer. Good Subjects are those who internalize the imperative to "be entrepreneurial," to "get with the program," to be silenced by the reminder that their salary and benefits constitute the bulk of university "expenses," to know in advance that, despite increasing enrollments, "there won't be money for new faculty positions so don't ask for them." Bad Subjects are those who just don't get it: who just can't seem to grasp that it's the way of the twenty-first century to expect taxpayers to invest in their own particular and immediate futures, to be free from investing in long-term and public ventures, and that it's the role of government to eliminate barriers to such freedom. In a conversation with a vice-president (research) (not at my home university) who noted the poor "performance" of an Arts and Humanities Faculty in the latest round of tri-council funding (i.e., by comparison to numbers of grants awarded to other Faculties on his campus), I pointed out that not only were there increased numbers of applicants for the same amount of funds but that structural changes in the SSHRC program roster also had a bearing on access and thus on success rate: that is, new envelopes for applications and new committees for adjudication of a wider array of proposals together means new competitors for those same or not-proportionally-increased funds. I also noted that the only new funds recently added to the SSHRC pot were explicitly targeted to business, finance, and management, or "business-related" proposals. For these observations, I was asked in mocking tones, "Why so defensive?" I answered in all seriousness, "Why construe analysis as defensiveness?"

WHAT (?) NEXT?

Readers may be wondering why this nostalgia for the good old days that weren't so good (or so old), why this loyalty to a national project that never was, or why this lament for a national project at all in these heady days of internationalism and the globalization of post-secondary education. Let me be clear: loyalty to an ethos of social welfare produced for, and productive of, a geopolitically defined citizenry is not the same thing as an unquestioning patriotism, nor is it nostalgic or elegiac to wonder when and why the social contract expired, or to want to assess, by contextualizing and historicizing, the damage between then and now. To continue "riffing" off the phrases and strategies of feminisms (the personal is the political, and the political is the personal), I think it's time to take back the nation, and to take back the university as a necessary means to that end.[5]

At the very least, I think it is time to understand anew what the philosophical role of a commission, such as Massey's, was after World War II, and to formulate what might be advocated in the Canadian post-secondary context in the Post-9/11 World War and the emergence of a wholly different security state. After all, Canada's report of the *Royal Commission on National Development in the Arts, Letters and Sciences* (1951) warned of the engineering of research and learning opportunities away from the humanities (e.g., 162, 358), of harm to curiosity or creativity-driven scholarship in the sciences (165–66, 168), of the deadly combination of limited funds and demand for rapid results (177), of how "in 1949–50...for every thousand dollars given to the universities for research, three hundred must be found from their own resources" (136), and so on. All of these citations, from more than half a century ago, sound absolutely familiar, and yet to speak, as I did in 1999 (in an analysis of the role of "culture" in federal foreign policy), of a strategic use for government funding of culture as security seems as remote now as the phrase "R&D" or the possibility of "job security" or a "social safety net" in 2009.

That the shelf life of such terms and possibilities should so quickly have expired speaks to what I believe is our most pressing infrastructural (and personal and political) need: time. Too much of our time is being diverted to survival of a few under terms that misconstrue accounting and accountability. Too much time is spent on managing a system that was intended to democratize education, too little time to ask what that might mean now or how to bring it about in future. Accessibility is narrowly construed as a financial concern when it is also an intellectual and a political concern. When universities are spending most of their time on exercises for measuring "quality" in increasingly constrained ways under increasingly constrained circumstances, are they still universities?

Those who are not listening carefully may hear university workers to be saying that we do not want to be accountable or do not want to be evaluated. As in every workplace, no doubt a few such folks can be found. But as Bill Readings said in the 1990s, "Arguing against the use of... standardized forms does not mean resisting the question of evaluation, merely the refusal to believe that the question of quality in education is susceptible to statistical calculation" (131). We need to reclaim the right and the responsibility to evaluate and to expect accountability from our employers, broadly understood. To the question of "quality," then, those of us engaged in the culture of post-secondary education and research need to respond with the question of the function of education, and to forge both new allies and new means (some of which may be old, but will be new in the event of their return) for answering that question. One of those functions of post-secondary education must be (Readings again) to "raise the question of accountability as something that *exceeds* the logic of accounting" (164).

But the question of the function of education needs to be formulated, and answers developed, by and for all of us in the academy, not just by and for those in the humanities and the social sciences. Researchers and teachers in all disciplines and fields need to know about each other's circumstances and particularities, to respect and appreciate our differences, while convening—to intervene—in the engineering of value for university-based cultures of research. People outside the academy need to hear not just what it is that we do, but the circumstances under which we make the attempt, and why. We have ready access to many of those people from "outside" in our classrooms: we need to teach, and to engage our students in research on the histories of higher education in Canada, so that they understand the circumstances under which they study, and help to shape the futures of education for themselves and others. Our students need to take it personally and politically, too.

NOTES

1.   Searching SSHRC's website for information about "transformation" and the "knowledge council" will yield, for non-Canadian academic colleagues and non-academic citizens alike, some of the history abbreviated here. See <http://www.sshrc.ca>.

2.   In 1999, Marc Renaud reported that "45 per cent of university faculty in Canada are getting only 11.6 per cent of public research funding" (qtd. in Whitton). In 2003–2004, Doug Owram, then-President of the CFHSS, reported that "69% of all undergraduates (81,000 students) and 67% of all graduate students (17,400) earn degrees in the humanities and social sciences," and "18,000 (53%) of all full-time faculty in universities are in the human sciences," but SSHRC's proportion

of research funding was only "11.2%" of the federal research funding available. At that time, 60% of the Canada Graduate Scholarships funding was allocated to humanities and social sciences disciplines (see"Bulletin," 20 February 2003, at <http://www.fedcan.ca/images/File/PDF/Federal%20Budget%20Previous%20 Years/budgetbulletin-e.pdf>). In the 2007 Federal Budget, while SSHRC received an increase of $11 million in funding (up from $5 million in 2005), the increase was targeted to business, management, and finance. In the same budget, of the very welcome increase of 1,000 new Canada Graduate Scholarships, 40% were allocated to NSERC, 40% to the CIHR, and only 20% to SSHRC (cited in "Bulletin," 19 March 2007, at <http://www.fedcan.ca/ftpFiles/documents/Budget_mar07.pdf>.)

3. A quick glance at the database for SRGs, accessible through the SSHRC website, demonstrates, for example, that: in 1995–1996, there were 16 committees (organized by disciplines and combinations of disciplines) and a total of 1,566 applications, of which 501 were funded; in 2000–2001, 17 committees adjudicated 1,542 applications, of which 642 were funded; in 2005–2006, 26 committees adjudicated 2,447 applications of which 981 were funded; in 2009–2010, 29 committees adjudicated 2,880 applications of which 941 were funded. For the last three periods on this list (2000–2001, 2005–2006, and 2009–2010), the success rate of applications (i.e., applications that were ranked fundable) was 41.6%, 40.1%, and 32.7% respectively. For the same competitions, the funding rate was 33.2%, 28.9%, and 22.2% respectively. New disciplines for eligibility during this same period, and/or accounted for under new (additional) committee structures, include Health Studies, Law, Accounting, Human Resources Management, and Business. For year-by-year data and these shifting disciplinary and other parameters, see <http://www.sshrc.ca/site/about-crsh/stats-statistiques/ tables-tableaux-eng.aspx>.

4. See the Council of Ontario Universities website <http://www.cou.on.ca/>.

5. See Giroux and Searls Giroux on the U.S. context.

THREE

Mining the Valley of Its Making

CULTURE AND KNOWLEDGE
AS MARKET COMMODITIES IN
HUMANITIES RESEARCH

Kit Dobson

WHAT DOES KNOWLEDGE DO? What is its purpose? Recent shifts in research in the human sciences, signalled by, among other things, the terminological shift from the "humanities" to the "human sciences," beg the question of the value of knowledge. The transformation of SSHRC, the primary Canadian funding body of such research, into what SSHRC terms a "value-added knowledge council" (*Knowledge Council* 25) is just one notable example. In the arts, both the targets and products of research can be seen as knowledge, for researchers do not merely produce knowledge; they sift through and analyze pre-existing products of knowledge to gain new ends. As a result, changing notions of what knowledge might be and how it operates directly affect both materials of inquiry and research outcomes—how these materials are regarded and analyzed, as well as their social valence.[1] The value of knowledge, therefore, and what it entails, is key to both the inputs and outputs of research in the human sciences. But how is "value" to be added to knowledge? And what does value mean in this context?

The SSHRC mandate, expressed in its strategic plan for 2006–2011, suggests that the value of knowledge lies in its social applicability, in its ability to connect citizens to one another and generate projects of ethical nation-building—what SSHRC calls the ability of research to "provide the understanding to build a truly successful, resilient, modern society" (*Knowledge Council* 7). In doing so, SSHRC asks that research be mobilized towards specific ends. I am not opposed to the applicability of knowledge; however, I do question the ways in which applicability is defined by SSHRC. As became apparent during the consultation process that SSHRC initiated in order to formulate its new mandate, SSHRC sought to promote a utilitarian concept of knowledge founded in applicability, a privileging strategy that could presumably prevent non-utilitarian forms of research from taking place or being funded. My primary concern is for research that falls outside the economic indicators with which applicability and development are often measured, especially anti-capitalist work; but this concern extends to traditional modes of research in the human sciences, such as historical textual scholarship and other modes that do not connect easily with the broader public. Pushing research toward adopting management models, SSHRC states that Canada is "in dire need of advanced humanistic and social scientific knowledge to manage our affairs in an increasingly complex and unpredictable world" (2). SSHRC is explicit, moreover, in stating that research must "invigorate the economy" (9). In this process of rerouting the function of knowledge, its use value risks becoming its exchange value (its economic benefit), perhaps a familiar turn that parallels some of the analyses of mass culture undertaken by the Frankfurt School of criticism. The extent to which knowledge can be applied to achieve a social good defined in developmental and economic terms is now set to become one of the key arbiters of fundability that SSHRC asks its adjudicators to consider.

This essay seeks to track the conceptual shifts underlying the notion of value operating in these recent changes to the ways knowledge and culture are deployed in Canada. Julia Kristeva has recently argued "for the reconstructive role that the humanities can play in the highly threatened social and political" contemporary world, a role that is played out through the expression of ideas (18). I worry that, today, the available scope of expressible ideas is being restricted by the increased application of a strictly economic model to culture. This essay, then, advocates the retention of a notion of value for knowledge and culture that exceeds that of mere exchange value. It does so as a means to ensure the continued relative autonomy of research in the human sciences. More specifically, assuming that there is more to research than economic and developmental applicability, it argues that there are more ends to research than the perpetuation of capitalism.

My own investment in these arguments comes from my still-recent and ongoing interaction with SSHRC. As a doctoral student at the University of Toronto (2002–2006), I was successful in gaining a SSHRC Doctoral Fellowship in my first year, one year prior to the introduction of SSHRC's more lucrative Canada Graduate Scholarship program. Midway through that year, discussions about the SSHRC transformation became a topic of general concern, and SSHRC representatives visited the university to discuss the proposed changes; I followed these talks with interest. It seemed to me that the Council's consultation process was already having an impact on the projects that were being funded, and I found myself, somewhat uneasily, allied with the new knowledge council's quest to "build understanding." Given the focus on research applicability in SSHRC's "Transformation," I became concerned that my own research was being valued for the manner in which it might be seen as developmentally useful—a form of utility that, to my mind, risks reducing the multiplicity of human struggles to an ultimately economic field. Given my leftist position and my research examining the transition from nationalism-as-radicalism in 1960s Canadian literature to the move away from these nationalist models of resistance in the contemporary era of global capitalism in Canada, such a direct form of applicability was, I felt, an uneasy match with my personal research goals.

The tensions, however, have not yet been irreconcilable; quite the reverse, they have been a source of productivity. But I do remain concerned. My research as a post-doctoral fellow, conducted under the aegis of SSHRC, and now as a junior faculty member, has focussed on the interactions taking place between federal arts funding initiatives and international trade agreements, looking at the outcomes of both for cultural workers. I am interested in the ways in which markets impact upon the cultural forms that literary critics analyze, as we often assume an alarming level of transparency between the process of artistic creation and the texts that we receive and analyze. My position is that such an assumption is naive in the current climate, in which economics—from funding sources to publishers—increasingly determine what can be produced and made available for general consumption. We need, increasingly, to step behind the book or cultural work and look for the ideologies that inform its very creation in material ways. The question of value—what literary value might be, and how it relates to economic value—is crucial in conducting this research. SSHRC, it seems to me, is also prompting a discussion of this question through its recent shifts.

My critique here is certainly aligned with SSHRC's goal of creating human sciences research that fosters policy development—in this case, perhaps SSHRC's own. For a start, SSHRC's policies are the necessary starting point for questioning value and how it is being rewritten in contemporary Canada. The arts are often considered (either negatively or positively) to be a bastion that stands against direct market applicability and economics—against usefulness, as Oscar Wilde maintained, or to mislead and deceive people, as Plato had it. Researchers will likely, even if reluctantly, situate the arts somewhere along this spectrum. This sensibility is expressed at its strongest in W.H. Auden's "In Memory of W.B. Yeats," to which I returned recently when teaching Richard Powers' 2000 novel, *Plowing the Dark*. Auden's line, "poetry makes nothing happen," so often invoked out of context, animates Powers' novel in its ongoing debate about the function of art in society. Auden's line is, of course, highly ambiguous, and is only made somewhat clearer when read in its immediate context; I quote it here because it points toward the problem that I am highlighting about transforming the abstract use value of culture/knowledge into an economic form. The stanza reads:

You [Yeats] were silly like us; your gift survived it all:
The parish of rich women, physical decay,
Yourself. Mad Ireland hurt you into poetry.
Now Ireland has her madness and her weather still,
For poetry makes nothing happen: it survives
In the valley of its making where executives
Would never want to tamper, flows on south

From ranches of isolation and the busy griefs,

Raw towns that we believe and die in; it survives,

A way of happening, a mouth. (248)

The immediate focus is Yeats' Irish nationalism, his ambitions for liberation from the English that are expressed in his own poetry, albeit with
reservations and mourning about the losses of a romanticized historical
Ireland. Auden alludes to the continuing oppression of the Irish, moving
on to his seeming dismissal of poetry. But this dismissal is also a positive valorization, in the several senses that critics have noted, from the
positive value of literally making "nothing happen"—as opposed to the
violence of those who would make things happen—to the exemption
of poetry from the world of the executives, surviving as an autonomous
way of being, an autonomy that may be increasingly difficult to locate. To
my mind, even being useless, in a Wildean sense, is useful in many ways.
Just not the ways that Auden's executives might like.

In Richard Powers' *Plowing the Dark*, Auden is repeatedly invoked
about the purpose and function of art. The novel is complex, but re-
volves in part around the character Adie Klarpol, a once-promising but
failed New York artist who recovers her inspiration while working for
an experimental virtual reality (VR) project in Seattle called The Cavern, in allusion to Plato's allegory in *The Republic*. The VR world is hailed
as the new space for creation, as the replacement of the traditional arts,
and as the breakdown of mimesis. But Adie is horrified to discover the
potential function of her new-found artistic medium at its public unveil-
ing: the prime investors turn out to be military contractors, interested
in developing VR for combat-training simulation programs. The novel's
conclusion seems to be that the independent arts risk disappearing in
the contemporary world of late capitalism. Adie's return to beauty and
the sublime, which has reanimated her spirit while she paints her three-
dimensional scenes in The Cavern, goes awry, and she destroys the work
that she has done. Whether the destruction of the art is a good or bad
thing, however, remains ambivalent. The novel calls art "that supreme,
useless, self-indulgent escapism" (398); art is said to contain "no formal
knowledge about the world," and is therefore not "capable of teaching"

(165). Powers queries the social responsibility of art, finding it often at fault and only capable of providing entertaining distraction, as it does for the character Taimur Martin who, in a parallel narrative, sustains himself while imprisoned in Beirut by reading the Koran, a reading that "tame[s] the abyss" (323). This use for art is shown to be worthwhile unto itself, as it keeps Martin sane in prison. The absorption of the arts into the market and the destruction of their autonomy, however, present Powers with a nightmarish future orbiting around the poles of senseless diversion and corporate militarism. My students were puzzled by Powers' artistic recourse to such a negative argument in a novel—a piece of art itself—and we spent a great deal of class time attempting to recuperate the arts from Powers' reduction of them to mere diversions or market commodities, a difficult task to achieve. Poetry, it seems, does have the potential to make things happen, as Auden's executives mine the valley of its making for military or propagandistic applications, for the ways in which it might mobilize citizens toward coercive ends—such as through advertising, Adie Klarpol's fall-back profession in *Plowing the Dark*.

This shift toward deliberately and directly making economic and developmental things happen as a result of poetry and, more generally, culture, the arts, and knowledge, is apparent in the changing climate in arts communities. These communities appear now routinely to capitulate to what George Yudíce terms "expediency." He defines the shift toward expediency as the process through which "the role of culture has expanded in an unprecedented way into the political and economic at the same time that conventional notions of culture...have [largely] been emptied out" because culture can be shown to be efficient in managing political and economic problems (9). Culture as an expedient to achieve development, Yudíce argues, has "displaced or absorbed other understandings of culture" (1) as culture becomes "a pretext for sociopolitical amelioration and economic growth" according to hegemonic Western capitalist norms (10). Culture is mobilized as a resource, used to manage differences, to create economically sound communities, and to foster the global interaction of citizens. His own investigation of the eclipsing of other views of culture by the culture-as-resource management model, Yudíce notes, signals a "caution regarding the celebration of cultural agency" (2). That is, the human sciences' and cultural studies' tendency to celebrate the arts' ability to provide autonomy or agency is seriously compromised when culture becomes the means through which societies are managed. The utility of cultural knowledge for many funding bodies and management groups today, then, is that it can be mobilized toward economic ends and thus become a value that eclipses other values. This process is worrying, Yudíce argues, because it involves "the conversion of nonmarket activity to market activity" (15); culture thereby becomes increasingly complicit with the expansion of the capitalist framework into new corners of the globe, further eliminating the possibility of any outside to economics (an "outside" that sounds increasingly romantic in our contemporary world). In this mobilizing process, culture may be used to bring about developmental ends with which we agree, but the evacuation of other uses of culture should pose serious questions for researchers.

Such an expedient argument for economic development is being called for increasingly by the funding bodies of cultural projects, as Yudíce notes of the World Bank, which has stated that "physical and expressive culture is an undervalued resource in developing countries" (Yudíce 13; World Bank 11). Further, the World Bank states, part of the challenge facing the world "is to analyze the local and national returns on investments which restore and draw value from cultural heritage" (Yudíce 13; World Bank 13). Similarly, the Canada Council's website section on advocacy for the arts quotes the following statement from the Canadian Chamber of Commerce as evidence for the usefulness of the arts:

> social value is created when resources are devoted to generate improvements in the lives of individuals or society as a whole. Thus, investment in the arts generates results with high intrinsic value, that is, a social return on investment that is not easily quantifiable. Quality of life issues are enormously important to business throughout the Provinces in order to attract and retain employees and their families to live and work in our communities. This factor is just as critical for a small mill town as it is for a big city competing for major head office reallocations. Families want to stay in communities that are rich and diverse with significant opportunities for personal development, including music, dance, drama, and visual arts.

So while the outcomes of cultural investment may be difficult to quantify, the Chamber of Commerce, along with the Canada Council, evinces a belief in the arts because they are connected in some way with economic development. Tyler Cowen, in his recent study of American Arts funding, cautions that making such an argument of expediency or efficiency in developmental terms is problematic, because it demands that we analyze the efficiency of the arts in spurring development at par with other such modes. "Social benefits are not unique to the arts," however, Cowen notes (15). He suggests that such economic arguments ultimately undermine the arts, as it is difficult to argue for investment in the arts in the face of economic indicators demonstrating that investing elsewhere can clearly contribute more to the survival of the poor or otherwise disadvantaged.

The Canada Council makes its case nevertheless, citing the arts as an efficient means of creating diversity and fostering productive forms of difference. Yudíce suggests that by exploiting local knowledges and cultures in the service of development, "artistic trends such as multiculturalism that emphasize social justice...and initiatives to promote sociopolitical and economic utility have been fused into the...'cultural economy'" (16). In Canada, these trends seem to mesh closely with government funding policies—multiculturalism being perhaps the most obvious Canadian example that has had an impact on how bodies like the Canada Council distribute funds—as the arts are mobilized to bolster specific state purposes. Yudíce argues that "representations of and claims to cultural difference are expedient insofar as they multiply commodities and empower community" (25); there is thus a resulting "rapprochement between consumer capitalism and multiculturalism" (161). Applying this argument wholesale to Canadian multiculturalism might seem unduly harsh, as it can be distinguished from, for example, the American model thereof (see Weisman), which is the basis of Yudíce's argument. But the reservations expressed by theorists such as Himani Bannerji about multiculturalism suggest that such a dubious assessment may not be entirely unfair. Bannerji argues that, as a state-sanctioned form, multiculturalism can be a means of "constructing 'the woman of colour'" from the outside, according to the pre-existing norms of the white nation (28), or a means to ensure sameness and compliance through legislating difference. Deploying culture as a resource within the capitalist state may render it little more than a means of decorating the landscape with diverse forms of diversion. The aesthetic function of knowledge may increasingly be to create happy and therefore economically productive consumers.

We have, according to Jeremy Rifkin, entered an age of "cultural capitalism" (7), in which access to cultural commodities defines our being. It is not surprising, then, that in this climate both SSHRC and the federal government talk about entering the "knowledge economy."[2] In this shifting economy, property is increasingly devalued in favour of access to cultural commodities. In other words, goods decline in value, while culture itself, in all of its diversity, is progressively commodified. For Rifkin, "cultural production represents the final stage of the capitalist way of life" (8), the final inclusion of all aspects of living within the economy, signalling an end to any form of "outside." Resistance movements, in this era, simply become part of the system, a shift epitomized for Joseph Heath and Andrew Potter by Vancouver-based "culture jamming" magazine *Adbusters*' 2003 decision to start selling branded anti-brand shoes in opposition to Nike's pervasive saturation of the market with sweatshop-produced footwear. For Heath and Potter, "countercultural politics" have been among the "primary forces driving consumer capitalism for the past forty years" (2). Cultural values become a component of the capitalist forces that they themselves may contest as they are commodified. The selling of anti-capitalist counterculture, Heath and Potter suggest, demonstrates the totality of contemporary capitalist space through what they term "the rebel sell," the commercialized field of action in which people are, as per the Beastie Boys, merely "fighting for their right to party" (322). The basic value of cultural knowledge to proponents of this era lies precisely in its marketability, in its ability to expend social energies in ways that are contained by the logic of the system and to direct impulses for change into channels that reinforce a diverse yet unified society under capitalism.

The economic rationalization of cultural knowledge therefore curtails the concept of value. Indeed, the value of knowledge was a recurrent topic in the SSHRC transformation discussions and runs parallel to the broader discussion. In the classic Marxist formulation, value is characterized by the modifiers *surplus, use,* and *exchange. Use value* denotes what value a commodity has once owned, while *exchange value* consists of a commodity's value as it is represented in the process of exchange. In Marx's model of industrial capitalism, labour is used in order to create a commodity that contains more exchange value than the exchange value of the labour itself, a commodity's surplus value. These processes, despite their seeming rationality, ultimately contain a modicum of arbitrariness, just as representational or signifying processes can be said to be arbitrary in the field of linguistics. Marx states that "when commodities are in the relation of exchange, their exchange-value manifests itself as something totally independent of their use-value....The common factor in the exchange relation, or in the exchange-value of the commodity, is... its value. The progress of the investigation will lead us back to exchange-value as the necessary mode of expression, or form of appearance, of value" (*Capital* 128). Exchange value is the symbolic representation of use value, a form of value that is quantifiable to the extent that the commodity provides a return to its purchaser. Art has, traditionally, been seen as exceeding this model. Its use value remains ephemeral; the surplus value that the artist's labour creates can be expressed as exchange value, but the correlation between labour and exchange value is highly arbitrary, and the use to which art can be put has been described as non-existent (Powers' "useless"). Marx attempts to measure use value "by means of the 'value-forming substance,' the labour, contained in the article," as "measured by its duration" (129), but the exchange value of the labour involved in creating a cultural work may not be reducible to the scale of wage labour.

Traditionally, and in the place of economic methods of ascribing value, art and cultural forms have been granted aesthetic value, which reduces art's counter-economic (or counter-capitalist) value to an oppositional notion of beauty that can be ascribed social worth beyond the forms of value ascribed to the commodity. However, in the belated recognition that their supposed universality is culturally determined by usually Euro-Western values, the deconstruction of dominant aesthetics means that decreasing numbers of researchers in the human sciences are inclined to position a resistance to economic measurements of culture through aesthetics, despite a recent softening in the tone of the "theory" that opposes aestheticism (as in Elaine Scarry's *On Beauty and Being Just*, inter alia). Alternatively, as I have suggested above, aestheticism may now be merely deployed toward creating a vibrant and pleasingly diverse world; as in the Chamber of Commerce's statement, aesthetics in art are still economically useful, a point that deconstructs the traditional divide of business and culture. Alternative aesthetics, such as feminist aesthetics, may promise social change, but the ready risk of their economic appropriation no longer renders the aesthetic a site of viable resistance. In the wake of aesthetics, or in its commodification, the model of the commodity exchange increasingly adheres to culture as it comes to be produced in a cultural economy. We have, then, to work through questions of value and use, rather than deflect them by defending the aesthetic.

But this dyad of aestheticism versus commodification is too easy—a formulation that assumes too much about how the concept of use value relates to culture and the exchange process. SSHRC suggests as much, for it acknowledges some of the problems of its mandate when it states that we need to think about other ways of finding value: "the challenge for the social sciences and humanities is to expand the idea of 'return on investment' to include benefits other than mere commercial ones" (*Knowledge Council* 12). Adorno, in his arguments about the culture industry, inaugurates the argument that mass culture leads to the eclipsing of use value by exchange value through the fetishization of the commodity and the commodification of art, but his response to this has been largely read as a romanticized defence of high culture. Though Adorno's critique strikes me as problematic, his notions of value are worth paying closer attention to, as his opposition of asceticism to aestheticism disrupts his basic equation of the non-commercial value of art with aesthetics. He argues in "On the Fetish Character in Music and the Regression of Listening" that asceticism suggests the negative manner in which autonomous art forms point toward the potential for pleasure by indicating its absence: "if asceticism once struck down the claims of the aesthetic in a reactionary way, it has today become the sign of an advanced art....Art records negatively just that possibility of happiness which the only partially positive anticipation of happiness ruinously confronts today" (33). Mass culture, in its promise of easy happiness through consumption, fails to live up to its promises, while what Adorno sees as "true" art, by recording the absence of happiness through asceticism, may provide a route toward it that aestheticism no longer can. Therein it has a social use that is neither a part of aesthetics, nor a part of the exchange relation.

Within this space, Adorno suggests, it might be possible to claim a value for art that goes beyond both the exchange process and aesthetics. Although his opposition between high art and mass culture is deeply problematic and unstable, the introduction of a third term into the possible range of values for art—aesthetics, ascetics, and exchange—might allow us to think about a space for art to retain a function that escapes the system of exchange without relying upon (readily commodifiable) aestheticism. That said, in a later essay, "Culture and Administration," Adorno recognizes that "the useful...is nothing immediate, existing for its own sake, but rather that within which the total system has its eye directed towards profit" (114). If use can be found in art, Adorno suggests, it can then be reified. The indication of pleasure through absence, for instance, can still be part of a work of art that is exchanged in order to produce value in society. Moreover, if that notion of happiness can be channelled toward specific ends, the function of serving capitalism in the cultural work itself might still be achieved. Asceticism or negativity, while promising a form of use outside of the exchange relation, can be turned to expedient ends, made to serve an economic function as an indicator of happiness that can, in turn, be commodified, reproduced, and marketed.

I find it useful to turn, as a supplement to Adorno's argument, toward Gayatri Spivak's struggle with the closely related issue of representation in her continued rewriting of her essay "Can the Subaltern Speak?" This essay is most fully reworked in her 1999 *Critique of Postcolonial Reason*, the version I use here.[3] The value of art has often been linked to its representational capabilities—especially in cultural arguments that advance a social justice model for the representational capacity of creative work— making the issues of artistic value and representation increasingly inseparable. They become even more inseparable when we think of exchange values as processes of symbolic representation. I want to address one of Spivak's concerns, in a relatively discrete section of her much longer essay. Here she is very specific: in working through the problem of representation, she returns to Marx's formulations in "The Eighteenth Brumaire of Napoleon Bonaparte" in order to juggle his two concepts of representation: *Vertretung*, political representation, and *Darstellung*, which she interprets as signification, the process of representation with which researchers in the human sciences often work. In the famous passage from Marx, in which he discusses the lacking class interests of small-holding peasants after the French revolution and wrestles with how to work with them on a political level, the problem of political representation veers toward a problem of symbolic representation. The passage is somewhat long, but is useful here in order to show this subtle movement from one form of representation to the other. Marx states that

> In so far as millions of families get a living under economic conditions of existence that divide their mode of life, their interests and their culture from those of other classes and counterpose them as enemies, they form a class. In so far as there is merely a local interconnection amongst peasant proprietors, the similarity of their interests produces no community, no national linkage and no political organization, they do not form a class. They are therefore incapable of asserting their class interests in their own name, whether through a parliament or constitutional convention. They cannot represent themselves, they must be represented. (177)

The problem for Marx is that such people cannot represent themselves politically because they do not have the class-based solidarity necessary to articulate a common interest. But this problem of political representation becomes one of symbolic representation when Marx considers the extent to which these peasants can form a class, since a class is a form of symbolic representation that differs from the political process of appointing delegates to speak in one's interest. This lamented lack of symbolic cohesion points toward a failure of political representability in an ultimately illogical jump when Marx states that no politics or lawmaking can take place on behalf of people who cannot be symbolically linked together. Spivak argues that it is key to "note how the staging of the world in representation—its scene of writing, its *Darstellung*—dissimulates the choice of and need for 'heroes,' paternal proxies, agents of power—*Vertretung*" in Marx and elsewhere (264). There is, she states, considerable slippage between the two. The processes of political action, along with the appointment of representatives, should not be reduced to the concerns of symbolism. Nor should the practices of representing value (political, use value) be reduced to abstractions (symbolic, exchange value). Critical practice, Spivak contends, needs to attend to the collapsing of these distinctions.

Value becomes representation in this process, Spivak suggests, because "value, as produced in necessary and surplus labour, is computed as the representation / sign of objectified labor" (263). Value is only represented in one form or another; it does not exist unto itself outside of the signifying chain. It is, as a result, vital for her that "the shifting distinctions between representation within the state and political economy, on the one hand, and within the theory of the Subject, on the other, must not be obliterated" (257). Should different forms of representation be reduced, the reduction favours, in her analysis, the signifying process, just as exchange value comes to eclipse use value. We need to maintain an awareness of these signifying processes and to remain dubious about their ability to transparently reflect the values that they are said to show. In the context of research in the human sciences, this means that we cannot simply allow the representational signifiers of exchange value—the signifiers of dollars and cents—to replace the subjects of research themselves: texts, people, and political struggles.

Spivak wrestles with this argument about representation in part because of the problem of the value of culture or knowledge that I am addressing here. Her anti-capitalist resistance cannot base itself in a traditional Western aesthetics, nor in the traditional methods of representation, as these exclude the subaltern women with whom her research is concerned. For Spivak, "the mode of production narrative"—the representational process of culture that derives value through productivity—"is so efficient because it is constructed in terms of the most efficient and abstract coding of value, the economic" (244–45). The signifying processes of the exchange relationship, in other words, are widely understood abstractions that might seem to represent culture and knowledge better than the things themselves. As a result, "the ground-level value-codings that write...women's lives elide us" (245). That is, "women outside of the mode of production narrative mark the points of fadeout" in history and culture (244), because traditional history and the forms of culture that get recorded interest themselves only—or at least primarily—in the economic. Thus women, like Marx's small-holding peasants, are written out of history. In the original version of Spivak's essay, this meant that, for her, the subaltern woman could not speak, since the knowledge that she spoke did not respond to the narratives of productivity; her speech was not intelligible to the powerful. Instead, in the 1999 rewriting, on the other hand, Spivak suggests that when the subaltern woman begins to speak and be heard by the world around her, she "has been inserted into the long road to hegemony" (*Critique* 310). She has become part of the symbolic structures of society and entered the mode-of-production narrative. This may be unfortunate, as the subaltern becomes engaged with yet another aspect of capitalist colonization, but it is also highly desirable because it seeks to render such women's lives livable, Spivak states. Reading the lives of women outside of the economic is, for her, a process of difficult and incomplete recovery. Her interest in grappling with forms of value beyond the economic derives, then, from this complex concern, one that is ultimately similar to Adorno's critique. While Adorno is staging a defence of high art, the erasure of autonomous forms of cultural expression through either the historical repression that Spivak notes or Adorno's market commodification is alarming and, today, almost instantaneous.

In Canada, the shift in the value of culture and knowledge reflects those changes witnessed in the recent transnational analyses of late capitalism by Yudíce, Rifkin, Spivak, and others. Literary critics here continue to document how value is recorded in ways that lie beyond the jingoistic processes of invigorating economies or interfacing across the new paradigms of the knowledge economy. In their recent examination of "Canada's radical poetries in English," Pauline Butling and Susan Rudy propose a shift in the way radicalism can be defined in Canadian writing, given that "the social meaning of radicality has changed dramatically in response to identity politics and the global imperatives of the 1980s and '90s" (xi). They leave the definition of the radical necessarily open, but acknowledge a difficult play with "the commodification of dissent" in Canadian poetics (xii). Contestatory writing maintains an awareness of the modes through which it circulates and the marketplaces that facilitate these exchanges; however, the exchange itself risks occluding the contents of what is being exchanged in the contemporary world of cultural capitalism, in which prestige—or Bourdieu's cultural capital—is gained through the consumption of cultural and artistic goods. Having, exchanging, and developing cultural knowledges, for researchers in the human sciences, may not be the same thing as investigating the ideologies that lie therein, especially when the contemporary exchange of knowledge asks that researchers assume the benefits (or benevolence) of the exchange model in the first place.

SSHRC states that "social sciences and humanities research is vital to building a just, prosperous and culturally vibrant world" (*Knowledge Council* 11). This notion of prosperity is, of course, the point with which I am concerned. SSHRC sees itself and Canada as actively participating in the global "knowledge economy," an economy in which, as I have suggested, more and more forms of "return on investment," that is, of value, come to be reduced to those that can be measured by economic indicators. If we do indeed live in a knowledge economy—or Rifkin's "age of access"—then we need to retain an awareness of the contours of the concept of value itself, especially as it is represented in the processes of exchange, lest knowledge, in all of its forms, be reduced to an economic bottom line in which the symbolism of the exchange value eclipses all others. The valley of poetry's making, as Auden had it, is now being trodden upon by executives eager to witness culture's expediency in managing our social conflicts. The valley is being mined, sinkholes dug in order to plumb for crude. The challenge to researchers in the human sciences is to retain a degree of autonomy lest we simply become the in-depth market researchers necessary for funding bodies to determine where they should invest their funds.

AUTHOR'S NOTE

Thanks to Aubrey Hanson, Sabine Milz, Jessica Schagerl, and Imre Szeman, who read and critiqued early versions of this essay, and to Smaro Kamboureli and Daniel Coleman for organizing the workshop "The Culture of Research: 'Retooling' the Human Sciences," for which this essay was prepared, as well as to the participants of the workshop for their feedback. My continued thanks to SSHRC for the support that made this essay possible, as well as to the Killam Trusts.

NOTES

1. Here I am thinking about knowledge and culture in one breath; that is, I see culture, the arts, and research as containing knowledge (albeit expressed differently), and I therefore treat them similarly. I think that it is fair to do so in the context of the humanities, although this might not be the case in other disciplines.

2. These rhetorics both imply a rupture from the past; still, I would argue that the contemporary moment exemplifies a hastening of processes that have been latent within capitalism for a much longer period.

3. Spivak's further essay, "Scattered Speculations on the Question of Value," underlies this analysis as well and is a further useful supplement.

FOUR

Taking a Place at the Table

Jessica Schagerl

Sometimes Ms. Mentor has to burst hopes, shred bubbles, and be the Grinch. While it is true that scholarly types can be generous, open-minded souls who'll share software, footnotes, and recipes for cat treats—they can also backstab, withhold, and compete to leave you penniless, naked, and shivering in the cold (metaphorically speaking).

> *—Emily Toth, a.k.a. "Ms. Mentor,"*
> *"They Will Not"*

INTRODUCTION

IN THIS ESSAY I AM INTERESTED IN how the shifting senses of academic labour in the humanities register differently for junior and untenured faculty, post-doctoral fellows, and graduate students than for full-time academic faculty. The voices of these untenured researchers are almost completely absent from debates and practices that are constructed in terms of future-oriented programs and policies with real bearings on how the coming generations of research scholars in Canada understand their position and the situation of the humanities. I am especially interested in how junior colleagues are introduced to and able to participate effectively in larger academic and political communities such as those increasingly sought after by SSHRC. Here, I argue that a productive emphasis might be placed on how mentoring can fit into the political and economic system of the contemporary Canadian academic community.

PERSPECTIVES ON ACADEMIC LABOUR

The thoughts that form the basis of this essay grew out of a hectic three weeks between mid-February and early March 2005, during which time I, as a graduate student, took part in SSHRC's "The Knowledge Project," an event that included a public research exposition as well as high-level discussions about granting formulas and the future of social sciences and humanities research in Canada. What is at stake in consultations such as these is not just that the social sciences and humanities should get their fair share of a publicly funded pie. At the root of this discussion are serious questions about when humanities and social science research stopped being seen as necessary for the development of a critical citizenry, when in the words of Domna C. Stanton it started "suffering from both a local assault on...already diminished resources and widespread indifference to [its] constitutive role in society's capacity to understand and to imagine" (3). At the same time, in addition to writing my dissertation, I was serving on a departmental hiring committee and acting as one of the chief organizers of a national conference. In my pre-PHD days, I worked for CFHSS, and that experience as much as any other has conditioned me to be curious about academic governance issues and who gets to speak for whom; I have also been involved in various discussions and interventions having to do with the directions of humanities research and the outcomes of large-scale research projects, including taking part in the Mid-Term Review of an MCRI. These experiences have sharpened my interest and experience in dealing with these types of questions.

In 2005, I was working as a research assistant for my doctoral supervisor, Diana Brydon, an opportunity that afforded me the chance to not only conduct research into the MCRI's themes of globalization, autonomy, and community but also to learn about "research management," including some aspects of how large-scale grants operate. I was asked to attend "The Knowledge Project" because I was, at the time, serving as the Elected Student Representative on the Project Management Board of the "Globalization and Autonomy" MCRI; Dr. William Coleman, the principal investigator of the MCRI, was invited to attend with one other member of his team—as were the Principal Investigators of all other MCRIS, other large-scale projects, and those successful in the hastily conducted "Clusters" competition of 2005. He chose to bring a graduate student to represent the Project because the "Globalization and Autonomy" MCRI placed a distinct emphasis on the training and research management capabilities of junior scholars.

I had two immediate reactions to my days in Ottawa at "The Knowledge Project." The first had to do with the sense that I was being given a unique opportunity by progressive senior faculty. My second, more visceral gut-reaction was related to my nagging suspicion that those who got to be seen as accountable for the success of promoting SSHRC were a self-selected cadre. I might have been the only graduate student in attendance, but I was now "one of them," a fact at once exhilarating and terrifying.

On the one hand, I was allowed, as a graduate student, rare access to discussions about the future of research in Canada, thus developing a clearer idea of what directions, perspectives, and approaches would be valued in the future. This type of early exposure to the intricacies of large-scale projects cemented my desire to try to stretch the boundaries of my own discipline, a task that I would first try to accomplish in my dissertation project. Writing about her own experiences as a graduate student who also "grew up" with a major research program, Lisa Maruca likewise notes the excitement of being "at the ground level of a project that would influence a variety of disciplines and scholars from around the world...It could not help but shape my own burgeoning academic identity" ("The SCE and Me"). In addition, this opportunity allowed me to understand better the many contingencies that influence how research is conducted, the variety of methodologies and discourse communities that need to be considered, and the challenges of developing granting formulas that are equitable. To the credit of many of the other participants, conversation did not cease when I appeared, nor did the vocabulary change. I had received careful and conscientious guidance in research management, professional development, academic governance, and questions about interdisciplinarity. As a result, I could understand what—for lack of a better word—I will call the specialized vocabulary employed by the Council and those who get to sit around the table.[1] To even enter into a discussion about the value and future of the SRG program, for instance, means that a scholar at the earliest stages of her academic career must be familiar with its terms, how it differs from other research grants, and what the various acronyms and initialisms at the institutional and SSHRC level mean. Without knowledge of the abbreviations used—MCRI, INE, CURA, SRG, etc.—a discussion can quickly turn into the equivalent of "blah blah blah blah, funding, blah blah blah blah, research." In practice, this means that a junior colleague is shut out of the discussion. There is no reason why graduate students should not be introduced to this language before they apply to one of these programs.

It is only a slight exaggeration to note that in the Canadian context "the odds of a PHD [in the humanities] landing a tenure-track position are slimmer than a reality star's figure" (Brassard 567). Even though there are lucrative scholarships available, most graduate students hold a precarious position as a result of the lack of any substantial investment by funding agencies in their research and publishing—even though in order to secure a tenure-track job they are asked to be just as productive as, if not more so than, seasoned colleagues. Graduate school trains students to operate within the context of the university, but it often does very little to negotiate expectations surrounding academic employment. Not surprisingly, there remains a "sense of discomfort among the graduate students and younger faculty...about their own future...in the academy in general" (Gilman, "Collaboration" 384). Teaching fellowships or contracts, for instance, can easily fall under the rhetoric of professional development but end up being convenient ways for universities to exploit junior faculty under another guise, forcing a continuation of the transient life of a graduate student but for someone with a PHD in hand. The scarcity of full-time tenure-track employment is often a greater concern to people caught in these positions than the future of research models. But what happens when these two concerns collide?

In October 2006, during collective bargaining negotiations, the University of Toronto unilaterally determined that it would no longer offer institutional support to sessional lecturers who were applying for research grants from SSHRC and other granting councils. In announcing the change in university policy, Angela Hildyard, Vice-President of Human Resources and Equity, claimed that "research is not a part of [the sessional's] employment relationship with the University," a claim that subsequently would be rigorously challenged by union representatives and those who support the sessional faculty (Hildyard). The university administration further argued that the administration of grants would have to continue past the term of employment; it went so far as to claim that sessional faculty "are not prohibited from obtaining other appointment status that would meet the University's requirements for grant applications" (Hildyard). In contesting the policy, union representatives from CUPE local 3902 (Unit 3) charged that the university was undermining its claims to scholarship by attempting to distinguish "between the 'real scholars' and the 'wage workers' who do much of the teaching" (Varughese 1). There was no acknowledgement of the important work that such scholars might in future do beyond the confines of the university or in something other than a tenure-track job, including diffusing research within and across various academic and non-academic communities. While the University of Toronto's policy would stand to have the greatest effect on the ability of contract faculty to conduct and disseminate research, it also stood to have significant consequences for graduate students, many of whom could benefit from grant-funded research assistantships (provided it was written into the grant and approved—another matter entirely!). Commentators noted that the policy also "jeopardizes the career development prospects of...newly-minted PHDs...trying to maintain the research profile demanded by tenure-track search committees" (Varughese 1) by consigning to the "sociopathological labor of the university" those who continue to have to "teach for food" (Moten and Harney 102). Ultimately, the University of Toronto administration was unable to uphold its gate-keeping; by late November 2006, it "restored the right of sessional lecturers to apply for external research grants in accordance with U of T policy" ("Update"). As the University of Toronto situation indicates, it is doubly important that junior scholars take an active interest in the "transformations" of SSHRC and the university, since these can coincide with movements to revalue and regulate various kinds of academic labour, thus adding to the overly competitive requirements of full-time academic employment.

I juxtapose my own experiences with those of the sessional lecturers at the University of Toronto in order to draw attention to the vagaries of the university system and the contradictory foundations on which both it and the granting council operate. Both examples point to questions about who controls the conditions under which academic workers operate. SSHRC promotes a future-oriented discourse, especially through its core values of "Learning" and "Building Capacity," where "the future" is expressly linked to young researchers who will eventually renew "Canada's research capacity" (*Knowledge Council* 7). Yet, there is a substantial gap between SSHRC's conscious acknowledgement of the role of young scholars and its planning in a practical way for a future that will embrace us. In SSHRC's published strategic plan, *Knowledge Council: SSHRC, 2006–2011*, for instance, which appeared in August 2005, the future directions for the Council were charted, and there was a justification for the Council's continued existence with increased federal funding for social sciences and humanities research. The strategic plan is often an uneasy mix of valorizing the status quo and leaving open the possibility for changing the research models privileged by the Council. Even though Marc Renaud, then President of SSHRC and Chair of its board, rhetorically asks, "We know how to shape our future, so what's stopping us?" there is a curious omission throughout the rest of the document of "the next generation of researchers and highly-qualified people who will build Canada's future" (7) beyond a cursory mention of "massive faculty renewal" that will bring "a new generation of professors into the academy who are increasingly expected—and expect—to be active in research and research training" (8). I remain unsure on what basis the authors of the Strategic Plan wrote this, especially when, immediately over the page, it is acknowledged that "there is still a lack of funding for graduate students in humanities and social science disciplines and few opportunities for those students to be actively integrated in research projects as part of their graduate training" (10). There is, for instance, no acknowledgement of the fact that this "next generation" is made up of contingent workers.

In "Youth, Higher Education, and the Crisis of Public Time: Educated Hope and the Possibility of a Democratic Future," Henry A. Giroux begins his discussion of the future of university education in the U.S. context by highlighting changing perceptions of youth culture. "Rather than being cherished as a symbol of the future," he ventures, "youth are now seen as a threat to be feared and a problem to be contained" (142). While Giroux is entirely focussed on the U.S. example, his conclusions have important implications for Canadian universities and cultural institutions like SSHRC, not the least of which is related to training students to recognize how citizenship, democracy, and ideas of the "public" are being shaped, ostensibly for the future, but in ways that limit what that future may bring. Chad Gaffield, the new president of SSHRC, also acknowledges the professional responsibility to "the future" of the academic research community in Canada. He envisions "moving SSHRC to be Canada's research agency focused on people, an agency not only supportive of the student researchers it funds, but also of the professors who teach those students and play such an important role in developing the next generation of scholars and thinkers of this country" (CFHSS, "Federation Applauds"). Gaffield's rhetoric differs only slightly from the rhetoric of SSHRC's "Transformation" documents: while the attention is rightly placed on the role of the more senior academic, who remains instrumental in fostering that elusive "next generation," there remains an assumption that students are primarily recipients of SSHRC funds—not co-creators of its future. What SSHRC's policy document does not, but should, say is that "future knowledge" means educating and fostering a new generation of scholars who are active in creating a "knowledge council" as part of the democratic public sphere, a generation of scholars who are able to connect their research, teaching, and administration with broader concerns over equality and justice. In this, as Jeffrey Di Leo notes, "the political dimensions of our affiliations are always already at work: it is up to us to decide if we are going to utilize them for progressive changes in academia or allow them to perpetuate structures of exploitation and inequality" (12–13).

The roles of young researchers in the development of governance structures are made more difficult by the perception of instability held by the next generation of scholars, from graduate student and post-doctoral fellow or sessional faculty to untenured junior faculty. Part of the reticence to acknowledge the potential of junior colleagues' participation in policy development has to do with the perception that graduate students, post-doctoral fellows, and sessional faculty are transient; they are usually on the way to "somewhere else." Ironically, this assumption of transience, with students going to new places, shifting their affiliations on a somewhat regular basis, is precisely what should be valued in the context of the knowledge exchanges and effective linkages increasingly promoted by SSHRC. In the next section of this essay, I explore how the "next generation" might gain a spot at the table; that is, how junior colleagues might be introduced to and able to participate in academic networks through a renewed emphasis on mentoring.

MENTOR/ING

The etymology of *mentor* in the *Oxford English Dictionary* charts a narrative of studied apprenticeship from private lessons conducted by a learned, older advisor to its equally common usage today as a trusted counsellor who can help an apprentice negotiate a professional milieu. As the term is commonly used, it represents a turn to individual guidance and counsel, an ethics of sponsorship and support, and a call to act as a "role model." Wrapped in the veil of efficacious pedagogy and personal support by someone who shares experiences, *mentor* has thus lost very little of the meaning it had when it entered into English from translations of Francois de S. de la Mothe-Fénelon's *Les Aventures de Télémaque* (1699), a political novel that gained currency in eighteenth-century Europe, including, in part, through numerous translations into English.

The political side of the word's roots should not be forgotten in a quest to make a mentor relationship synonymous with an apprenticeship relationship, for the knowledge gained from a mentor can all too easily become a tool that can be used for an identifiable end such as financial reward, socio-economic advancement, and the chance for security. This kind of recognition of the term's instrumentality need not be seen as entirely negative. Most obviously, the value of an academic mentor includes the improvement of the material conditions of graduate students, post-doctoral fellows, and junior faculty. Junior colleagues who have a degree of familiarity with granting structures and the process of application, for instance, are those who will more likely be successful in securing grants. To talk about being a mentor is necessarily to involve oneself in a discussion of the future. She who is mentored is generally seen to benefit from the wisdom, knowledge, and expertise of a trusted guide who shares experiences. "Words of Wisdom about Academic Culture" may come from a dissertation supervisor, the professor in the office next to yours, or, as the epigraph to this essay suggests, from *The Chronicle of Higher Education* ("They Will Not"). As a noun, *mentor* has a rich history in English; the verb form *to mentor*, in contrast, is a more recent addition to everyday parlance.

The OED lists the first instance of *to mentor* from 1976: "Dr. Gould has... mentored several graduate students." Appropriately enough, considering the root word's links to pedagogical structures, the example foregrounds an academic and affiliative relationship. Arguably, the academic roles negotiated in the mentor relationship are influenced by how the humanities, in this instance, are conceptualized. In the words of Geoffrey Galt Harpham, "a clearly articulated rationale for humanistic inquiry would... help to displace the attention from the professor to the profession, and also to focus the profession's attention on the community that it inhabits, whose support it seeks, and whose long-term interests it serves" (22). The affiliative relationship of mentoring can help to confer value on one's academic self-identity. An academic has affiliations, "[relationships that confer] value and identity on individuals, disciplines, and institutions" (Di Leo 1), with her institution and her discipline—as well as with her mentors. Although the OED example does not say in what the students were mentored, it is reasonably safe to assume that, in 1976, the mentoring relationship had to do with the creation of disciplinary identities; this process of creation, of course, assumes the "legendary wholeness, coherence, and integrity of the general field to which one professionally belongs" (Said, *The World* 228). Thus, a service interest in mentoring has as its basis the end goal of helping a student become a professional in a designated field.

The addition of *mentor* as a verb signals, in part, the shift from a formalized one-on-one hierarchical relationship to a network of professional relationships, some of which may indeed mimic sanctioned power structures but others that are informal, collaborative, and participatory. As I understand mentoring in the academic milieu, it involves a process whereby a senior colleague works collaboratively with a junior colleague or a student in order to negotiate, both on a practical and conceptual level, the various roles of an academic. A mentor might help a young professor navigate through the various stages of professional life such as promotion and tenure, or she might help a student prepare for the job market. Jeffrey Theis is only partially correct, therefore, when he infers that graduate programs of necessity create individual scholars. While it is true on a strictly literal level that "the newly minted doctorate cannot bring graduate school friends and faculty members to the new job" (88), she will almost certainly bring her network of relationships with her, thus extending on-campus and inter-campus networking opportunities and creating spaces for informal mentoring relationships to develop. These opportunities include doing the kind of work and performing pedagogical projects that would be done after the completion of the PHD (see Hudnall, for instance). It also means getting involved with meta-scholarship, such as taking part in questions of academic governance, "transformation" discussions, or departmental representation, instead of sticking to narrowly defined research.

Mentoring can help to clarify an otherwise opaque culture of research that for too long has not directed its attention to the productive relations between its various members: "This mentoring in collegiality would probe practices of dialogue and personal interaction in the academic setting critically; in so doing, it would perform the very kind of professional conversation that exemplifies collegiality" (Lewis 78). Collegiality, of course, is a tertiary factor that influences mentoring in very real ways. Because faculty "social[ize] their students in attitudes to the profession" (Dubrow 58), it is important that relations between faculty and younger researchers operate on visible professional and personal levels. It is no longer enough to discuss the state of the field and one's future in it over drinks in a bar. As Emily Toth ('Ms. Mentor') makes clear, the days of historian Stephen Ambrose receiving twenty-five job offers in his final year at grad school are long gone: "Today, a Stephanie Ambrose would be delighted with *one*" (Toth, *Impeccable* 22). Not only does the "sweatshop atmosphere" of continual CV-building (Tumbleson 60) create divisions between senior and junior colleagues (who are pressured to begin publishing earlier and more often), it often leaves graduate students wondering how to cope with the demands of the workplace. This atmosphere also complicates efforts to make the university a more equitable place. Many young female graduate students, post-doctoral fellows, and faculty, for instance, face what one commentator aptly calls "inordinate demands on their time at the start of their careers" (Lewis 81), largely due to the child-bearing and child-rearing years falling at this time. A greater proportion of academic women than men also care for elderly relatives (CFHSS, "Feminist"). Although many argue that gender equity has been a priority for universities for years, data about the recruitment and retention of female faculty from Statistics Canada remain sobering: female professors continue to be "underrepresented and paid less than their male counterparts," with women making up only 14 per cent of new appointments to the most senior rank of Professor (Perkel). Ms. Mentor's comment about Stephanie Ambrose's one potential job offer is thus about more than the competitive academic job market. It also speaks to gender, academia, and just how limiting a university system can be when based on the ideal of a productive male academic who can devote all his mental and physical energies to his work. In reality, the "drinks in the bar" approach to mentoring only works for an individual who has the time and inclination to career-building in this way. It does equally little for the young female academics who choose to have a child (or children) and for the male academics who play an increasingly significant role in child-rearing and household-keeping. Thankfully, the vestiges of the masculinist mentality about who constitutes a "proper" academic are slowly melting away, although not fast enough for many of us. What a real process of mentoring makes clear is that there are challenges at every level. Untenured faculty are not in a position to stick their necks out any more than graduate students (and perhaps even less), and, even when they become tenured, change can be slow and painful.

A scholarly interest in mentoring also seeks to foster the professional development of junior humanities scholars; in addition, it aims to push against the limits and boundaries of research methodologies, for example, by promoting interdisciplinary and often intergenerational research. Senior faculty are often better equipped to alert their junior colleagues to (potential) changes in research formulas—simply by being more "in-the-know." Increased dialogue (across generations as well as disciplines) is necessary for creating institutional paradigms that are more equitably future-oriented. I see, therefore, a parallel between the push for collaboration and interdisciplinarity and the increased involvement of junior scholars. Much as interdisciplinarity involves dialogue across different fields of knowledge, mentoring involves dialogue across generations. It means revisioning the model of solitary academic work that is often fostered by the university system and to a lesser extent by granting agencies. Where interdisciplinarity and collaboration allow a researcher to confront critiques that emerge as different disciplines and individuals contest each other's theoretical frameworks, perspectives, and practices, the encouragement of junior faculty in helping to chart future directions of the humanities can produce new models of research.

Almost by its dictionary definition, *mentoring* suggests an emphasis on collaboration as part of academic development. Collaboration with a junior colleague models professional competence and collegiality (Theis 90). These collaborations will likely first take the form of working with a faculty member who shares similar disciplinary research interests. Eventually an academic who has had a productive experience of collaboration at an early stage in her career will be able to undertake the "cross-disciplinary, cross-referential kinds of writing" that are increasingly sought after by institutions such as SSHRC (Chow 52). Even though many junior scholars relish the opportunity to work in groundbreaking, interdisciplinary ways, there are still very real disciplinary hurdles to doing so. Chief among these hurdles is the perception that disciplinary expertise might be lacking. Certainly, there is the perception among junior researchers involved in interdisciplinary endeavours that they face another level of challenge in securing academic employment, notwithstanding SSHRC's emphasis on the value of interdisciplinary collaboration. The experience gained in research management on an interdisciplinary project may be limited if departments and institutions do not follow the lead of SSHRC in recognizing its importance.

My discussion here reflects my own personal experience working on a large-scale interdisciplinary project, the "Globalization and Autonomy" MCRI. I had the opportunity at the MCRI's mid-term review to discuss the role of mentoring and its relationship to interdisciplinarity at some length. What ended up happening at our review was that the SSHRC reviewers—all of whom were generous to the graduate students and post-doctoral fellows who were speaking—ended up acting in the role of cheerleader. They attempted to assuage the anxieties of the speakers by making note that "there will be jobs for people versed in interdisciplinarity." Even with statements of support such as these, disciplinary affiliations remain paramount; the young researcher who pursues knowledge in interdisciplinary and collaborative ways requires equal mentoring to ensure that her real disciplinary strengths are apparent to departmental hiring committees and then promotion and tenure committees.

It is no great stretch of the imagination to see those aspects of mentoring—such as involvement, where possible, in research networks—that make good pedagogical and professional sense. However, in my experience, most faculty are less inclined to think of involving junior colleagues, especially those at the graduate and immediate postgraduate levels, in policy and strategy discussions at departmental, faculty, and institutional levels, for example in writing funding applications, dealing with knowledge-based institutions, or coping with institutional constraints. There is, as the work of Gerald Graff makes clear, plenty of good (teaching) value in bad debate; that is the gist of what he calls "teaching the conflicts," as I understand it, and it is likewise central to a successful mentoring relationship that privileges participation in the contested nature of one's field. Notwithstanding my own involvement in that one round of discussions, young researchers are rarely, if ever, consulted about the future research models to which they are expected to apply and that they may one day administer. However, there are a surprising number of faculty members and policy developers who believe, as I do, that the "next generation" of research scholars in Canada funded by SSHRC should have a stake in discussions about its future. Pragmatically, these future funding guidelines will have to be negotiated by anyone, including sessional faculty, who undertakes a research project. Philosophically, incorporating the perspectives of junior scholars into the discussions about new ways of producing innovative humanities scholarship—rather than expecting them to reinforce and acquiesce to programs determined on their behalf—seems pressing. How can one "learn the ropes" of large-scale research projects if student and junior faculty involvement is not integral? And at what point does SSHRC itself have an obligation to model the kinds of research behaviour and patterns it expects successful researchers to adopt vis-à-vis actively integrating young researchers?

What we need, therefore, in addition to rethinking the nature of humanities research more generally, are structural and philosophical changes to granting programs that will increase opportunities for junior colleagues to take part in shaping institutional paradigms. This involvement could come from funds targeted specifically to facilitate mentoring: in research management, in grant writing, in dealing with institutional questions at a micro and macro level. Importantly, these funds targeted for mentoring should be above budget lines for research assistance by graduate students. It certainly fits SSHRC's mandate to allocate funding to student researchers; this provides experience in research methods but does not necessarily encourage preparation for the part of the researcher's profession that involves negotiating grant applications and collaborative research models. In addition, there should be greater recognition of mentoring roles in academic and tenure reviews and in grant applications. My suggestion of greater involvement perforce places yet another demand on younger scholars. The investment of time and intellectual energy on the part of younger scholars, together with a genuine financial investment in the "next generation," will pay dividends as the "millennial" generation shifts from being students to being teachers. This shift has already taken place (Johnson 7), and its effects will only become more pronounced as greater numbers of students make the transition from the undergraduate to the graduate classroom and then complete the doctoral degree. At the same time, however, we also need to assess how mentoring can help across the range of academic positions (see Andrew Martin).

It is not my intention here to enumerate the various ways in which one can be mentored. No list I could compile could be exhaustive; furthermore, it would read as prescriptive when I firmly believe that in order for a mentoring relationship to be successful it must be relational and flexible. Instead, I want to reinforce one key point about discussions of mentoring by making reference to the useful work undertaken by CFHSS on mentoring. "Notes on the 'Next Generation: Mentoring in Universities' Workshop," a workshop moderated by Donna Palmateer Pennee, underscores several areas in which mentoring could play a more substantial role in the development of Canadian academics who work in the humanities and social sciences (CFHSS, "Notes"). It is the kind of discussion that needs to take place more frequently—and with greater input from a wider range of scholars, since the interests and preoccupations of graduate students, post-doctoral fellows, contract and junior faculty might shift the terms of debate. Ultimately, not only should transparent, shared decision-making take place, but this decision-making should involve junior colleagues since "at both the institutional and departmental level the advantages of involving untenured colleagues in administrative work entailing substantive decision-making outweigh the disadvantages" (Dubrow 57). Chief among these advantages is the fact that "the institution can benefit from the expertise and new ideas of a younger generation, and its members can acquire a sense of involvement in, even ownership of, the institution or department that will encourage many other types of collegiality and also discourage them from leaving should the opportunity arise" (57). The kind of involvement

I am advocating would also have real effects on institutional memory, helping junior colleagues understand the historical trajectory of certain courses of action, while also creating opportunities. While I agree that in academia "some knowledge must be reserved for privileged individuals because it is sensitive and would cause embarrassment or dissension if it were disseminated" (Lewis 83), there are plenty of opportunities to draw on the ideas of the younger generation. If mentoring is to be successful in helping to enable a generation of younger colleagues to not only take part in but eventually chart the directions of future research in Canada, then it must also help the senior generation of scholars develop perhaps new ways of relating to graduate students and junior scholars.

CONCLUSION

The kind of research culture I envision takes as its central retooling strategy the everyday practice of mentoring—a practice centrally concerned with learning the vital strategies of how to make and keep intellectual relationships across universities and departments. This essay has argued that junior colleagues should be placed in positions where they can have an influence on the future of the programs offered by granting agencies. Enshrining mentoring as one of the broader set of competencies encouraged by granting agencies might mean that more senior scholars involve junior colleagues in the decisions that will shape both of their careers. The inclusion of younger voices in the debates about the future of humanities research, scholarship, and funding will only serve to strengthen communities of research. Mentoring in the vagaries of academia can be a real complement to individual intellectual merit. By encouraging collaborative affiliations across generations, disciplines, universities, and countries, mentoring provides a productive way for junior scholars to gain research leadership expertise and be able to effectively comment on the future directions of the profession.

AUTHOR'S NOTE

I gratefully acknowledge the financial support of SSHRC (Fellowship Division). Thanks to Daniel Coleman, Smaro Kamboureli, and the other participants of the Culture of Humanities workshop. Warm acknowledgements of one's mentor are usually seen as a sign of affection, proof positive that the lessons learned have been good ones. So it is with great fondness that I mention my mentors, who have helped me negotiate a career in research and teaching and who continually inspire me: Diana Brydon, Irena Makaryk, and Daniel Coleman. Kit Dobson, Helene Strauss, and Heather Snell read drafts of this essay as it was being prepared, and I thank them all for their generous feedback.

NOTE

1. The specialized and often initialism-filled vocabulary used by SSHRC is not just a concern for younger scholars who might be concerned about being excluded from discussions; it is also a concern SSHRC feels with regard to the public. The vocabulary used in these sorts of discussions often excludes the very researchers who potentially stand to benefit from the policies and, at the same time, risks alienating the non-academic public.

FIVE

Employing Equity in Post-secondary Art Institutes

Ashok Mathur &
Rita Wong

BY THE LATE 1990S, THE FIVE MAJOR art schools in English-speaking
Canada had begun the transition from diploma-granting colleges to specialized universities where students could earn undergraduate degrees
in fine arts, media arts, and design. While this did not occur simultaneously—degree-granting and university status came at different
times depending on provincial and national shifts in education priorities—the leadership of these institutions worked together so that this
status transition encouraged a concomitant cultural expansion from a
discipline-specific, teaching-heavy focus to one that engaged interdisciplinarity and research. This expansion was not without its problems
or detractors. As with any institutional change, there can be an accompanying fear of loss that small gains that have been hard won (such as
class sizes) would be erased rather than strengthened. For instance, the
opportunity for developing "research" at an arts institution carried with
it the taint of a "more-work-for-the-same-pay" clause, not to mention
setting off alarm bells that a research-based institution would be less
attentive to pedagogical concerns. Indeed, the very term *research*, traditionally the purview of so-called academic disciplines, is a challenge
within arts spaces where production is more often seen as creative

output, even though it goes through many of the same processes of specialization, background investigation and preparation, student training, site-specificity, and peer review. It was in part this perceived schism that gave rise to the implementation of the Research/Creation program in SSHRC, an eventual recognition that artists in post-secondary institutions are deeply involved in research and should not be prohibited access to the same forms of support available to their colleagues in different disciplines and faculties. Prior to this new program in 2003, artist-researchers were limited to the more modest resources available from the Canada Council, whose grants provide temporary subsistence for artists to pursue specific projects; those in university posts, however, sought equality within their institutions. The five major art schools in Canada—the Emily Carr University of Art + Design (ECU),[1] the Alberta College of Art + Design (ACAD), the Banff Centre, the Ontario College of Art & Design (OCAD), and the Nova Scotia College of Art & Design University (NSCAD)—made the arguments that research would become integrated with current workloads (i.e., that ongoing arts practices were also part of that research) and that such new opportunities enhanced teaching opportunities, but it is a claim still hotly contested because teaching loads, in many cases, have not diminished from those of the college days. The demands of research, too, particularly in media-rich disciplines, have had an impact on pedagogy where faculty must keep up with technology changing at unprecedented rates. Given this climate of institutional change and challenge, it is no wonder that employment inequities persisted in art schools that self-defined as oases of creativity but often reflected a Eurocentric garrison mentality.

SSHRC defines *research/creation* as follows, in its description of the research/creation grants that are part of its fine arts programming:

> any research activity or approach to research that forms an essential part of a creative process or artistic discipline and that directly fosters the creation of literary/artistic works. The research must address clear research questions, offer theoretical contextualization within the relevant field or fields of literary/artistic inquiry, and present a well-considered methodological approach. Both the research and the resulting literary/artistic

works must meet peer standards of excellence and be suitable for publication, public performance or viewing. (SSHRC, "Research/Creation")

Before a book of poetry is written or a sculpture made or a painting completed, much scholarly investigation often can and does occur. Questions of racial equity and decolonization are not separate from such processes as research/creation but form important reference points from which to understand how normative cultural frameworks are either reinforced or challenged. It is through the stories that we tell about our work, and how we situate ourselves, that culture comes to be reinvented in the process.

This essay arises from the activities of a research team (professors, artist-researchers, undergraduate and graduate research assistants) investigating, in part, equity issues at post-secondary schools of art and design in English-speaking Canada. Through a joint initiative between the SSHRC and the Department of Canadian Heritage, members of the team (Ashok Mathur, Aruna Srivastava, and Rita Wong, with the assistance of Rennard Lusterio and Louis Cruz) interviewed students, graduates, faculty, and administrators from the five aforementioned schools to determine both the effect of previous and the potential of current equity work to address changing demographics and social conditions in arts training in this country. This essay is the result of coalescing the disparate ideas of the team into a collaborative narrative. We follow the principles practised in critical pedagogy, namely, storytelling and counter-storytelling, to articulate the challenges of pursuing equity in these particular sites. Empirical evidence and statistics indicating systemic inequities are, of course, important in making the argument that change is needed, but, beyond the numbers, the stories we tell each other and ourselves are, we argue, what might cultivate the will and personal investments to implement changes in our lived realities.

Each of Canada's post-secondary art institutions has made some efforts, ranging from feeble to vigorous, to address employment equity, the officially designated groups being women, Aboriginal people, visible minorities, and people with disabilities. However, none of these institutions, as our research ultimately showed us, has done nearly enough to incorporate an anti-racist pedagogy and practice into the warp and woof of its fabric. When considering the implications of such slowness of progressive movement within the various cultures of research these schools attempt to champion, it becomes apparent that, unless concerted, systemic changes occur, there will be little to signify any progress in matters of equity in the shift from teaching-college to artist-researcher-institute. It remains to be seen how art schools will meet the challenge to nurture a vibrant and multi-faceted research environment that speaks to and from a variety of minoritized positions. From hours of transcribed interviews, we see a picture emerging: one of hope, but one somewhat dampened by what Pierre Bourdieu would call the position of the oblate—that low-level priestly order that is invested in keeping things as they are because that's the way they always have been (100). We would not begin to suggest that this was an overarching tone; indeed, most people we talked to voiced a need for progressive change. But to what order, in what manner, and at what speed—these are the questions. As one interviewee phrased it, "We're not doing 'terribly' but we could do better." Rather than languish in the half-hearted realm of "not terrible," we have suggestions about how "better" can happen immediately. With the collating eye of research assistant Kathryn Sloan, we developed a number of action points, originally delivered to a diversity session at an OCAD symposium in early 2006. It is critical that these points be embraced in order to foment substantial and immediate, rather than cosmetic and glacial, change. These points are interspersed in the essay, and we explicate them as best we can. While we acknowledge that there will be resistance to such implementation, we also feel that, without a radical movement, the current post-secondary art and design scene will remain mired in both an unrecuperable past and a technologically driven future.

A critique of multiculturalism can begin with the question of how to align and organize toward the goal of decolonization. If multiculturalism is not to circulate people of colour around an undeclared but still dominant white centre, it needs to be reoriented in terms of how it speaks to historical and contemporary power relations, particularly around issues of indigeneity. This ongoing need to build alliances was brought home to us during a panel at the ECU called "Define Indian," which explored connections between "Indians," as in First Nations artists, and

"Indians," as in South Asian artists.[2] At one point, one of the co-ordinators, Lori Blondeau, explicitly stated that educational institutions are colonial spaces that have historically been used to colonize Indigenous peoples—through residential schools, for instance. She was questioned by someone in the audience: "Did I hear you right? Did you say that educational institutions might be colonial instruments?" Her assertion that no, she had not said "might be," that such institutions *were* unquestionably colonial instruments, raised laughter and appreciation as well as discomfort from quite a few people in the audience, which consisted of members from the general public as well as ECU students. The moment stands out for us—where a voice of resistance speaks back to the institution, contributing to the process of shifting the oppressive patterns that mark colonization.

That exchange also reminded us of our responsibility to name and examine the mechanisms of colonization, so that this burden of work does not rest solely on First Nations people's shoulders. How does one act as an ethical ally? As one of the panellists, Dana Claxton, pointed out, all of us who come to this continent, regardless of race or relationship to different colonialisms, are implicated in the imperialist subjugation of Indigenous peoples. Acknowledging that we are implicated does not have to be a negative, stagnant place; it can be the springboard for action and consciousness. Claxton, who saw the connection between red Indians and brown Indians (the very term a problem in the context of geography and nationalism) to include a common, long-term battle against the British empire, emphasized the importance of knowing the histories of the land on which we live and recognizing the differences, including levels of class oppression, that continue to make it difficult to organize together. Claxton expressed dismay at how, when she started teaching, students were ignorant of basic history such as the outlawing of Native customs, like the potlatch (1884–1951), and the sexual sterilization acts under which thousands of Native people were sterilized from the 1920s to the 1980s. It is ongoing, difficult, and necessary work to point out how such histories (de)form the norms of what gets taken for granted. While we are grateful that voices like Claxton's and Blondeau's have at times resonated loudly in the classrooms of ECU, on unceded Coast Salish land, we are all too painfully aware that ECU, like other art schools across Canada in 2006, has not had permanent First Nations professors to develop curriculum or teach these critical histories and practices, but has instead relied on sessionals.[3] In 2007, ECU finally hired two First Nations faculty members, and it is quite possible that other art institutions may also slowly address this gaping lack. Still, the problem, as we know, is systemic; it has to do with not only small gains through employment equity, but Eurocentric curricula, questions of student support, inadequate funding, labour conditions, the need to strengthen connections to communities that are underserved by art schools, and much more.

To this end, two of the key recommendations coming from this research address course content and delivery.

I. *Curriculum audit to determine where and how to offer more inquiry- and research-based courses that allow students to match material and content to a more culturally valid approach.*

The trend at all the four degree-granting schools (The Banff Centre is considered a post-secondary institute but does not have a full-time undergraduate or graduate body, nor does it grant degrees) has been to "up the ante" in pedagogical scope, all moving from diploma programs to undergraduate degree-granting and now graduate institutes. This shift toward a university model is thwarted by teaching loads that are, in some cases, more than twice as heavy as those in universities, and by a general resistance to a culture of research (ranging from an evident split between "academic" and "studio" courses, or inadequate financial support and course releases necessary for an effective research model, to resistance by some faculty to perceiving their work as "research" rather than as art/design production). Without this paradigm shift that also needs financial resources, it is difficult to support research-based approaches that incorporate the multiplicities of cultural difference. Curriculum audits, done in tandem with a continued push toward artistic-research (as is currently supported by SSHRC, for instance) can facilitate the changes necessary to move research from a Western neo-imperialist project to one that addresses the needs of Indigenous and racialized communities.

Research, carefully aligned with decolonizing processes such as those described by Linda Tuhiwai Smith in *Decolonizing Methodologies*, could be a way to engage systemically marginalized students. Smith documents how research has historically operated in the service of imperialism, resulting in a great deal of suspicion and mistrust toward the concept of "research" among Indigenous communities. At the same time, Smith recognizes that Indigenous researchers and communities are pursuing urgent, valuable forms of research, whether or not it is called this by name or recognized as such in neo-colonial frameworks. Smith proposes ethical and respectful ways of conducting research that acknowledge power inequities and hold researchers accountable to their communities.[4] Research- and inquiry-based courses, in such a context, would take into serious account the concerns of Indigenous and racialized peoples.

2. Add courses and course materials that are specifically geared toward more diverse approaches to representation. This means remodelling how art history is taught as an exclusive or mostly European domain.
Graduating and senior students at the institutions where this research project was undertaken expressed a strong need for a diversified curriculum, as did administrators and faculty. The tricky part is how to include without overloading, how to add without the perception of losing something in the process. This is not dissimilar to curriculum development in university liberal arts programs in the 1960s, 1970s, and 1980s where the hue and cry was how the inclusion of new courses and programs (women's, queer, ethnic studies) would detract from a "classical" education. But the counterpoint was, and continues to be, that in order to keep up with contemporary issues, curricula must constantly evolve. This cannot happen by insisting that students take on more, but that they be able to determine the course of their own education. Again, the dilemma here is how to effectively incorporate such remodelling without creating the impression that "something has to go," or that students will be receiving a less-than-comparable education when up against their university peers. Part of this problem comes from the historical imperative

of the art and design schools that, for years, served as an alternative structure for students who did not wish to engage with the non-studio environment of university art departments. Indeed, in order to qualify for granting degrees, all these schools, perspicaciously wary of losing the art-production side they were so well known for, chose to "add on" the academic courses, such as art history and critical/cultural studies, to the extent that many programs require as much as 20 per cent more course-work than university equivalents. In this environment, for instance, art history professors teaching at art/design schools (many of them products of university programs and conscious of the breadth of their own edu-cation) lament the fact that their students are already being given short shrift and become protective of the more conservative categories of art history offered in traditional degree programs. How to add into the mix, say, courses on First Nations art history when current contemporary (albeit Eurocentric) art history courses are either unavailable or already folded into what some see as impossibly compressed compromises? Our recommendation, of course, comes from an argument for rele-vance in contemporary art practices; the students at these institutions are not developing themselves as art historians, but as critical think-ers and artist-researchers who will require an adaptive mindset around complexities of history, culture, and communication, not as addenda to studio programs but integrated into them. This seems to be the key: inte-gration rather than an addendum, a revisioning of what it means to study art and design. This integrative approach may be working better in some disciplines and areas than in others; those teaching in media and design programs, for instance, and instructors from a variety of disciplines often offer complementary studio and academic components within a single class. This approach, both interdisciplinary and inclusive, allows for a greater integration of ideas, politics, multiplicities, and practices, and it affords students the opportunity to move fluidly between contexts.

When tackling the problem of how to address and remedy historical injustices and exclusions, it is important to have an anchor as we negoti-ate the demands and pressures of institutions. Cornel West notes that if there is no

social movement or political pressure from outside these institutions (extra-parliamentary and extra-curricular actions like the social
movements of the recent past), transformation degenerates into mere
accommodation or sheer stagnation, and the role of the "co-opted progressive"—no matter how fervent one's subversive rhetoric—is rendered
more difficult. (qtd. in Creighton-Kelly 112)

As activists who have worked both in and out of institutions, we recognize that institutions need the interventions and contributions of artists
from diverse communities if they are to succeed at their public mission of
providing an education that meets the needs of students and society. The
questions that then arise include these: What would constitute meaningful institutional recognition of historically excluded or marginalized
artists? How do we translate theories of democracy into institutional
practices? If decolonizing public education is a value we hold dear,
how do we implement it? Chris Creighton-Kelly's essay, "Bleeding the
Memory Membrane: Arts Activism and Cultural Institutions," reminds
us that "we ought to get over our Canadian 'niceness' and bring more of
the details and everyday oral accounts of institutional functioning under
the microscope" (110). Returning to "Define Indian," we want to clarify
that such a directly anti-colonial moment is still relatively rare, and
that Sharon Fernandez's statements in 2002 continue to be relevant and
accurate:

If the arts and humanities are marginal, and public space shrinking like the
water table, the space for critical debates by artists of colour is even more
invisible. How do you nurture the next generation of artists, when critical discourse is inadequate and connections to politically active mentors
are tenuous? How does one do this in institutions of learning such as art
schools and universities when the diversity of cultural practices and histories of anti-racist struggle within the Canadian cultural scene are absent
from most curriculums? The renewal of vision that comes from grounding
in quotidian communal realities is disappearing as the significance of the
local that nurtures community is being reconfigured. What we need are
new forms of localism that are imbued with the subversive potential

of multiple points of origin amidst the common intersections we all experience. (76)

In the context of art schools, a possible way to cultivate such multiply origined and dynamic localism could be to strengthen community-based education (see Melanie Fernandez's article on community art practices). This leads to two more recommendations that seek to address the insularity of institutions.

3. Serious resource-allocation for outreach to racialized artistic communities outside the institution.
In times of fiscal restraint, it is difficult to argue for resource allocation, but there are inroads being made in certain quarters. For instance, OCAD is the first of the art schools to hire a director of diversity and equity, whose role is to liaise with a variety of communities and report directly to the president, giving the position both weight and character, and creating the possibility for meaningful rather than cosmetic change. While other schools are slower off the mark, ECU does have a part-time Aboriginal Liaison Officer, ACAD is beginning to roll out its Systemic Change Initiative (SCI), and NSCAD is looking to local racialized communities for recruitment.

4. Exchange programs for students and faculty.
Institutions are already under pressure to "reach out," but largely within the corporate model of finding external sources of funding, to liaise with business communities and bring in dollars and, in turn, place their students in well-paying jobs. Given these priorities, reaching out to racialized and otherwise marginalized communities seems to reap minor benefits, other than, of course, to do what post-secondary institutions should have as their primary focus—to create environments that foster progressive and critical thinking and practices. In terms of exchange programs, again, many do exist, but largely within Eurocentric networks. Fostering possibilities in and around Indigenous and racialized communities globally needs more attention. Indeed, only recently (and led by its equity office) did the Canada Council institute artistic

residency programs outside the London/Berlin/New York/Paris model. Much work still needs to be done (Port of Spain in Trinidad is the only non-European locale thus far), but this is a step in the right direction, one that art and design schools can learn from.

Indeed, there has been some enthusiastic discussion and research into strengthening community-based education at schools like ECU and OCAD. Courses such as ECU's Interdisciplinary Forums (which provided a temporary platform for Tribe and the South Asian Visual Arts Collective, SAVAC) are one example of efforts to bring community practitioners into the halls of the art school. However, much more is possible and necessary. One major challenge will be to ensure that outreach to First Nations communities and communities of colour is an integral component of courses and programs being contemplated. Rather than replicating historical, colonial marginalizations, the education system can offer a potential space of transformation. What is at stake, more mundanely, is the school's climate, the ongoing need to translate good intentions, of which there is an abundance, into daily operations, which are constrained by budgetary and labour pressures. It is crucial that administration and faculty seriously explore differences in cultural practices and values if art schools are to transform to meet and match the diversity they aspire to respect (consider the efforts at ECU). This is long-term, time-consuming work that requires patience and dedication; it also requires more resource allocation that acknowledges the value of what community partnerships contribute—not easy, given the financial pressures on educational institutions.

Administrative leadership is also important; for instance, OCAD's Employment & Educational Equity Task Force (EEETF), chaired by Wendy Coburn and Richard Fung, with consultant Sharon Fernandez, reports directly to OCAD's President, Sara Diamond, and its stated mandate includes "climate, curriculum, recruitment, faculty recruitment as well as employment and sexual harassment policy" (Diamond 78). Equally important, the EEETF's work is viewed as a critical component of OCAD's strategic plan in its efforts to address and integrate into the diversity that forms Toronto. In OCAD's 2006–2012 strategic plan, cultural diversity may prove to be an underlying thread in the four complementary strategies it lists: developing "a New Ecology of Learning (NEL); an integrated approach to research and graduate studies; a reciprocal community of local and global relationships; and new funding goals and models" ("Leading" 3). There is clearly support for having OCAD's staff and faculty reflect the diversity of the city that surrounds OCAD as one key component of serving students in their pursuit of excellence. Yet, upon reading the summary, we find that the question of how decolonization translates into administrative structures remains to be tackled. Would, for instance, the new funding goals involve partnerships with First Nations communities? Perhaps with the hiring of a director of diversity and equity such questions might be addressed. Further, the optics of such a plan, replete with a director, allows for those both inside and outside the school to understand the will and possibility for change. Such a plan might encounter a skeptical gaze, and, given the histories of art institutions, not unwarranted wariness, but it does open the door to systemic change—perhaps only a crack, but that is, as Leonard Cohen would say, how the light gets in.

Meanwhile, ACAD is mobilizing its SCI, its stated mandate being to "analyze the behaviors, attitudes, policies and practices throughout the college regarding issues of diversity, with a goal of becoming culturally competent both on an individual and institutional level." While its projected outcomes of "fostering diversity" are amorphous, with no specific language about practical changes in hiring or inclusiveness, the SCI is at least now part of the consciousness of ACAD and has the potential to foment actual change, given the will of leadership and grassroots alike. For instance, in the spring of 2007, the SCI led a number of workshops on the question "what does diversity mean to us?" ("Systemic Change Initiative"). The hiring of an SCI co-ordinator, while a step toward progressive action, is perhaps hindered by a rather sweeping definition of diversity, although, as the plan is implemented, both the definitions and the actions might become more concrete if given adequate resources and strong leadership. This is, after all, the crux of the matter: making effective change fluidly and with significant impact. Striking the balance between having accountable, transparent, and fair procedures and having flexibility to make quick decisions is not easy. At times change moves more slowly than one would like, to the degree that one either commits to a process with no guarantees or decides to focus one's energy elsewhere. As Creighton-Kelly puts it:

> Activist engagement in institutions must take into account democratic, participatory processes, even when they are tedious. It is messy, fiddling work, like constantly tinkering with a machine that has been designed by nine different people, knowing you will never get it in tune. It is work that has none of the grandeur of totalizing theories, none of the romance of "revolutionary" action, none of the comfort of institutional embrace. It is hard to imagine someone doing it for their entire career without burning out or eventually dulling their critique. (112)

The hope is that policies—be they around employment equity, affirmative action, curricular diversification, or harassment—are widely implemented in a school's culture, so that the burden of always standing up for "diversity" does not fall solely upon the few, still-struggling-not-to-be-token, faculty of colour while everyone else goes along, business-as-usual. As Richard Fung asked in 2002, "How many people of colour do we have within the boards or senior management of our large cultural institutions? We think it's a victory if there's one! And what this does is produce a burden on those individuals to be representative, to speak on behalf of race or ethnicity" (*13 Conversations* 78).

This brings us to the crux of the matter and the importance of recommendations that directly address racialization and equity issues within the ranks of the art school system.

5. Hire more racially/culturally diverse faculty and administrators.
6. Make hiring criteria interdisciplinary to meet this need.
7. Go outside the safety of our institutions for hiring expertise.
8. Implement affirmative action until equity is achieved.

The question of hiring and retention might seem an obvious one, but how to achieve such ends? More importantly, while there's often a will, or a rhetoric, of approval, it only counts if the end results are the hiring of diverse faculty. However, focussing on and practising radical interdisciplinarity has the potential for rapid change. While hiring criteria are often drafted (or finalized) in the boardroom and through Human Resources, a faculty/student/administrative movement to shift into the future (or try to keep pace with the present) is critically important. This can and will mean going outside the institution's walls and metaphorical insularity to bring in external consultants for hiring committees—not headhunting firms that tend to toe a conservative line, but members from racialized and disenfranchised communities who can walk into a hiring situation and assist with the difficult process of institutional change. The recommendation we land on, then, is an official implementation of equity hiring. We call this "affirmative action," a principle that has rarely been deployed in a Canadian setting that tends to favour a more polite, but relatively toothless, employment equity plan. That is, instead of casting a wide net and seeing who might apply, the suggestion here is for institutions to recruit actively and aggressively, taking into consideration factors such as the gaps among current faculty and demographics of student populations as well as those of the city, region, and nation.

NSCAD's employment equity policy provides working definitions to distinguish equal opportunity and affirmative action. It states, "Employment Equity is partly achieved when equal opportunities are provided through the removal of discriminatory barriers to employment and promotion, including the elimination or modification of all practices and systems, not authorized by law, which cannot be shown to be bona fide occupational requirements." However, employment equity by itself does not address historically inherited inequities that come with white supremacy. More is needed:

> Employment Equity is further achieved when affirmative action measures are promoted to reverse the historic under-representation in faculty, staff, and administration of women, aboriginal peoples, visible minorities, and the disabled. Affirmative Action measures include the introduction of positive policies and practices and the establishment of internal goals and timetables towards the achievement of employment equity by increasing the recruitment, hiring, training, and promotion of these designated group members. ("Nova Scotia College")

So, the explanation about why affirmative action is needed has been officially posted; the question that then remains is whether resources are devoted to identifying quantifiable goals and timetables.

Even if institutions manage to hire a few designated group members, what remains structurally daunting is the need for healthier redistribution of workload. We are thinking here of the depressing economics of higher education; basically, there are not enough permanent positions, and a systemic reliance on sessional faculty exploits the fact that there are more people available than jobs. This situation is endemic to the entire post-secondary sector, and art schools are no exception. What we observe is regular faculty with heavy teaching loads who are overworked and don't have enough time for their creative practice and research during the school year, and sessional faculty who are financially pressured to accept as many courses as possible because they work from contract to contract each semester. There are, of course, exceptions to these scenarios, but it remains a general pattern that we find disturbing and demoralizing.

There needs to be more attention given to how to retain, not just recruit, faculty from underrepresented groups, by addressing work-life balance, for instance. Better policies around sabbaticals and leaves of absence for personal reasons, as well as more support for faculty development (through exchanges, for instance) could perhaps help reduce turnover rates. People work at art institutes because they love those schools' environments, their subjects, their students, and so forth, but it is important that faculty not be burnt out. Coming up with solutions to this problem involves a radical redistribution of workload, paying attention to alternative models of job-sharing, team-teaching, and other labour issues. These kinds of readjustments could help to make working at art institutions more attractive to First Nations faculty, and artists in general, for that matter. An economic model that redistributes workload and resources more equitably could make art schools healthier and move them one step closer toward the decolonization that is so urgent yet still so far away if schools are to work toward being ethical, creative, and healthy places that foster innovation. This project of redistribution also speaks to the necessary development of a culture of research, one that is both inclusive and supportive, and that incorporates histories, practices, and methodologies previously excised from the curriculum and the very body of these institutions.

The glaring underrepresentation or absence of permanent First Nations or other racialized faculty in art schools raises questions: is it merely that employment equity policies are glacially slow, or is the colonial structure these institutions have inherited doing the work of normalizing marginalization and exclusion without needing to be explicit about it? For an art school to be truly welcoming, how does it need to change culturally, economically, and politically? "Cultural diversity" cannot be contained to surface notions of race, exemplified and foregrounded by four-colour glossy promotional brochures. In order to be ethically engaged, we need to turn our gaze toward the colonial inheritance that still haunts the halls of the art schools. While we might joke about renaming ECU as the Sophie Frank Institute, Sophie Frank being the Squamish basket maker who Emily Carr befriended,[5] the project to decolonize art schools needs active imagination on both a daily basis and at a structural level. As one (white) faculty member phrased it, "Coming out of the imagination of colonization is like learning how to walk again—so much undoing, and so much unfamiliar territory, and we don't have the training for it. It's about being open to thinking and seeing and perceiving differently than what we're used to" (Anonymous interview). Can art schools be made more welcoming at every level, from student to faculty to governing board, so that this process of evolving perception can occur? We certainly hope so, because such a welcoming would benefit everyone. In terms of sustainability, our long-term survival might well depend on how well we can adapt to the First cultures of this land and understand how privileges have been shoddily built upon losses and gaps. The challenge isn't merely how to employ First Nations faculty in tenure-track positions (though that seems to be already such a big hurdle), but how to learn and implement models of organization and processes that make institutional spaces more democratic and participatory in an embodied, daily way, so that the institutions work *for* communities rather than *on* them.

The most difficult, then, but concomitantly important recommendation is that of changing ways of thinking, which would include this component:

9. *Compulsory diversity training for existing faculty and administrators.*
Various training models have been applied at several schools, largely through student and faculty initiatives. In one of the initial forays into such planning at ACAD, we were struck by the desire and commitment of the student body, unfortunately unmatched by faculty or administration to the same degree. For effective transmission of ideas into action, of course, such plans require support at the highest administrative and the deepest grassroots levels. Indeed, because of the nature of shifting demographics and new hirings, there are varying levels of significant support among student and faculty at all the schools studied. We might be encouraged by the knowledge that several of these schools have increased faculty of colour and First Nations faculty by, in some cases, 200 or 300 per cent, until we recognize that this amounts to going from one to two or three people! But we also have to realize that even these small changes have come about only after significant groundwork by those already part of the institution, through volunteer or funded initiatives, local activism, and awareness-building projects that range from student lobbying to faculty professional-development workshops. However, until there is a shift in administrative sensibility, most likely taking the form of strategic equity hirings at the top levels, the status quo will likely continue. Initiatives such as OCAD's equity plans and ACAD's SCI are critical benchmarks, but will they have the tenacity to create actual and significant change within the foreseeable future, or will they, as have so many plans before, collapse on themselves when push comes to shove?

Overt or malicious racism is relatively rare in our day-to-day dealings in art schools, thankfully, yet neglect, polite indifference, complacency, overwork, and inadequate funding all contribute to our sense that we're in an unsatisfactory holding pattern, that more is possible—indeed necessary—to re-energize the halls of art schools, to sustain and improve their ability to serve many communities, not only the relatively privileged ones that have historically had access to them, despite the fraught and often marginalized position that generally comes with the word *art*. Andrea Fatona's warning echoes strongly:

> There's a certain face to institutions that suggest the work on equity has been done. This closes any kind of discussion on the fact that it's not just something that you do and it's done, but it's a continual process. This discussion must be ongoing. The discussions by people of colour have evolved and now take place in a host of different places and tones. The issues might be framed differently, but the actual fundamentals of representation haven't necessarily changed. One of my fears is that issues of representation are now falling outside of public discourse because of the ways in which they have been co-opted, particularly by institutions. I believe these issues need to be out there in the public sphere. Otherwise, they get sucked into spaces where they are no longer visible or important, and as a result of the "it's been done" attitude certain bodies and voices continue to be left out of the conversations. (41)

Imagine what it would take to make art schools healthier, inspiring, decolonized spaces. The kind of research produced in these spaces would value and incorporate cultural diversity as part of a larger shift from short-term economy to long-term ecology.

NOTES

1. Before May 2008 (during the time of the research for this essay), its name was Emily Carr Institute.

2. The event was part of a series of events collaboratively organized in 2005 by two artist-run collectives: Tribe—A Centre for Evolving Aboriginal Media, Visual, and Performing Arts, and the South Asian Visual Arts Collective (SAVAC). Both Tribe and SAVAC are artist-run collectives without a permanent space. They deliberately chose to intervene in educational institutions in Vancouver, Saskatoon, and Toronto—relatively permanent spaces that need to shift from assimilation to transformation.

3. This is slowly changing; as demand increases for First Nations art content in educational institutions, schools (such as Emily Carr University) are beginning to address these concerns in their job postings.

4. Curriculum development could, for example, directly address the questions outlined by Smith. She states that:

> In a cross-cultural context, the questions that need to be asked are ones such as:
> Who defined the research problem?
> For whom is this study worthy and relevant? Who says so?
> What knowledge will the community gain from this study?
> What knowledge will the researcher gain from this study?
> What are some likely positive outcomes from this study?
> What are some possible negative outcomes?
> How can the negative outcomes be eliminated?
> To whom is the researcher accountable?
> What processes are in place to support the research, the researched and the researcher? (173)

5. Someone who lived in poverty and lost nine children to the colonizer's diseases, Frank deserves to be remembered for her example as much as Carr.

SIX

SSHRC's *Strategic Programs, the Metropolis Project, and Multiculturalism Research*

THE CULTURE OF NO CULTURE, GOVERNMENT PARTNERSHIPS, AND CHALLENGES FOR THE HUMANITIES

Marjorie Stone

TWO KEY REPORTS, READ IN TANDEM, speak to the challenges the humanities increasingly face in a neo-utilitarian environment. One is the 2005 strategic plan for the SSHRC, *Knowledge Council: SSHRC, 2006–2011*—a primary impetus for this collection of essays. The other is the 2006 report "Large-Scale Research Projects and the Humanities" prepared by a working group for the CFHSS. The SSHRC document identifies "clustering research, building modern tools, mobilizing knowledge and connecting people" (16) as the strategic directions that will transform SSHRC from a granting council to a "Knowledge Council"; it also unequivocally states the Council's intent to focus "the largest relative increases" in an augmented budget on "clustering research, building research capacity and intensifying knowledge mobilization" (23). The Federation report draws on SSHRC's own statistics to document the growing underrepresentation of the humanities in the strategic and/or large-scale "clustering" and collaborative programs that increasingly dominate SSHRC's vision, values, and funding distribution. Its authors conclude that, while the humanities have maintained an equitable representation within the SRG Program, "between 1998/99 and 2003/04" there is "a noticeable trend that favours the social sciences as the ratio of expenditures as a percent of total research expenditures between the humanities and social sciences goes from double...toward treble" ("Large-Scale" 9). In the MCRI category, the humanists who constitute 28.2 per cent of the SSHRC community were represented in 14.7 per cent of projects between 1999–2000 and 2005–2006 (11); in the CURA and the strategic programs, percentages run from 10 per cent of the projects and 12 per cent of the researchers or lower (12). Moreover, such statistics obscure the degree of marginalization because a relatively limited range of humanities disciplines tend to be represented in large-scale funded research, and often these "span the boundary between humanities and social sciences," such as "history, communications & media studies, library and information science" (33–34).[1]

The environment for the humanities is especially threatening because the SSHRC strategic plan is clearly a manifestation of the larger government culture within which the Council functions under the federal Ministry of Industry. In other words, it reflects SSHRC's attempt to position itself favourably within the funding priorities determined by the Treasury Board and changing bodies of federal legislators in a politically fragmented and mutating environment. The pressures Department of Industry priorities can exert on SSHRC, together with high-level interventions in the use of its budget, have intensified since 2005, with any additional funding increasingly tied to programs in business and finance or applied research on the Canadian North.[2] I thus do not argue here that humanists' most effective recourse, in light of the Federation report, is to assail SSHRC for the neo-utilitarianism that underlies its strategic vision. A more comprehensive investigation is called for within the contexts that shape the changing institutional cultures in which humanists must adapt if they are to survive and thrive. In other words, we require analyses of "governmentality" in the fuller sense of Michel Foucault's term, incorporating conduct at differing levels, within individual subjects and particular cultures, not just technologies of power associated with the state (see Mitchell Dean).

This essay considers what humanists can learn from the Metropolis Project about the governmental structures and cultures shaping SSHRC's programs and research opportunities. While many humanists may have seen the Metropolis booth in passing at the Congress of Social Sciences and Humanities, most (to my knowledge) are relatively unaware of the project and greatly underrepresented in its extended policy-research networks. Why do such absences matter? They matter first of all because the Metropolis network engages in research on many subjects of great concern to humanists and the Canadian public, but it largely proceeds without participation from several humanities disciplines. As a key early model for SSHRC's large-scale partnering initiatives, the Metropolis Project also casts considerable light on the competition and consultation protocols for networked research, the interventionist role of government in targeted research programs, the marginalization of less applied humanities disciplines in such programs, and the challenges as well as the potential benefits of partnering with government and community organizations. While I focus on research programs relating to im/migration and multiculturalism, the structures and issues explored here have broader ramifications. Humanists should be especially concerned about the ways in which the marginalization of the arts, together with the disciplines that study them, is masked by the use of the omnibus term *culture* to signify a culture without culture. This phenomenon occurs in the Multiculturalism Program of the Department of Canadian Heritage (commonly referred to as "PCH," combining "Patrimoine canadien" and "Heritage Canada" in one initialism), the Metropolis Project that it helps to fund, and in SSHRC's 2005 *Knowledge Council* strategic vision. At the same time, the adversarial stance assumed by many humanists toward "official multiculturalism" is not without its own occlusions, a point I note briefly below, before proposing some strategies for humanists at the present time.

THE METROPOLIS PROJECT

The Metropolis Project is a joint-strategic program for research and public policy development on "migration, diversity, and immigrant integration in cities in Canada and around the world," as the website states as of July 2009 under "About Us" (<http://www.canada.metropolis.net>). Whereas MCRIS are normally limited to two five-year funding cycles, the Metropolis Project was awarded funding for a third five-year phase in 2007 to support its five national/regional centres (in Atlantic Canada, Montreal, Toronto, the Prairies, and Vancouver) and its international networks. The project provides a window on the federal government and its interface with granting councils because, while major funding for it comes from SSHRC, partnering funding as well as research themes and objectives are shaped by a consortium of a dozen or more federal departments and agencies (as of July 2009, fourteen—see the "Partners" link on the website). The number and mix of these partners has varied over phases of the project, as have the research agendas, but Citizenship and Immigration Canada (CIC) and the Multiculturalism branch of the PCH have consistently played leading roles. Co-ordinated by an Ottawa "Project Team" working in conjunction with a federal Interdepartmental Working Group and the Directors for the five Metropolis centres, the project also works with government partners at the provincial and municipal levels across the country, as well as with non-governmental organizations (NGOs) working in immigrant settlement, refugee services, and regional economic development, as well as in multiculturalism, anti-racism, and diversity organizations or programs.

One dimension of Metropolis activities that may be alien to many humanities researchers but that contributes to its vitality as a policy research network is that all of the project's activities are tri-sectoral, involving not only academic researchers, but also government and NGO partners. Within each of the centres, the research carried out is also tri-sectoral and organized into "domains" that vary to some degree among centres, although not in terms of core domains (for example, all five centres have an Economic Domain, although only one has a Domain on Gender and Women). The academic researchers come from diverse disciplines and, in each of the centres, from multiple universities. However, following the pattern analyzed in the 2006 Federation Report on large-scale research, the social sciences heavily predominate (especially political science, economics, sociology, anthropology, geography, economics, law), with some representation from more applied interdisciplinary studies (e.g., education, applied linguistics, urban studies, media and communication studies, religious studies, gender and women's studies). The social science focus of the project is reflected in the backgrounds of the dozen or more Metropolis Directors. During my own term as one of three Directors for the newly established Atlantic Metropolis Centre from 2004 to 2007, the latest centre to join the network, I was one of two humanists among the group initially, then the sole humanist. In other longer established centres, Directors all came from the social sciences.

WHY THE METROPOLIS PROJECT MATTERS
TO HUMANISTS

A primary cause for concern about the underrepresentation of several humanities disciplines in the Metropolis Project is that each has produced a great deal of research relevant to the issues the network investigates in its annual national and international conferences, regional workshops and colloquia, and its numerous publications. These issues include cultural identity and heritage, multiculturalism and intercultural understanding; racism, race relations, and human rights; economic, educational, and language training opportunities, and programs for immigrants; media representations of immigrants and minorities and their political representation; refugees, asylum issues, human trafficking, temporary worker programs, border surveillance and migration flows; transnationalism and diasporic networks; citizenship and its transformations with globalization; intergenerational dynamics in immigrant families; religious diversity; immigration history; immigrant health and well-being; and what might be termed migration ethics. Within the Metropolis Project, migration ethics is much less well developed than health ethics is outside of it, in part because philosophy is not well represented in its networks. However, especially in the form of political philosophy, it is much better represented than literary disciplines including English, French, Spanish, and Comparative Literature, as well as interdisciplinary areas such as post-colonial studies and cultural studies; disciplines that study the fine and performing arts are even more underrepresented. Research opportunities for many humanists are diminished by their lack of involvement in a large-scale strategic network of this kind, and there are attendant effects on funding for graduate students in their disciplines and the future of their programs. The Metropolis Project is also stunted in key dimensions by the absence of less applied humanities disciplines and its lack of attention to the arts, in particular. The similar marginalization of humanists within other SSHRC strategic programs means that their voices can be seriously underrepresented in Ottawa, as at "The Knowledge Project"—the February 2005 "knowledge fair" held by SSHRC in preparation for the release of its *Knowledge Council* strategic plan. For this event, SSHRC funded the attendance of delegates from MCRI, CURA, "Clusters," and strategic projects such as Metropolis, but not executive representatives of the sixty-plus learned societies that operate under the aegis of the CFHSS.

On a broader front, the Metropolis Project matters because the transformations in its agendas over its three successive five-year phases register the increasingly interventionist role of government departments in SSHRC-funded research, the intensified retreat from multiculturalism to "integration" following 9/11, and the "securitizing" of government discourses that occurred across a range of federal departments in a period when the Canadian Border Services Agency (CBSA) was created out of the border surveillance, policing, and migration control sides of CIC. This last development, a major restructuring, was imposed in a top-down, ad hoc manner with very little public debate and, ironically, very little input from researchers in the very Metropolis network created to provide government with policy-relevant analysis on such subjects. Both the integration agenda and increasingly directive role of government partners in the project were especially evident in the policy priorities set out in the Memorandum of Understanding (MOU) for the third five-year phase of the project beginning in 2007. In the MOU, the words *integration* or *integrating* recurred in the terms of reference for three of the six domain areas across the project's five centres; for this phase, the research priorities as well as the resultant domain areas were also more centrally determined by the consortium of federal partners. In contrast, in the first two five-year cycles, domain names and formations were articulated by academic researchers within each centre, although there was also an obligation to address identified federal priorities in a stated percentage of the research. The increasing emphasis on integration in phase three was accompanied by a declining emphasis on multiculturalism and diversity in the MOU; while multiculturalism is still mentioned in the document, it is framed as Canada's "multicultural approach to inclusion." The shift to a securitizing agenda in phase three, in combination with the "integration" model for managing immigrant populations, was especially evident in the requirement that at least some of the centres create domains focussed on justice, policing, and security aspects of im/migration. This requirement was a direct result of four new federal funders joining the consortium of partners for the project (departments and agencies dealing with justice, security, border control, and policing). In addition, structures were put in place in phase three that required more cross-country co-ordination and centralization of research by the five centres and more effective knowledge mobilization by the project's academic researchers.

Another reason why the Metropolis Project matters to humanists is that the competition protocols used to award funding differ substantially from those used up to 2009–2010 in the SRG program with its system of discipline-specific juries and reviews from peers. Moreover, the differences point to some of the challenges involved in obtaining independent assessment of large-scale networked and partnered research, especially when the research is targeted. While SSHRC maintains its usual rigorous standards of peer review through assessment by national and international groups of experts and by the requirement that each of the Metropolis centres submit detailed annual reports on activities (averaging over 100 pages), the presence of multiple government partners for the Metropolis Project results in mid-term reviews for the project that are in some respects akin to that used for the MCRI program, but in other respects closer to the process used in assessing government programs. For example, unlike the MCRI mid-term review process I have engaged in, the Metropolis mid-term review process is managed not by academic researchers but by professional consultants or auditors trained in program review; effective dissemination of research to government partners is also greatly stressed. In addition, the fact that the project is so extensively networked—indeed, a Canadian success story in terms of its global presence—presents challenges, since most Canadian researchers working on the issues it investigates are already part of the network, and many leading international social science researchers on migration have affiliations with it. There may be fewer differences in this respect than there appear in relation to the "blind" review in the SRG Program, since the group of specialists on a particular topic (e.g., a particular author within the field of Victorian poetry, to name my own principal special-ization) may not be large. That said, there are important procedural as well as quantitative distinctions between the system of individual peer reports SSHRC draws on in the SRG and the committee and consultant re-ports employed to award funding and to assess progress in strategic and large-scale projects.

As the Metropolis Project illustrates, the competitions for new fund-ing in networked research with government partners can, furthermore, move away from an open toward a closed system, more akin to a system of government tender or the applied research model of working for cor-porate partners that has proven to be a very mixed blessing in the case of the sciences. In this respect, it is instructive to consider the competition to create a fifth Atlantic Centre in the Metropolis network midway through the second cycle of the project, to join the four existing MAW centres (Atlantic-speak for Montreal and West). The competition was only creat-ed by SSHRC following several years of intensive lobbying and sustained investment in regional Metropolis-planning workshops and conferenc-es by the Ottawa Metropolis secretariat; Atlantic Canadian researchers on migration and diversity and interested university administrations; Atlantic immigrant settlement and multiculturalism agencies and asso-ciations; provincial and municipal government partners with the goal of attracting more immigrants to Atlantic Canada; and sympathetic federal partners in provincial offices and agencies such as the provincial offic-es of CIC, PCH, the Atlantic Canada Opportunities Agency (ACOA), Status of Women, and others. As the first Assistant Dean for Research in Arts and Social Sciences at Dalhousie University from 1999 to 2002, I was the "point-person" representing the university in this protracted series of multi-player, bridge-building regional negotiations. Contrary to the long odds many skeptics placed on the endeavour (given the challenges of working across four provinces, more than ten universities, multiple disciplines, community-university divides, and two official language groups), we ultimately developed a harmonious regional partnership, with Saint Mary's University acting as the lead institution among university partners. The formation and lobbying by the Atlantic consortium that this process precipitated, however, was not enough in itself to ensure any opportunity to compete for Metropolis Project funding. SSHRC could not proceed with the top-level commitment from the project's principal partners in Ottawa, and as so often occurs in such matters, there was opposition in some quarters to the financial investment at stake. Approval to make the partnership investment on the part of CIC, the lead federal partnering department, finally came among other legislative commitments in the last days of the Chrétien government, in part as a consequence of additional lobbying, in this case, by Atlantic Members of Parliament. A competition was then opened in which the Atlantic consortium for a Metropolis centre could compete. Although this was an open competition, it was also one in which there was only one competitor and in which we were given less than a month to prepare an application.

The absence of competitors did not, however, mean that the application to establish an Atlantic Metropolis Centre escaped rigorous peer review, since support for an additional centre among researchers within the four existing centres was mixed. On the one hand, some supported an Atlantic Centre and extended their aid and insider advice to colleagues in the Atlantic; researchers from the Prairies Centre with its similarly dispersed regional model of operation were particularly supportive, in part because in the first round of application for Metropolis Project funding in the 1990s they had been positioned as outsiders relative to the clusters from Montreal, Toronto, and Vancouver. On the other hand, some Metropolis researchers from the MAW centres saw the establishment of a fifth centre as a potential drain on funding they already found insufficient to support the kinds of activities and knowledge transfer their government partners were demanding. It is interesting to note that this opposition occurred despite the fact that numerous Metropolis social science researchers routinely carry out research on the importance of "social capital" networks to successful immigrant integration in the economy and Canadian society: that is, the critical role played by social networks and bonds in what is ostensibly a "free market" society. Ironically, however, they did not apply a "social capital" critique to the process involved in integrating "outsiders" into their own project. What the Metropolis Project therefore indicates is that "social capital" analysis—extended and enriched by a "cultural capital" analysis, I would add—may be particularly important to assessment of large-scale, networked research.[3] In fact, the larger the network, the more it may be necessary for sshrc to conduct an intensive social and cultural capital audit of the project's benefits and its openness to welcoming new members of the network. Much as a key research theme in Metropolis networks is creating "Welcoming Communities" for newcomers, sshrc should ensure that large-scale projects it funds are "welcoming" research communities.

The need for "social capital" audits of the inclusiveness of large-scale research networks is underscored by the further light that the Metropolis Project casts on sshrc's behind-the-scenes relationships with government partners and the closed loops that can be created when consultation processes (regarding suitable research themes, for example) are confined to an existing strategic network of partners. The likelihood for such closed loops to develop is compounded by structural "silos" within some of the very large government departments that sshrc collaborates with in its strategic programs. As in universities, the passive structural metaphor of the "silo" does not capture how differing branches of large government departments, with diverse histories, mandates, cultures, and visions, may operate as dynamically contested and competing domains, with all of the territorial rivalries and anxieties such conditions breed. These internal divisions are often invisible to those outside, in the academy or the general public, for whom government, especially at the federal level, constitutes an intimidating totality, much as the academy as the stereotypical "ivory tower" does. What academic has not at some point pictured government as Arthur Clennam does in Dickens's 1854 novel *Little Dorrit*? For Arthur, it is a labyrinthine, yet monolithic "Circumlocution Office" into which he ventures, accosting one official after another with the question "I want to know..." (Dickens 87, 95).

Although I regularly asked regularly asking Clennam-like questions of government policy workers, it took me some time to begin to grasp how SSHRC's consultation protocols, compounded by divisions within PCH, helped to explain the relative absence of several humanities disciplines from the Metropolis Project. These structural factors also contributed to the narrowly defined research objectives that made SSHRC's 2003–2006 Multiculturalism Joint Strategic Program (a separate program from the Metropolis Project) so alien to humanist researchers who investigated it as a source of potential funding. The research objectives of this program focussed heavily on quantitative social-science analysis of the Ethnic Diversity Survey (EDS) produced by Statistics Canada in collaboration with the Multiculturalism branch of PCH, a survey that also included very few questions related to diversity manifested in the arts.[4] Conversations with various PCH officers first led me to discern some of the structural and systemic factors underlying the Multiculturalism Joint Strategic Program's narrowly framed approach. One of the keys to the Metropolis Project's partnerships with federal departments is the "interdepartmental" meetings it hosts in Ottawa. At one of these in 2004, where I was invited to give a presentation on "culture," I buttonholed a PCH officer from the Multiculturalism branch that partners with Metropolis and bluntly asked him why the culture of the creative arts and the disciplines that studied them were so peripheral to the project. The first explanation he gave was that the Multiculturalism Program focussed on issues that have policy levers. When I questioned this explanation, pointing to the importance of the arts and culture sector to the economy, among other things, the officer then said that a primary objective of the branch was the promotion of social tolerance. In other words, he seemed to imply that works by Rohinton Mistry, Dionne Brand, M.G. Vassanji, Wayson Choy, Joy Kogawa, George Elliott Clarke, among many others, were unrelated to fostering social tolerance, and that the publication, dissemination, and study of such writers, involving hundreds of thousands of Canadians, did not connect to policy levers.

A subsequent, less direct encounter with this same PCH officer cast further light on the institutional cultures shaping the 2003–2006 SSHRC Strategic Program on Multiculturalism. In 2005, as one of the Metropolis Centre Directors for the newly established Atlantic Metropolis Centre, I received a letter from the Multiculturalism branch of PCH inviting input regarding themes for the next year's competition in the program. While the program as presented on the SSHRC website appeared to be distinct from the Metropolis Project, this letter indicated that it was more interconnected with the latter than such appearances would suggest. At the time, I noted this point with some concern, but seized the invitation as an opportunity to network with several Canadian literary and cultural scholars outside the Metropolis network with much more expertise in Canadian literature, multiculturalism, and ethnicity than I had (including Diana Brydon, Smaro Kamboureli, Christl Verduyn, and Winfried Siemerling, with whom I had earlier discussed the problems that the Multiculturalism Strategic Program posed for literary and cultural researchers). Together, we submitted a slate of themes that we thought would be more inclusive of the humanities while also suited to social scientists, and we were happy to see what we judged to be a more open set of research objectives for the program in its third year of operation. Some time later, I discovered that the author of the letter was the very policy officer to whom I had posed my questions at the 2004 Ottawa forum. Regarding the officer in question, I was well aware in this instance that one officer's take on multiculturalism did not a policy make—or unmake—having by this point met numerous members of Canadian Heritage's federal and Atlantic offices, many of them deeply committed both to advancing cultural interests and to the role of the arts in preserving and enhancing the multicultural heritage of Canadians. The larger question arising from the consultation letter, however, was the suitability of a consultation process drawing on a predominantly social science network of Metropolis Centre Directors to determine themes for a Strategic SSHRC program ostensibly intended to be equally accessible to humanists and social scientists. Would not the consultation process for such a program's themes be broadened, for example, by sending letters inviting input from presidents of learned societies in both the humanities and the social sciences?

Additional consultation and then collaboration in writing an essay on cultural citizenship with senior policy analysts from PCH (Sharon Jeannotte and John Foote)[5] helped me to understand further the institutional history behind the "culture without culture" in the Multiculturalism branch of PCH. They pointed me to a history of the department in a 2001 report by Greg Baeker et al., titled "'All Talents Count.'" As this report indicates, PCH was created in 1993 out of the merger of "Multiculturalism and Citizenship" with "the arts, heritage, culture and broadcasting sectors of the Department of Communications," along with programs for "official languages, Canadian Studies, native programs and state ceremonial responsibilities" from the former Department of the Secretary of State; amateur sport from the "Department of National Health and Welfare"; and "National Parks and Historic Sites from the Department of the Environment." As a result, Baeker comments, "the new Department found itself responsible for addressing issues of 'culture' and 'cultural diversity' in two contexts": "policy areas inherited from the Department of Multiculturalism and Citizenship and from the Department of the Secretary of State were concerned with Canada's commitments to 'culture and diversity' in the deepest, socio-cultural sense," whereas "policies and programs inherited from the Department of Communications interpreted 'culture and diversity' more narrowly in terms of policies related to arts, heritage, and cultural industries activities" ("All Talents Count'" 8). In a similar overview of the history of PCH in a 2000 report on "Cultural Policy and Cultural Diversity in Canada" for the Council of Europe (16, 25), Baeker comments on the "potential for policy confusion and disconnection between these two distinct policy arenas" and how it "may have been further exacerbated by the (false) public perception that early multicultural policy had been primarily concerned with funding for 'ethnic festivals'...[or] the 'three S's of saris, somosas, and steel bands'" (16). As his reports suggest, the marginalization of the arts within the Multiculturalism Program, and in turn within the Multiculturalism Strategic Program and the Metropolis Project, thus grows partly out of the structures of accountability and internal silos within PCH.

CULTURE WITHOUT CULTURE: THE METROPOLIS
PROJECT AND THE MULTICULTURALISM PROGRAM

The PCH internal silos the Baeker report describes have serious repercussions beyond the department for organizations, agencies, and groups
both in the cultural sector and the academy. These repercussions are
compounded by the more externally visible institutional gulf between
SSHRC (operating under the Department of Industry), and the Canada
Council (operating under a branch of PCH that is separate from its Multiculturalism branch). Together, these visible departmental barriers,
combined with the less discernible internal divisions within PCH, may
help to explain the absence of SSHRC Strategic Joint Initiatives in the area
of arts and culture aside from those involving new technologies. Chronic
underfunding for arts and culture is another undeniably major factor
in this instance, exacerbated by the cutbacks to funding for arts and
culture programs by the Harper government publicized by Yann Martel,
among other writers, in *The Globe and Mail*. Both these budget cuts and
the internal departmental divisions within PCH that I am describing are
especially difficult to delineate and resist because they are obscured by
the conceptual fuzziness of the omnibus terms *culture* and *cultural*. Thus,
in 2008 the Harper government could maintain that it was not making
cuts to the federal budget for arts and culture because, while it was
reducing funding for PCH branches in these areas, it was also investing in
sports, another form of culture for which PCH is responsible.

In a subtler manner, I would argue, the term *culture* functions to
mask the relative absence of the arts together with the disciplines that
study them in the Metropolis Project, funded by the Multiculturalism
program of PCH, and to a lesser degree in SSHRC's *Knowledge Council*.
In all of these contexts, we encounter references to "culture." While it
is clear that a "culturally vibrant world" and a "vibrant cultural and intellectual life" *are* valued in the context of the SSHRC *Knowledge Council*
document (4, 15), the strategic plan does not mention writers, artists,
or the disciplines that study their cultural expression. Since the keyword, *culture*, is, as Raymond Williams notes (80), one of the most
complex terms in the language, its umbrella use in a document directed

primarily at senior bureaucrats and decision-making ministers is understandable. Both historically and in the present, *culture* is possessed by what Michel Foucault describes as a "polyvalent mobility."[6] It is the lack of concrete terms associated with "culture" and its alternating presence and absence in the SSHRC document that give rise to more disquiet. For instance, there is no mention of the literatures disciplines, aside from a passing reference to the study of "modern languages" in the Appendices (20), which foregrounds the more utilitarian dimension of language study (also prevalent in the Metropolis Project), not literature, and shears away a substantial part of what most "modern languages" departments do. The one use of the word *literature* in the *Knowledge Council* report is an allusion to the need to reassess the status of "grey literature" (22): that is, writing that, like many government reports, takes the form of non-refereed, policy-driven materials. The absence of the term *literature* in its dominant humanities sense in this key SSHRC document occurs despite the fact that the growing number of researchers investigating literatures recently necessitated the creation of a second "Literatures" committee in the SRG Program in the period preceding SSHRC's *Knowledge Council* strategic plan.

Dick Stanley's categorization of the "three faces of culture" within the policy contexts of PCH helps to illumine some of the specificities the catch-all term *cultural* tends to swallow up in the SSHRC strategic plan as well as in PCH's mandate and operation and in the Metropolis Project. In a tripartite classification that overlaps with Williams's breakdown of the three principal senses of *culture* in *Keywords*, Stanley distinguishes among "Culture H" (the repository of past meanings and symbols, traditions), "Culture C," the making of new meanings and symbols through discovery and creative activity in the arts, and "Culture S," the set of symbolic tools from which individuals construct their "ways of living" (22–23).[7] Writers and humanists such as Roy Miki would no doubt find Stanley's lack of attention to the power dynamics at play in these categories problematic: Miki, for example, distinguishes the "cultural as a matrix for the social imagination of embodied subjects" from "'culture' as an achieved state to be possessed, commodified, or otherwise treated as a privileged container," emphasizing that the latter is more likely to "be found in complicity with political and economic regimes in power" ("Inside" 1). Stanley's monolithic definition of "Culture H" is furthermore predicated on an assumption of internal cultural homogeneity called into question by the work of philosophers such as Seyla Benhabib (3–4) and research on the complex dialogic forms of double consciousness, "fusion" culture, and diasporic forms of cultural citizenship by Winfried Siemerling (*New North American Studies*; *Writing Ethnicity*), Smaro Kamboureli (*Scandalous*), Gerard Delanty (*Citizenship*), and many other scholars.[8] That said, Stanley's simple tri-partite distinction is useful for my purposes because it brings into view the absence of "Culture C," in particular, from the sshrc 2005 Strategic Plan, *Knowledge Council: sshrc, 2006–2011*. Aside from a passing mention of "cultural 'outputs'" (7), it is "Culture S" that predominates. This more dominant meaning may help to explain why, in the all-caps preface to the plan's peroration, *cultural* disappears entirely from the list of modifiers, displaced (or covered over) by the term *social*: "TODAY, MORE THAN EVER, CANADA AND THE WORLD NEEDS ADVANCED KNOWLEDGE TO DEAL WITH OUR MOST PRESSING SOCIAL, POLITICAL, ECONOMIC AND ENVIRONMENTAL PROBLEMS" (25).[9]

The same conceptual fuzziness of the keyword *culture* that masks the marginalization of "Culture C" within the sshrc's *Knowledge Council* document also operates within the Metropolis Project. For example, at a 2001 Metropolis conference on "Identity" in Halifax, jointly sponsored by the Canadian Ethnic Studies Association, a background paper was commissioned on identity in "Sport" and another on "Culture," the latter covering identity and diversity in the four fields of literature, film, theatre, and music.[10] In the international context, we find collections like *Writing Across Worlds: Literature and Migration* (King et al.), which seeks to combine "the social scientist's concerns with explanation and the student of literature's expertise in the handling of text," arguing that literary works focus "in a very direct and penetrating way on issues such as place perception, landscape symbolism, senses of displacement and transformation, communities lost and created anew, exploitation, nostalgia, attitudes towards return, family relationships...and many more" (x). In the Canadian context, however, I have not encountered a comprehensive, interdisciplinary Canadian counterpart to this collection produced by the Metropolis networks. Nor is "Culture C" very visibly represented in annual national and international Metropolis conferences, which commonly involve eight hundred to one thousand participants. My own attempts, in collaboration with Sharon Jeannotte, Winfried Siemerling, Carrie Dawson, and others to organize a series of Metropolis workshops since 2002 involving literary and cultural researchers, representatives of NGO organizations like PEN Canada's "Writers in Exile" program, and government officers with a strong interest in the arts have seemed like so many drops in a succession of lagoons of policy-relevant social science research. At the 2005 International Metropolis Conference in Toronto, out of 104 workshops, only three featured any attention at all to literature and the arts. While the representation of film and media studies especially has been better at some national conferences, as of 2009 the participation of literary studies in the Metropolis Project has not greatly changed since 2002, despite the fact that literary disciplines lobbied SSHRC for more inclusion in the Project at that time, when the network was applying for a second five years of funding.

While I have found the Ottawa secretariat of the Metropolis Project as well as numerous PCH officers to be generally supportive of more participation from humanities disciplines and the arts, the attempt to address their underrepresentation encounters numerous obstacles. For example, for the 2008 tenth annual national Metropolis Conference in Halifax, the Secretariat and the organizing committee agreed to incorporate a statement I drafted into the Conference "Welcome" announcement and call for workshop proposals: "Recognizing that arts and culture often reflect emerging issues, events related to these themes will run throughout the conference, including film showings, theatre, visual arts exhibitions, dance, and readings." For the conference itself, Bruce Barber of the Nova Scotia College of Art & Design and others organized a series of visual arts exhibits, while others organized workshops related to the art.[11] However, finding funders to support such conference activities among the Metropolis Project's federal sponsors and provincial and municipal partners was very difficult, given the demand on Canada Council and PCH programs in the cultural sector, restraints governing the use of funds, the chronic underfunding of the arts and culture sector noted above, plus the absence of bridging networks uniting arts NGOs with immigrant settlement and multiculturalism organizations (the primary NGO partners of Metropolis).

CRITIQUING HUMANIST CRITIQUES OF "OFFICIAL MULTICULTURALISM"

It is also true that between 2002 and 2007 I did not encounter many literary and cultural researchers vociferously arguing for entry into the "big tent" of the Metropolis network, in part because for many it remains a relatively alien space where they will encounter so few of their peers in their own disciplines. Many humanists also have very little practice in partnering with government (as opposed to NGOs such as writers' federations), and in relation to "official multiculturalism" (hereafter OMC), in particular, they have assumed an oppositional stance to the state. There is no need to rehearse here the critiques articulated by figures such as Neil Bissoondath and Himani Bannerji, or explore the ideological differences among them. Bannerji can be taken as representative, however, in reiterating in *The Dark Side of the Nation* the view she earlier articulates in the 1990 anthology *Other Solitudes*: that OMC functions as an "ideological elaboration from above" in which immigrants are "ethnicized, culturalized and mapped into traditional/ethnic communities" in order to mask "structural and economic inequalities" (Hutcheon and Richmond, 44–45). Critiques of this kind, and they are legion, often rely on "ize" formations to present OMC as an ideological apparatus that marginalizes, ethnicizes, ghettoizes, minoritizes, essentializes, co-opts, domesticates, dehistoricizes, and fetishizes cultural groups (an array of the terms typically employed). This kind of approach is epitomized, for example, in Eva Haque's paper at the 2005 "TransCanada: Literature, Institutions, Citizenship" conference, the first of three important conferences co-organized by Kamboureli and Miki (<http://www.transcanadas. ca>). Like many before her, Haque argues that "language and culture are mobilized through the national formulation of multiculturalism within a bilingual framework in order to incorporate subjects into the current racialized hierarchy of belonging and citizenship rights" ("Multiculturalism"). Since Haque's paper draws on her OISE PHD thesis in sociology, it indicates that such characterizations of OMC are by no means limited to humanists. One encounters similar critiques within the Metropolis Project, like Colin Mooers's 2005 Working Paper "Multiculturalism and Citizenship," published by Toronto's Metropolis Centre, CERIS.

While such critiques make important points about the intersections of power, state agendas, neo-liberalism, and capitalism, they tend to reproduce OMC as an abstract, monolithic entity, functioning as a reified Other against which the critics define their own positions. They also anthropomorphize the "state" in ways that emphasize technologies of power from above more than the "governmentality" influencing differently positioned subjects acting from localized positions—often with somewhat conflicting agendas—both within government departments such as PCH and outside of it. In relation to literary and cultural studies, for example, they overlook the benefits that flowed from the Writing and Publishing Program (WPP) operated by the federal Multiculturalism Program for a period of twenty years, beginning in 1978–1979, before it was terminated, partly as a result of the massive restructuring that attended the creation of PCH in the 1990s, partly as a result of repeated attacks on the ghettoizing effects of "OMC." As Judy Young, the WPP director for many years, points out, the program provided 1,600 grants to individual writers, scholars, small presses, and community associations to support the publication of works by or about writers conveying "a specific cultural experience." She notes that many of the writers who entered the pages of the *Oxford Companion to Canadian Literature* between the 1970s and the 1990s were funded by or connected with the WPP at some point. It also funded a special 1980s issue of *Canadian Literature*, publishing what Young describes as the first major conference on literature, multiculturalism, and identity in the country, as well as *Other Solitudes*, the 1990 collection of Canadian "multicultural fictions" edited by Linda Hutcheon and Marion Richmond. Young rightly observes that literature is "a field in which debates and questions about diversity, ethnicity, race, [and] gender started earlier than in the other arts"—a point that makes its marginal status within the Metropolis Project all the more troubling. She argues too that literature is "an area in which Multiculturalism, both as government program and as social reality, has made significant advances" (6). A complete list of the subventions of the WPP over its final ten years that I obtained from PCH officer Austin Cooke indicates the role the program played in small presses in every region of the country. When Cooke gave a similar, though briefer, overview of the WPP to Young's in a session on "Literary Studies and the Metropolis Project" that I organized at the 2002 Congress, the thirty Canadian Literature and post-colonial specialists present seemed to agree on the important contribution the program had made, and expressed dismay at its termination (Cooke in Stone et al., "Literary Studies"). There is a striking contradiction, however, between this response to the WPP and the oppositional views on OMC I have noted.

While such oppositional critiques are vital to democratic institutions (even a responsibility, one might say to be effective, at least some of this criticism should be constructively engaged with and addressed to policy makers themselves. In addition, it would be helpful to see more inclusion of essays by policy makers like Young in academic anthologies and more attempts to include current government policy makers in conferences in literary and cultural studies, which, for the most part, take place without the participation of either government or NGO representatives. For instance, Young's essay on the WPP provides a counterpoint to the excerpts from Bissoondath and from Daniel Stoffman's glib but disturbingly reactionary essay on "The Illusion of Multiculturalism" included in Elspeth Cameron's anthology, *Multiculturalism and Immigration in Canada* (2004). Whatever one's views on Canadian OMC, it is important to keep in mind the larger context formed by the backlash against multiculturalism in many countries including our own. As Ella Shohat and Robert Stam point out in the "Introduction" to their 2003 collection, *Multiculturalism, Postcoloniality, and Transnational Media*, the "polysemically open" concept of multiculturalism is in some ways "an empty signifier onto which diverse groups project their hopes and fears." Unfortunately, they add, "At this point in history it is largely defined by its enemies from both ends of the political spectrum" (6). Often, too, critiques from the political left and right converge. The risk of reifying critiques of Canadian

OMC from the cultural left playing into the hands of critiques from the political right is particularly high at the present historical juncture. In an article posted on Open Democracy entitled "Remaking multiculturalism after 7/7," Tariq Modood cites some of the "waterfall of commentary" attacking multiculturalism in Britain as "misguided," "dangerous because it destroys political community," and "sleepwalking to segregation." Modood saw Canadian multiculturalism as resisting this backlash, but this is less and less the case.

PARTNERSHIP CHALLENGES AND RETOOLING STRATEGIES FOR HUMANISTS

The participation of more humanists in tri-sectoral conferences like those held by Metropolis might provide avenues for humanists to join the many social scientists expressing concern about more reactionary attacks on multiculturalism. Diana Brydon's characterization at a TransCanada conference of both the "Metropolis networks" and PCH as "toil[ing] on 'integration' continually" is prescient in discerning the "securitizing" and "integrationist" federal agendas I have noted as more pronounced in phase three of the project.[12] However, her monolithic characterization of both Metropolis and its PCH partners overlooks one of the valuable dimensions of the Metropolis Project. In my experience, the network's conferences and workshops "continually" provide forums of exchange in which NGO delegates (including members of cultural minorities, representatives of the Canadian Council for Refugees, anti-racism workers, activist lawyers, and union leaders, for example) can and do challenge "integrationist" agendas, as well as immigration and refugee policies, either through the plenary or workshop panels in which they are speakers, or through the "open mike" Q&A sessions that follow all conference plenaries (which often address controversial issues such as the French government's policies on the hijab, for example, or living without citizenship status.) Furthermore, many social scientist researchers within Metropolis have sharply critiqued the increasingly interventionist role of the federal government in determining the research priorities of the network.

While there is much to criticize in the marginalization of the humanities within the Metropolis Project as it currently operates, strategic networks of this kind also provide an opportunity for humanists to learn more about the challenges of policy-driven and/or partnered research, even for social scientists engaged in the kinds of quantitative and applied forms of research that government partners often emphasize. For humanists, as I note above, these challenges are compounded by the probability that both the government programs and the NGOs that provide the most likely sources of partners (for example, arts councils, writers' federations, small publishers, regional theatres, and PEN Canada's Writers in Exile program) are often the most likely to be significantly under-resourced. That said, in many instances the difficulties that academic researchers must negotiate in policy research and knowledge mobilization are common to the human sciences. These challenges include: (1) reconciling pressures for policy-driven research with the vital academic and public need for curiosity-driven research, and balancing government priorities with the public good; (2) developing productive partnerships with policy officers only to find key contacts rotated to another department or portfolio, and recognizing that both government workers and NGO partners work within different institutional structures of accountability and often lack the job security and protection of academic freedom enjoyed by tenured researchers; (3) acknowledging that, as a corollary of this lack of security, government and NGO partners may need to negotiate the language in which critiques of policies and programs are articulated even when they strongly agree with them; (4) balancing the differing reward systems of the academy and government (peer-reviewed articles vs. "grey literature" reports) and addressing knowledge-mobilization demands that entail packaging complex, nuanced research issues and results into encapsulated policy "outcomes" that can be presented to a Deputy Minister in summary form.

An important question that sometimes arises in the context of such partnerships is whether it is always quantitatively measured "findings" and "data" that federal partners most desire or need from academic researchers, delivered in the kinds of "outputs" that SSHRC's knowledge-mobilization agendas emphasize. In fact, Meyer Burstein, the visionary founder of the Metropolis Project and a former senior bureaucrat in CIC, has observed that SSHRC may have overshot the mark with its emphasis on "transferring" targeted, policy-driven research outcomes to its government partners.[13] Such an emphasis, in his view, risks undermining the very dimensions of academic research (its paradigm-questioning, for example) that might be of most value to policy makers. At Metropolis centre annual planning retreats and Centre Director meetings, I have also often heard senior government policy makers—both at the federal and provincial level—give less emphasis to quantitative findings than to the conceptual value of academic research in bringing them up to date with new knowledge and in assisting them to "re-frame" complex policy questions. As the Canadian Federation for the Humanities and Social Sciences report on "Large-Scale Research Projects" notes (although in the context of social sciences research), in many government agencies, "conceptual use of research...is more common than instrumental or symbolic use of research," a finding that suggests "less solution-oriented research from the humanities also has the potential for broad impact within government" (8). While this may indeed be true, the potential for such "broad impact" may never be realized, of course, if the partnerships and communication channels that facilitate it do not exist in the first place.

Among the changes in the culture of the humanities that may be important at the present time, the creation of networks, forums, organizations, and other mechanisms for generating and facilitating such partnerships seem to me to be especially critical. There is a special need for partnerships that cut across silo formations within government or departments of government (e.g., the differing branches of the PCH), or bridge the structural and governmental gaps that separate educational curricula in post-secondary institutions from those in high schools (resulting in a troubling lag in the incorporation of "new" multiethnic writers into high school curricula). Critiques of government policies such as multiculturalism or integration (sometimes masked as *interculturalism*) also need to go beyond totalizing constructions of the "state" to draw on consultation with individual program officers and investigation of specific programs and policy implementations, as the example of the WPP suggests. Within programs like the Metropolis Project, more inter-disciplinary collaborations with social scientists might permit a fusion of qualitative and quantitative approaches, combining "stats with stories," or macro statistical data with investigation of individual creative and social expressions (e.g., studies of changes in curriculum or increasing production of works by immigrant writers and their connections to more wide-ranging social and/or political changes). These kinds of collabora-tions are often facilitated by what Mieke Bal terms "bridging concepts," which many humanists are well versed in (e.g., employing narrative or metaphor as methodologies to work across disciplinary boundaries or differences between academics and NGOs and policy makers), or by the development of new interdisciplinary fields (e.g., "migration humani-ties," on the model of "medical humanities," in relation to Metropolis research). Within text- and author- or artist-centred disciplines, more investigation of developments that involve communities and trends might act to foster productive partnerships between the humanities and social sciences (e.g., sociologies of reading communities,[14] surveys of cul-tural texts as indicators of shifting values; creative cities research, and the mapping of "culturescapes").

This essay is not wholly directed at humanists themselves, however. As I have indicated above, I believe that it is also incumbent upon SSHRC to carry out "social and cultural capital" audits of the larger research net-works it funds to ensure that they are "welcoming" and inclusive across the full spectrum of disciplines covered by its mandate. It would further be useful to analyze SSHRC collaboration protocols and structures in light of collaboration theory developed within various humanities disciplines in order to tease out and address issues of hierarchy, hegemony, agency, access, authorship, and ownership. Co-ordinated requests by human-ist learned associations to SSHRC might call upon Council to ensure that consultation processes for identifying research themes in its Strategic Joint Initiative programs involve humanists as well as social scientists; or that "Requests for Proposals" for targeted research on policy issues from federal departments are more widely disseminated (possibly through a set of links or an RFP "bulletin board" on the SSHRC site), as opposed to within particular research networks like Metropolis. SSHRC might also do more through its strategic programs to create incentives for humanists to engage in more tri-sectoral forums that bring together academics, community representatives, and government representatives (forums on, for example, the emerging concept of "cultural citizenship" or the effects of Canadian cultural diplomacy). And as SSHRC and Federation officers have often remarked, humanists need to work to change university tenure and promotion cultures that do not adequately recognize and reward the dissemination of research in policy papers and magazines that may have a wider circulation and employ more accessible language than that used in traditional academic publications.

I advance these "retooling strategies" not as someone whole-heartedly wedded to them, but as survival strategies worth investigating by humanists in a world where new alliances and approaches may be critical to the preservation of what we value most. Is it dystopian at the present moment to imagine a future government directly intervening to redesign SSHRC's granting programs or even to dismantle the Council as we know it? I wish that I could believe it was. Likewise, just as the PCH was formed out of other departments and agencies in the early 1990s, it can also be disaggregated or dissolved and reconfigured into a new formation. What might be the consequences of such developments within university programs that study literature and culture, and the research programs that inform these and support a new generation of researchers? In his famous defence of poetry, Shelley defined one function of literature as helping us "to imagine that which we know." It is also useful to seek to imagine what we do not yet know.

NOTES

1. See Appendix A of the Federation report for more detailed statistics and breakdowns.

2. The Canadian government's spring 2007 budget allocated $11 million in additional funding to SSHRC, all of it specifically targeted to research in finance, business, and the economy. This state intervention in the funding allocations of SSHRC has occurred under a minority government; a majority government with a similar

vision might intervene even more directly in SSHRC's established budget to direct research funding allocations among differing disciplines and fields of research. It also occurs in a period when the success rate of 29 per cent within one of SSHRC's two Literatures Committees compares to a success rate of 49 per cent for applications adjudicated by the Economics Committee.

3. For a summary of definitions of *social capital* and *cultural capital* as these concepts have been articulated by Robert Putnam and Pierre Bourdieu respectively, see Stone, Destrempes, Jeannotte, and Foote, pp. 109–10.

4. For more information on the Ethnic Diversity Survey, see the link to "Ethnic Diversity and Immigration" on the Statistics Canada website: <http://www41.statcan.ca/2007/30000/ceb30000_000-eng.htm>.

5. Sharon Jeannotte, now senior fellow at the Centre on Governance at the University of Ottawa, was senior advisor to the Canadian Cultural Observatory in the Department of Canadian Heritage from 2005 to 2007. From 1999 to 2005, she was the manager of International Comparative Research in the department's Strategic Research and Analysis Directorate. John Foote was a member of the department's Policy Research Group at the time of my collaboration with him.

6. Foucault's term is cited by Stoler (376), and applied by both to racial discourses.

7. I am indebted to Sharon Jeannotte for directing my attention to Stanley's essay. The conceptual slipperiness of "culture" is more fully addressed in "Immigration and Cultural Citizenship: Responsibilities, Rights, and Indicators" by Stone, Destrempes, Jeannotte, and Foote (104–06).

8. For a summary of recent theories and concepts of "cultural citizenship," see Stone, Destrempes, Jeannotte, and Foote (106–09).

9. The omission of "cultural" from this list seems an especially curious omission at a time when some of the most high-profile issues, controversies, and "problems" in recent times have turned on cultural representations (for example, the targeting of Salman Rushdie's *Satanic Verses* by Ayatollah Khomeni's fatwa, the murder of Dutch filmmaker Theo van Gogh, Danish cartoons, the Redress movement by Japanese Canadians stimulated by Joy Kogawa's *Obasan*). Accompanying this disappearance of the term *culture*, humanists also disappear in the paragraph this statement introduces, where "scientists" and "social scientists" are identified as those who can deliver "real lasting solutions to terrorism, AIDS, poverty, global warming."

10. The paper, "Culture and Identity: Ideas and Overviews," was capably dispatched by Liane Curtis, Dipti Gupta, and Will Straw. As one might expect, however, there were multiple gaps and absences in a background paper of standard article length seeking to cover all of these fields. Two literary and cultural specialists in Canadian literature who participated in the conference—Christl Verduyn and

Barbara Godard—confirmed my sense that the paper omitted a large amount of relevant work on identity in literary and cultural studies, where interest in this theme had developed two decades before this particular "Identity" conference took place (on this last point, see also Judy Young below).

11. Bruce Barber worked with Halifax curators and with Mern O'Brien of the Halifax office of PCH to organize a Newcomers Art Exhibit, running through the conference; Susan Walsh, of Mount Saint Vincent University, organized a workshop incorporating presentations by immigrant artists and by Shahin Sayadi, creator and director of One Light Theatre; and Chedly Belkhodja, a political scientist and film maker at Université de Moncton with a strong interest in cultural expression, organized film showings. Unexpected illness meant that I could not follow through on co-ordinating the organization of more workshops and events featuring the arts in the conference.

12. See Brydon's "Metamorphoses of a Discipline: Rethinking Canadian Literature within Institutional Contexts," given as a conference keynote, and published in Kamboureli and Miki, *Trans.Can.Lit.*

13. Burstein's comments were made at the annual strategic planning retreat of the Prairies Metropolis Centre in Edmonton in February 2005, in the same month when SSHRC held "The Knowledge Project" fair in Ottawa noted above.

14. One example of such a project is the transatlantic Beyond the Book project (<http://www.beyondthebookproject.org>), headed by Danielle Fuller (University of Birmingham) and DeNel Rehberg Sedo (Mount Saint Vincent University).

"everything wants to hang together"

RE-IMAGINING ROY KIYOOKA'S
ACADEMIC SUBJECTIVITIES

Paul Danyluk

> "pedagogy" is an act of faith these maladroit days when Whitman's, not to
> mention MacLuhan's, Democratic Vistas have turned into a cancerous eco-
> nomics. there's a pall hanging over our whole Education system and i suspect
> it has something to do with more than the economic morass, the stab-in-
> the-back "cutbacks" in funding at all levels—it has something to do with the
> surmise that "we" as educators have been complicit in the very inequalities
> we are besodden with.
>
> —Kiyooka, Pacific 304

> Tho I am in my way "adept" at playing the part of a man at large in the wide
> world and tho I wouldn't dismiss the myriad rituals of any Citizen's public
> office, I know for myself that the endless machinations of our public offices are
> fundamentally heartless.
>
> —Kiyooka, Pacific 207

THAT TODAY'S INDEPENDENTLY-MINDED, though never truly independent,
humanities scholars are forced to negotiate their professional identity in
an academic environment increasingly shaped by corporate notions of use
value is not a new phenomenon. As Roy Kiyooka's observation on the state
of bureaucracy reminds us, such "machinations" might be "heartless,"
but those privileged enough to critique their operations are themselves
complicitous and must choose, if they so desire, how to mitigate that

complicity through critical resistance. Faced, as we are in the humanities, with no chance of professional survival outside the public structures this volume is designed to examine, it has become necessary to find ways to activate responsible critical perspectives so that we do not risk disengaging from either our object of study or from society at large. Embracing a future of uncertain job markets and governmental calls to change the ways we research, this essay looks to Roy Kiyooka as an academic, artist, and teacher from a previous generation in an attempt to trace the trajectory of what has changed in the profession and understand what remains in the always-shifting corridors of academia. Getting behind the epigraph to appreciate Kiyooka's understanding of his own complicity in the structures of academe promises to offer a productive model of critical engagement with the structures that shape our professional lives.

Attempting to respond to some of the overarching concerns raised by the contributors to this volume, this essay offers an evaluation of the present academic environment with its reliance on research profiles and quantitative measuring of academic success. Not suggesting a revolutionary move away from present methods of performing academically, I believe that success in the academy arises from an equal share of diligence and creativity, mixed with a healthy dose of ambivalence. The ambivalent academic is aware of the machinations surrounding his or her work and is able to negotiate them without losing sight of personal, intellectual, and creative growth. Rather than a subject position of stagnant indecision, the responsible academic's ambivalence extends from and engenders broader perspectives by encouraging a holistic approach to research and pedagogical practices.

Linking literary analysis with structural critique I gauge this ambivalence by employing Roy Kiyooka as a paradigmatic instance of a multidisciplinary artist in academe whose concern with professional issues anticipates SSHRC's current mandate. Kiyooka's letters present him as an idiosyncratically responsible academic who integrates interdisciplinarity and collaboration, though close readings of his letters suggest that he would not be an ideal SSHRC candidate. His oftentimes-irreverent interactions with authority figures and a desire to remain independent of the "system" render him not professional enough for research grant funding. Such an imaginative projection is supported by Kiyooka's posthumously published *Pacific Rim Letters* that invites us to read it in relation to the current university research environment that his career predates. Not merely a nostalgic look back at a supposedly simpler time, this analysis considers those aspects of critical and creative work that are jeopardized through the standardized awarding of career-building grants through SSHRC's professionalizing discourse of producing, and widely distributing, knowledge.

A RESPONSIBLE ACADEMIC

Roy Kiyooka's *Pacific Rim Letters*, a collection of letters he wrote between 1975 and 1985, and edited posthumously by Smaro Kamboureli, can be read as autobiography, but also as literature and cultural commentary "in which Kiyooka expounded on photography, pedagogy, capitalism, 'art biz' in general" (Kamboureli, "For What" 335). The correspondences that emerge from this text between Kiyooka's roles as poet, artist, intellectual, and professor of fine arts at the University of British Columbia reveal a subject whose pedagogical and academic actions are grounded in a multidisciplinary art practice that, in turn, reveals the imperative to remain alert to the "always alternate perspectives" that should inform academic teaching and research (Tsang 91). These alternate perspectives become apparent in Kiyooka's letters to the dean of his faculty and the letters of reference he wrote for colleagues and students. The often conflicting roles Kiyooka performs as "disciplined" university instructor and radical educator dramatize the tensions and complicity characterizing the different institutional narratives with which he engages. Kiyooka's ambivalent relationship with the academy, as evidenced in *Pacific Rim Letters*, and his earlier collection, *Transcanada Letters*, provides a case study for examining the intersections between artistic practice and academic subjectivity in the Canadian university system.

Negotiations with power structures mark Kiyooka's subject formation from an early age, beginning with his family's relocation from

Calgary to Opal, Alberta, during the Second World War. Designated an *enemy alien*, Kiyooka was forced to quit high school and help support his family, first finding himself "transformed from an agile city kid with soft hands into an ungainly but tough as nails farm boy," then later working "on the killing floor" of a meat processing plant in Edmonton, followed by summers as a fish processor in the North West Territories (Kiyooka, "Dear Lucy" 22). Indelibly shaped by these experiences, Kiyooka "was rarely bitter" according to Daphne Marlatt, though he often displayed a perceptive cynicism toward "bureaucratic small-mindedness...[and] sleazy inauthenticity" (Marlatt 14). This cynicism, drawn from keen observations of the world around him, certainly did not preclude Kiyooka taking great care of the lives of everyone he knew. Reading through recollections from friends and colleagues leaves one with the distinct impression that Kiyooka thrived on the energies of conversation and revelled in the foibles of others, while never being mean-spirited, never judgemental: "he gently and generously teased, probed and poked. He could be personal yet not personal simultaneously in his friendship...he would drive right into the core of the issue with an all-encompassing perspective" (Itter 27). The playful seriousness that marks his friendships with lovers and students alike is reflected in the art that first brought him public notice and the teaching that secured his influence among generations of artists and writers.

Kiyooka began his life in art under the tenets of abstract expressionism, studying under painters J.W.G. MacDonald and I.H. Kerr at the Provincial Institute of Technology and Art (now Alberta College of Art) in Calgary from 1946 to 1949 (Kamboureli, "For What" 350; O'Brian 150). Though starting his career in the painting mainstream of the 1950s, Kiyooka's creative practice would not remain stable, as he would soon make his own way through the art world, influenced by the changing cultural landscape of the 1960s where "conceptual ideas began to take precedence over the art object; the new media of performance art, installation, and video emerged; [and] artist-run centres sprang up across the country" (Vida 10). Kiyooka gave up painting in the late 1960s (10) in reaction to what he saw as the increasing consumerism of the Canadian art scene. Progressively more interested in the collaborative possibilities across art forms and among various artists, Kiyooka began to explore new forms and new ways of understanding the world through art and creative collaboration. As John O'Brian, Naomi Sawada, and Scott Watson note, "increasingly [Kiyooka] saw the position of the artist in opposition to the institutions of art" (150). This oppositional stance was not only reflected in his creative practice, but was also an integral part of his pedagogical practice that extended beyond coursework to embrace the mundane, the unexpected, the fantastic.

Kiyooka's university teaching saw him crossing the country from Regina to Vancouver, from Montreal to Halifax, and back again to Vancouver where he ended his teaching career at the University of British Columbia in 1991 (O'Brian, Sawada, and Watson 150). Far from conforming to the expectations of his institutional locations, Kiyooka performed his role as university teacher in idiosyncratic ways, as highlighted in Henry Tsang's anecdote about the first class he took with him:

> He [Kiyooka] tilted his head sideways to consult the ceiling, then back to us, then to the ceiling again, finally shaking his head and muttering, "No, no, there's far too many."....Then he said, louder, projecting, "There are too many of you for this class. Some of you will have to leave."...He just stood there....We waited...for something else to issue forth from him...but he was finished, he had said all that he needed to say. So eventually everyone left. And when it was time for class the following week, there were four of us. (Tsang 84)

In an essay on Kiyooka's pedagogical practices Tsang reveals Kiyooka's non-standard methods of teaching art, especially painting, as advocating a close engagement with the self as essential to creativity. Tsang's image of Kiyooka demanding a manageable class size presents him as a teacher not concerned with the institutionalized commodification of learning, but with real human interaction as integral to teaching and learning. In doing so, Tsang sets up Kiyooka as a resistant academic, a figure who will not submit to institutional demands at the risk of jeopardizing educational value. Tsang notes how in the classroom Kiyooka thematized the everyday realities of life as an artist and an academic when he "spoke of the nitty-grits like buying groceries, making meals, washing the dishes and the challenge of finding the balance between the incidentals of living in this world...with that of being an artist" (85). This refusal to dismiss the mundane from the teaching of art demonstrates a critical need to engage with the complications of living and learning that Donna Palmateer Pennee introduces through the trope of the "not negligible." As an academic practice this trope involves "mobilizing different kinds of representations...to teach and learn differentiation while also teaching and learning similarities that are not reducible to sameness" ("Literary" 82). In this way the quotidian distractions Tsang refers to constitute an integral element of Kiyooka's pedagogy; the quotidian is distinctive yet shared. By highlighting everyday life as "not negligible" within the realm of academia, Tsang shows Kiyooka to be a teacher with a complex understanding of self, and as an educator who insisted on the uniqueness of the people he encountered within and through the bounded sites of the academy.

The process of constructive and all-encompassing critique that Kiyooka's teaching performs is an important element of what I term the responsible academic. A responsible academic asks penetrating questions and pushes limits of knowing and teaching in ways that leave the whole community, be it local, scholarly, ethno-racial, or national communities, enlightened, invigorated, and eager to continue asking questions. I approach this understanding of academia from a site of multiplicity and "critical intimacy" as encouraged by Diana Brydon. In discussing the ethics at play in the post-colonial classroom, Brydon argues that "post-colonial pedagogy looks ahead through looking critically and intimately at the learned forgetfulness and complacency built into the educational project as we know it and its complicities with both imperialist and nationalist projects" ("Cross-Talk" 63). As a classroom practice, Brydon adopts the pedagogical position that, "through postcolonial pedagogy, the teacher will be changed along with her students, and the commitment to changing cannot end with the end of the school year" (64). This implication that the student and teacher are treated as whole beings necessitates a move away from scholarship and teaching that produce authoritative readings of texts to scholarship and teaching that are open to the play of signification within texts, the classroom, and within one's own self as student, teacher, and scholar. This multiplicity creates a personal critical engagement with the object(s) of study that encourages reflection while inviting an interventionist reading and learning practice.

Kiyooka's strong advocacy for art as personal exploration under-scores an insistence on the role of intuition in critical thinking (Tsang 92). This idea is complemented by Tsang's description of Kiyooka's art as a multidisciplinary practice that enacts "a continuation of an ongoing dialogue" (90) through which "there were always alternate perspec-tives" (91). The "not negligible" status of Kiyooka's daily activities intersects with the importance of art and pedagogy that mark his role as a responsible academic teacher and researcher. Understanding academic engagement with the "not negligible" "as method, as a set of relations, as potential" (Pennee, "Literary" 79), requires the critical practice of recog-nizing, accepting, and engaging with the differences that inform human experience. Such attention to the particularities of difference encourag-es a wider frame through which to view the academic, both as a complex human subject and as a professional institutional construct.

ON THE INSIDE, ACTING OUT

The drive to understand the self and/as other results in a need to artic-ulate one's own image of the self as clearly as possible. This need for a re-articulated conception of the academic subject drives Kiyooka's attempts to describe the role of the artist/academic/critic in a 1983 letter to the University of British Columbia's Dean of Arts, Robert Will (*Pacific* 203–05). A response to being denied a year-long sabbatical, the letter is a showcase of rhetorical flourish and critical condemnation of the sys-tematic containment and control of faculty in the early 1980s. Directly challenging the false notion that the university professor must function as a specialized tool to be used by the faculty, Kiyooka asserts his own academic subjectivity as a direct response to his artistic and personal experience:

For what it's worth, I want to say that the notion of the unspoken institutional containment, e.g. "you were hired as a painter to teach painting
and you had better stick to it, etc.," doesn't make much sense to an inside
practitioner. Furthermore, it seems to me wholly unwarranted by the very
nature of art with its myriad transformations. For what it's worth, I have
from the very beginnings of my life in art/pedagogy held to an ideal which
goes like this: any faculty member's own intellectual (albeit creative)
growth ought to find a forum in the domain of pedagogy. All the more so
in the Fine Arts where the unspoken mandate is: "cast a keen eye on the
riddled universe and paint or speak of its coruscations." (203)

Kiyooka's insistence on the role of pedagogy in art and research critiques
institutional and, when read in today's climate, sshrc practices that
value a useful product over the craft of teaching new ideas in the classroom or outside strict curricular definitions. Kiyooka's discussion of
academic and creative constructs foregrounds the complexity inherent
in the academic subject position he occupies. By articulating his holistic
position, he asserts the right and responsibility of the academic intellectual to occupy multiple subjectivities at once. (He was granted the leave
he had requested, but only after an exchange of many memos, the letter
quoted above appearing to be the one that helped resolve the issue.)

The ambivalence of the academic subject is highlighted by the shifts
in tone and self-reflexivity that signal Kiyooka's difficulty in comfortably inhabiting the spaces of academia. Beginning the letter by listing the
contents of his "bag of perturbations" (*Pacific* 203), Kiyooka continues by
explaining that he tried to let go of his frustration: "'So be it. It ain't the
end of the world. It ain't nuclear missiles'...even as something in [him]...
whispered 'Tell it the way you feel, you have nothing to lose speaking on
behalf of your sense of art'" (203). This radical desire to tell a personal
truth within the institutional frame of the fine arts department is tempered by Kiyooka's need to nonetheless accede authority to institutional
power read in his frequent repetition of the phrase "For what it's worth"
(203, 204). Marking the beginning of the two middle paragraphs of the
letter, this phrase is a critical interjection of Kiyooka's academic subjectivity into the logic of the academy, which he clearly aims to correct and

enrich, not abandon or considerably restructure. Its first use, seen above, establishes what he sees as a problem with the containment of creative and critical practice within the confines of his department. In the second instance, this containment is thematized through a critique of the practice of artistic specialization, as it "indenture[s] the artistic impulse": "For what it's worth, let me assure you that the painter you thought you hired was much more than that all along" (204). This assurance reveals that his particular type of scholarship, the act *and* art of teaching and learning art for himself and others, is grounded in a counter-modern impulse. This impulse views the fact that the "Industrial Revolution with its grand procession of magnificent machines spelled the beginning of the end of a hitherto 'ambidextrous' human being": "bit by bit his varied skills got translated into a particular kind of quantification machine" (204). This machine mentality denies the "relevant dialogue" (204) that constitutes pedagogy, and that is the basis of art as Kiyooka sees it and practises it. While accusing the dean of promulgating and practising the heartless machinations of bureaucracy, the letter's efficacy lies in the idea that depersonalization is not total, and can be resisted by a deeply personal analytical reckoning of one's professional academic self.[1]

Offering a view into the changing professional academic landscape, Kiyooka laments what he sees as his status as a second-class academic.[2] Having sat on the "tenure and promotion committees" and advocated for younger colleagues whose art and critical practice were in conflict with "the conservative art historians and their dominant views" (*Pacific* 203), he watched younger, accredited colleagues receive sabbatical leaves while he was routinely denied (203). Feeling he has "fallen head over heels into a large credibility gap which is to all intents and purposes not of [his] own making" (203), Kiyooka nears the end of his career in the early years of hyper-professionalization; his anger and frustration record the changing field of Canadian academia in the 1980s. Kiyooka's institution, like other Canadian universities, was undergoing a radical shift that would see the adoption of increasingly corporate models of governance, progressively more funding from private business donors, and the realignment of the university as a customer service–driven entity concerned with maximizing student turnover and encouraging research production based on performance indicators and needs often defined from outside the academy.

Kiyooka's view of himself as essentially an outsider operating on the inside of academia reflects Brydon and Pennee's depictions of the academic as a multi-faceted social thinker. This model of the academic is comparable to the figure of Edward Said and his construction of the academic intellectual. In a series of lectures collected in *Representations of the Intellectual*, Said examines the image of the intellectual in Western culture. Borrowing from a diverse range of representations, from pre-revolutionary Russia, through early Modernism, to the late twentieth-century non-European academic figures of Salman Rushdie and himself, Said presents the intellectual as always socially bound yet imbued with an awareness of his or her boundedness. In establishing a social reality whereby "every human being is held in by a society, no matter how free and open the society, no matter how bohemian the individual" (69), Said highlights the interconnectivity that demands a multi-perspectival approach to life, work, and art. Adopting a multi-disciplinary approach to the intellectual, as I have been arguing, allows for an understanding of a socially engaged artist, writer, and academic, like Kiyooka, as an intellectual presence unbound by rigid disciplinarity or bureaucratized careerism. In arguing that this intellectual figure necessarily occupies an institutional site, either the academy or social sites such as the media, Said recognizes that the intellectual is complicit in the very constructs he or she critiques. Not content to merely accept this complicity, Said suggests ways that academia can offer a position of power from which to speak and act against inequality and injustice:

> the intellectual does not represent a statue-like icon, but an individual vocation, an energy, a stubborn force engaging as a committed and recognizable voice in language and in society with a slew of issues, all of them having to do in the end with a combination of enlightenment and emancipation or freedom. (73)

Attempting to avoid complacency, Said's academic intellectual is energized by the world that he or she inhabits, and not merely the content of disciplinary research. Not simply a position acquired through the awarding of certain degrees—Kiyooka lacked "formal" education—the academic intellectual achieves, and must maintain, that status through critical reflection and action, such as the support of social causes or the exposure of critical failings in dominant socio-cultural systems of control, including the university.

In his diagnosis of the contemporary academic intellectual, Said critiques the "inevitable drift towards power and authority" (*Representations* 80) that professional academics experience. Because professional advancement entangles academic intellectuals with power structures that often lead to structural inequalities, they are not always able to speak with an uncompromised voice against injustice, tyranny, and oppression. To counter this Said advocates for a professional amateurism "fueled by care and affection rather than by profit and selfish, narrow specialization" (82). By adopting an attitude of amateurism, the academic intellectual, according to Said, is free to explore beyond disciplinary and ideological boundaries both without and within the academy.[3]

Unlike Kiyooka's pedagogical foregrounding of the "not negligible," Said's academic intellectual operates not as a whole, but as a constantly reconstituted subject unable to fully integrate an understanding of the self into the multitude of ways he interacts with the world. In his critical review of Said's image of the intellectual, Jeffrey Williams argues that the amateurism and freedom that Said so values are inconsistent with his intellectual position as an acclaimed scholar of great influence. Emphasizing how Said avoids discussion of social privilege in his definition of free intellectual activity, Williams writes, "Said ascribes a free-floating quality to an intellectual who by his definition speaks to a public sphere, but he fails to account for the channels through which one even has access to that public sphere" (403). Using Said's status as an amateur commentator on Middle East affairs as an example, Williams problematizes amateurism by stating that "it is Said's position as an exemplary professional that provides validation and legitimation for his political views and gives him a privileged public location from which to make his political interventions" (403). Though comparable to Kiyooka for his focus on the extra-disciplinary, Said fails to acknowledge the diverse range of his subjectivity, ultimately reinforcing hierarchies of expression Kiyooka opposed from the inside out.

"TO REACH OUT BEYOND SPECIALISM / TO BE TRULY RESPONSIBLE"

The particularities of Kiyooka's experiences as an academic insider are marked by his specialization as a painter and his subsequent inability to be defined by any singular label outside of very particular moments. Kiyooka's earlier collection of correspondence, *Transcanada Letters*, originally published in 1975 and reissued in 2005 with an afterword by Glen Lowry, provides a rare view into one artist's conceptions of the 1960s and 1970s arts and culture scene in Canada. As Lowry notes, the collection "deals explicitly with Kiyooka's exhibition, collaborations, and aesthetic ideas" (371), but it is more than a catalogue, as Kiyooka's letters "articulate a new poetics that is akin to the work of Charles Olson or the New American poets" (371). Like *Pacific Rim Letters*, this earlier collection bears witness to the action and thoughts of a critical social observer. Acutely aware of the machinations surrounding his work, Kiyooka's letters present him as an artist self-confident in his art and status, though always anxious that the Canada Council, "the C.C. our Medici might bless" him with grants (*Transcanada* 37). Kiyooka's anxiety places him at odds with the bureaucracies of the federal grants he needs to do his work. In frustration Kiyooka writes to a friend, "I'm pisst off at / having to substantiate the terms of my / seriousness after all these years" (302). Despite displaying a playfulness often at odds with the conservative bureaucracies of granting agencies and the academy, Kiyooka takes very seriously the role of the artist/teacher as one who approaches his or her work with "nothing less than 'wholeheartedness'" (39), the unequalled and total engagement with the object at hand as it has come to be. As he implies in a letter "To a Young Painter who wld be a Teacher," attention to detail, sensitivity, and concentrated focus are the hallmarks of seriousness in art and teaching: "1 teacher to 1 painting to 1 student at 1 time each time we are given the time to attend to the particulars" (39). This attentiveness to the particular goes against the models of cost efficiency and commodification that characterize current trends in post-secondary education. For Kiyooka, the commitment to particularity—"1 teacher to 1 painting to 1 student at 1 time"—suggests at once the gravity of pedagogy and a seriousness that manifests itself in the appreciation of the art object, in the nurturing of the artist/student, and not in the machinations that surround, and create, space for the "time we are given" to honestly and seriously construct (new) meanings.

Never content to voice his irritation at bureaucratic entanglements in private, Kiyooka's "open letter to the C.C.," the Canada Council, is just as vehement in its indignation at his having to provide references to vouch for his capacity as an artist: "the artifacts I have already caused made in the past / 20 yrs ought to be adequate proof / of my seriousness—beyond mere good intentions" (*Transcanada* 298). Kiyooka's use of colloquial and poetic language in a letter sent to an official agency about the importance of sculpture integrates the value of the carefully crafted form of poetic language into the stultifying discourse of granting agencies. It is worth noting how he makes a distinction between sculpture and language: "These words wont accomplish more than words enable. What- / ever theyre abt they are not sculpture—its / afterall sculpture that I am talking abt" (298). By highlighting the incommensurability of words to convey the seriousness carried through art that does not use language, this statement signifies the gap between art and the economics of art. Similar to the importance of paying close attention to the particulars of a student's work, the self-reflexivity in this letter that requests support of his art belies a generalized approach to the evaluation of art that such national granting agencies demand. While funding for art (and academic investigations) is granted based on the systematic filing of identifiable products, Kiyooka suggests that the fact of art as intentioned creation is proof enough of the artist's value as an artist, since to be an artist itself presupposes seriousness. Such an attitude of resistance toward the standards of the Canada Council application procedure gives way to an even more complex self-representation in his comments on academia.

Kiyooka's letters regarding his academic subjectivity occupy a space between self-assurance and self-critique. Not containing as many references to academia as his posthumously published collection, *Transcanada Letters*' secondary narrative arc, after the business of art, focusses on Kiyooka's attempts to get a teaching job in Vancouver. Though there are not many letters to that effect, several of Kiyooka's correspondences about academia foreground his personal desire to again live and teach on the West Coast. These letters, dated from 1966 to 1971, state his desire for a job and show the academic job market, or at least Kiyooka's conception of it, as a site where one may get ahead simply by sending the right letter to the right person. Writing how he is "keen abt teaching at UBC" (212), and wondering if he "can be of use to SFU" (122), Kiyooka's letters show a casual approach to the academic job market that was successful, as his cross-country itinerant existence ends with an appointment at UBC in 1972. In getting there, though, Kiyooka reveals the complexity of his academic subjectivity as he both appeals to the right people in the right institutions while subtly deconstructing the hierarchies and bureaucracies that they inhabit. Kiyooka begins a 1971 letter to Simon Fraser University's Vice-President Academic, Brian Wilson, on a wistful note: "I've been thinking How shall I find a / teaching position in Vancouver where I wld prefer / to be.... where my / family and friends not to mention the mountains / the trees and the ocean preside" (122). This poetic invocation of landscape and loved ones is followed by a stanza devoted to recent artistic projects, and followed by another that attests to his abilities as a teacher—"I know how to tell the ABCs of Art" (122)—that, when read together, construct a holistic academic subject seeking the perfect constellation of place and people in which his work—art and creative writing, as well as pedagogy—can co-exist. Though the overarching academic narrative of *Transcanada Letters* winds down on a hopeful note, it is important to note that Kiyooka's lengthy struggle to find employment in the city of his choice suggests that getting ahead in the 1970s world of Canadian academia was no less challenging than it is today.

The shift from the 1970s into the 1980s saw the emergence of an anxiety at Canadian universities as the public spending of previous decades declined, causing universities and granting bodies to turn increasingly to more private and corporate dollars that would reshape academic life. During the time Kiyooka was writing what would become his second collection of letters, the idea of the university as an isolated site of knowledge production continued to be challenged in light of subjective realities and postmodern, post-colonial constructions of Western culture and society (Fulton 233). These challenges sparked a move away from excessive specialization toward an interdisciplinary approach that continues today. The 1986 critical essay collection *Universities in Crisis: A Mediaeval Institution in the Twenty-First Century*, co-edited by William Neilson and current SSHRC President Chad Gaffield, offers an historical look into the period of disenchantment in which Kiyooka wrote *Pacific Rim Letters*. Margaret Fulton's essay in the collection on the need to restructure and reorient teaching and research notes that the university risks obsolescence by failing as a social model in a society increasingly dominated by the economics of corporate ideology: "we have failed abysmally to produce the pool of trained graduates that the economy requires" (239), while also being unable to productively extract itself from the "classical scientific and educational paradigm" inspired by the Greeks and Romans (245). In response to this perceived failure of the university to respond to social and intellectual values and needs of the 1970s and beyond, Fulton argues the university does not understand that "excellence must stem from an element of synergy rather than single-mindedness" (239) in ways that can "accommodate the spiritual and recognize the visionary" (245). She argues "professors and students alike must learn to do many things at once in order to do one thing well" (239). This "one thing" leads back to a discrete discipline, but a discipline now positively charged with the ideas of other disciplines and other modes of thinking. Also advocating increased interdisciplinary interaction as a meaningful response to corporate pressure and a flagging academe, Donald A. Michael argues there is great potential in the uncertainty inherent in any cross-disciplinary search for answers. Taking uncertainty, "being able to psychologically and cognitively recognize what specifically it is about [a] situation that one does not know" (206), as the basis for intellectual growth, Michael imagines an academic landscape where error does not equate to failure (207) and the individual is recognized as integrated but not contained,

where like Kiyooka, the everyday, the "coruscations" of the "riddled universe" (*Pacific* 203), play an acknowledged role in creative and critical
work. This stance demands a holistic approach to teaching and research
much like Kiyooka's approach to art and pedagogy: "across disciplines to
embrace contexts larger / than art's largesse seems to be how i / function
best" (*Transcanada* 240). Calling for a structural shift toward greater in-
terrelating and less rigid disciplinarity, Michael and Fulton demonstrate
a desire for the kind of changes in the configuration and the approach to
academia that Kiyooka himself writes of throughout the 1970s. Taken together, these writers and thinkers anticipate the shift at the millennium
towards interdisciplinary critical practice that ascribes to the scholarly
researcher an important role in today's society.

MANDATING KNOWLEDGE: "CALLIT, THE ACTS OF AUTHENTICATION"

The mass-culture economic modelling of the humanities currently
underway under the auspices of sshrc's new mandate as an agent of
knowledge production and distribution risks sacrificing *"unbound curiosity, that is one unconfined by any a priori notions (rationalizations?) of
relevance or simple-minded usefulness"* that Kiyooka strongly advocates
(*Pacific* 203–04). In the same 1983 letter to the ubc dean of Arts mentioned above, Kiyooka argues for the non-categorical nature of creative
research and the importance of the everyday in pedagogical practice:

> I have no intention of trying to prove to you that my 8 books of prose and
> poetry, plus a couple of hundred poetry readings throughout N.A., have
> a special relevance to my effectiveness as a teacher or even painting if
> you haven't already got the mind to deal with it. The true pedagogy, if
> such a beast is possible in these crazed '80s, consists in, callit, the acts of
> authentication of all we are called upon to witness in our lives. (204)

Kiyooka's authentication manifests itself in a flexible artistic and professional practice as an academic intellectual with a "lack of credentials" (201), who approaches all his work from the perspective that "an artist's life work intersects at all points with the body politic" (210). Kiyooka's construction of the self and other in relation to public dynamics foregoes uniform practice and calls for a holistic and collective understanding of the individual and his or her specificities, an understanding that offers a creative model for socially, pedagogically, and critically responsible academic practice.

Employing the sweeping language of nationalism and pluralist freedoms in its 2005 policy document *Knowledge Council: SSHRC, 2006–2011*, SSHRC outlines its mandate to make social science and humanities research relevant to a larger segment of society by "implementing four key new strategies: clustering research, mobilizing knowledge, connecting people and building tools" (*Knowledge Council* 16).

> All this will make Canada a more connected nation that reaps unprecedented benefits from both the scale of its geography and the rich diversity of its population. The great availability and systematic sharing of ideas and research insights will also support, both directly and indirectly, the fullest expression of Canada's particular approach to participatory democracy. (24)

These strategies encourage a type of research that enables Canadian society to reflect upon the problems it faces while offering public knowledge that "must inspire and inform real world debate, enrich intellectual and cultural life, and invigorate the economy" (7). As a "knowledge council," SSHRC is interested in the distribution of "hard-won knowledge out into the world, to families, community groups, policy-makers, legislators, and the media" (2). This emphasis on distribution interprets university teaching as a form of dissemination, and constructs the university classroom as a "birthplace and training ground for the next generation of researchers" (7), a site for building a highly skilled workforce. This paradigm ignores pedagogical and learning desires at an individual level that do not focus upon social use value as the bottom line. This adoption of social use value as the ultimate goal of research risks transforming university researchers and teachers into mere social functionaries, entangled in a rigid discourse of economic nationalism geared to prosperity through research as a directed social good. By building such directives into policy, SSHRC assumes a much greater role in the creation of new knowledge than it has in the past while paradoxically imperilling not only research independence but also its role as a federal agency. Unlike the "Women and Changes Strategic Grants," offered from the mid-1980s to 2000, that facilitated multi-year, and often collaborative projects, with long-term goals (Heald 90), the language of "Strategic Partnerships" that SSHRC has adopted reveals an imperative toward a patchwork of intellectual engagement that has value (literally currency in this case) as long as private partners and public interest hold. In contrast, Kiyooka's engagement with the academy, creativity, and with knowledge itself rests on the idea of the deeply personal, decidedly non-strategic uncovering of the self in relation to everything else.

As a critically and creatively aware academic, Kiyooka's declaration that "everybody is a bona fide member and an activist (each in their own way) in the ongoing histrionics of a given culture" (*Pacific* 110) critically undercuts the societal privilege he holds as a university professor, a published poet, and a renowned, award-winning artist. In his lecture "We Asian North Americanos: An unhistorical 'take' on growing up yellow in a white world" (*Pacific* 108–10), Kiyooka presents himself as an activist greatly influenced by his family and language. The significance of the mother tongue as a form of learning, of knowledge acquisition that presages even "the thot of *learning* anything" (108), is paired with the learning of "the efficaciousness of silences" modelled by his father (109). This referencing of personal history leads to Kiyooka's assertion that "we have to attend to our own pulse and extend our own tenacities" (110) as a direct response to "growing up [and subsequently living] yellow in a white world" (108). Having imposed himself upon the White Anglo-Saxon Protestant dominated structure of the academy, Kiyooka understands that academics and artists of colour "shall have to remain vigilant if we are to insert ourselves in to the W.A.S.P scheme of things" (110). Kiyooka's friend, fellow poet, and SFU professor, Roy Miki notes, "political efficacy in the university is, then, constrained by various academic and administrative procedures that neutralize, or otherwise devalue, critiques of racism, sexism, classism, and ethnocentrism within the system" ("What's a racialized" 162). For Kiyooka, vigilance against such devaluation manifests itself through a proactive pedagogy and radical professionalism that re-forms its commodified texts (e.g., letters of reference) and resists an urge toward easy recognition and celebrity: "i'll never make images to sell anything: the artist in me long ago made a pledge to use whatever medium that came to hand to divine the callit sacral ground of all our image making" (*Pacific* 227). In so doing, he refuses the effacement of his Japanese Canadianness, and the "riven path" (201) of his artistic sensibilities, against the dominant white society, and its vaunted institution of knowledge, the university. By constantly re-figuring his place within the structures he operates, Kiyooka rejects academic stereotypes through the textual performance of a non-quantifiable self. In this way, the incidental constructs of the Japanese Canadian academic artist intellectual that his speech constructs cannot be contained in any single frame.

In a poem that concludes a letter he wrote concerning poet Barry MacKinnon's teaching position at New Caledonia College in Prince George, BC, Kiyooka critiques the connections between bureaucracy and pedagogy that sidestep creative, and therefore difficult to categorize, knowledge:

> pedagogy has bitten the dust, again
> long live all the un-copyrightable things in the world
> i'd like to live till the dawn of a new
> literacy, one rooted in a non-ideological world class
> consciousness: ethnic superiority is
> given the lie everyday through chinks in the media
>
> Ah! the thraldoms of New Caledonia!
> ignorance is an invisible best stalking the hallowed
> corridors of pedagogy and power. (*Pacific* 35)

As a critique of media and the challenges of teaching in his day, Kiyooka's protestation, written in the prose part of the letter, to "keep all the channels, not to mention the network, open," is amplified by how "ethnic superiority is / given the lie everyday through the chinks in the media" (35). The double entendre on *chink*, as gap admitting a slice of light and as an ethnic slur against Chinese people, exposes the media as a machine of meaning-creation not dependent on its parts, operating within and beyond its own gaps and erasures. From Kiyooka's perspective, therefore, SSHRC's mandate to distribute, and thereby tailor, academic research to mass media in a way that implicates the researcher in a system of fabrication would constitute "the lie" (35) that undercuts the value of research as "unbound curiosity...unconfined" (204) by a politics of economic productivity and control. Like Said's warning that intellectuals must avoid the enticements to power encouraged by specialization, Kiyooka's letter exposes how social structures can limit the range and practice of intellectual activity. This idea is best reflected in the last two lines of the poem where the phrase "invisible best" welcomes a reading and a misreading around the theme of sanctioned ignorance. This reader who, when reading the word *best* expected the word *beast*, assumed it was a typographical error by Kiyooka faithfully transferred by his editor. Careful rereading, though, does confirm the appropriateness of *best*. As an invisible beast, ignorance adopts an exteriority as something destructive that infiltrates the academy in a clear and present manner. Conversely, ignorance as an "invisible best" constructs success as a product of sanctioned ignorance whereby the unquestioning acceptance of institutional power dynamics is the path to promotion. Brydon's definition of sanctioned ignorance as being "the forms of ignorance we feel no need to remedy" ("Cross-Talk" 68) links to Said's notion of academic specialization as a method of intellectual containment. Like specialization that is characterized by an intense focus on a discrete area of knowledge to the exclusion of other perspectives, sanctioned ignorance permits a lack of perspective as long as one's uncritical position upholds the dominant discourse within which such ignorance is expressed.

Returning to the economics of our present day, I suggest that sanctioned ignorance can be applied as a critique of the focus on the standardization of descriptive language that SSHRC encourages. As grants play an increasingly important role in scholarship, hiring, and advancement decisions, academics are pressured to conform not only by using a standard grammar and syntax much maligned by Kiyooka, but also to adopt key words and ideas, such as "partnerships," "research capacity," and public knowledge, in research descriptions (*Knowledge Council* 7). This streamlining not only affects the language, but also the ways in which researchers think of their work. This upholding of a dominant discourse excludes certain voices, while encouraging a homogenized intellectual landscape that values sameness and success over personal and creative intellectual risk. SSHRC's practice of awarding grants "based on peer-review judgment of the probable significance of the contribution to knowledge in the social sciences and humanities" ("Apply") does not necessarily ensure diversity of research as all humanities scholars strive to fit SSHRC's critical frame. The question of probability that peer review raises is a good one to consider in light of Kiyooka's embrace of probability, as a gathered impression of success based on casual observations and friendly analysis. This personal, and potentially more intellectually honest, approach to evaluation runs against the impersonal evaluative model SSHRC requires by relying on records of research achievement, institutional authorization, and bureaucratic tangles of online applications with paper attachments and submission policies that must adhere to pre-established categories of what matters. Clearly not replicating such a system of impersonal evaluation through his letters of reference, Kiyooka's issuance of academic currency may not hold up to the rigours of contemporary academia but stands as an avant-garde push against encroaching rigid professionalism required to support the career growth of colleagues in an increasingly bureaucratized academic world.

For Kiyooka, the university was a site for personal exchange of creative and critical acts. To him, interdisciplinarity was not a *hot* collaborative model but simply a way of performing academically and creatively, of living his life. From Kiyooka's perspective, the function of academia is to assist people, through ideas and practice, toward an understanding of themselves and the various spaces they inhabit. Kiyooka took his critical creative practice beyond the singular and often confining spaces of artistic disciplinary bounds to expansive spaces of photographic, poetic, and musical collaboration with artists, musicians, and friends.

Never driven by strict rules, Kiyooka often took an impromptu approach to forms of expression with which he was not familiar, such as in his playing of the zither under the "'apprenticeship' with New Music composer (now playwright) Don Druick" (*Pacific* 353). Through two years of weekly-recorded sessions, Kiyooka was only "Interested in 'self-instruction,' and a kind of 'shamanistic sound-making,'...[refusing] to 'learn musical skills or how to tune'" (353). This particular act of creative collaboration, though structured and recorded, lacks the objective aim of direct purpose so desired by academic granting agencies in the economics of academia.

As a model for practical action, Kiyooka may seem out of date in relation to present academic realities, but his practice of being a scholar who is alive to the artistic, pedagogical, and research ideas around him offers promising ways to consider the always changing priorities of critical academic practice. Not yet in the throes of the tenure-track gauntlet, my observations still find inspiration in Helen C. Chapman's essay on the figure of the young academic as someone whose task is to unsettle the "solidification of thought into fixed motifs and ideas" (38) that strict disciplinarity and bureaucratic rigidity entail. A type of responsible action, this Kiyookan model of academic engagement encourages the unity of teaching, learning, and research. It is that idea of the academic space as one of wholeness, where "everything wants to hang together" (*Pacific* 111) and nothing is unconnected, that Kiyooka offers us—a place of responsibility where the person in the role of researcher is not merely a tool at work, but an instrument at play: where "to touch the bottom of the well (of self) [is] never an intention, never a programmatic thing" (185).

AUTHOR'S NOTE

A shorter version of this essay, entitled "Multiple Subjectivities: Roy Kiyooka and Academic Citizenship," was presented at the Narratives of Citizenship conference at the University of Alberta, 23–25 March 2007. A copy of that essay, along with a video recording of the presentation, is available on the conference website: <http://www.arts.ualberta.ca/~gsea/conf/>.

1. Kiyooka's ambivalence toward institutional structures is made clear in letters written to department chair Jim Caswell apprising him of his progress during the sabbatical year (*Pacific* 244, 264). These letters present an academic subject invested in the quantification of creative practice who, despite an effective rhetoric of resistance, is comfortably enmeshed in and complicit with the very structures he critiques.

2. Kiyooka received a Diploma in Fine Arts from the Provincial Institute of Technology and Art in Calgary in 1949 (*Pacific* 350). In a letter to his department chair Jim Caswell in 1983, Kiyooka writes, "I didn't intend to be a teacher of any sort given my lack of credentials, etc. but I soon discovered I had a knack for it and, about this time, I discovered that my knack for it was, shall we say, 'entwined' with my propensities as an artist. I am one of those who have really never been anything else but an artist/teacher" (201).

3. Said cites the case of his own lecturing on the topic of Palestine, despite his formal training in literature (88). More critically, he references linguist Noam Chomsky's longstanding and respected commentary on politics and warfare (*Representations* 100).

EIGHT

Making the Reference Personal

QUESTIONS OF
ACCOUNTABILITY WITHIN
THE "DE-REFERENTIALIZED"
UNIVERSITY

Melissa Stephens

*The remaining problem then is: Does she or he have the strength
to persist in light of the tremendous pressure to conform to what her colonizers have defined as intellectual excellence?*

—Marlene Kadar, "Coming" 12

DEBATES CONTINUE TO SURROUND the role of personal experience in
scholarly research. In this essay I discuss the significance of testimonial
practice to academic discourse and the necessity of articulating intersections between personal and professional life. I also suggest how terms
such as *excellence* and *accountability* are politicized and theorized for
the purpose of institutional critique. The pedagogical effects of experiential discourse should continue to be questioned as personal memory
and institutional history inform various stages of research. During times
of global economic recession and increased job insecurity, it is particularly urgent to assess how testimonial scholarship enables teachers and
researchers to critically bear witness to their lives and location(s) within
the post-secondary institution.

While uses of personal narrative in scholarship do not guarantee
the production of effective institutional critique, I am interested in how

self-reflexive modes of inquiry put into crisis conceptions of truth and objectivity by demanding that we question ourselves and our methods of accountability in research.[1] Through the course of this discussion, I revisit Bill Readings' *The University in Ruins*, for his critique of the corporatized university continues to raise ethical questions about the relations between professional accountability, academic pedagogy, and institutional practice.

In Readings' view, *excellence* has become a regulatory term used by universities to ensure performance efficiency and the marketability of knowledge; it circulates in academic discourse as an empty signifier bearing little relation to the content or quality of education (21–43). The "structure of corporate administration" manages teaching and research— intellectual life within the university—through the process of what he calls "dereferentialization," reducing the educational experience to a results-oriented account based on statistics and evaluations (29). Students, in turn, are "encouraged to think of themselves as consumers rather than as members of a community" (11). As "the logic of consumerism" (134) emphasizes efficient knowledge production, it limits and devalues the time for critical analysis and intellectual debate; in turn, it may also signal "the loss of the subject-referent of educational experience" (126).

Intellectual activity and knowledge production seem at odds in the consumerist logic that dominates Readings' vision of the University of Excellence. Although this particular narrative of the university resists an attack on specific institutions, many students and professors could likely confirm some of his claims based on their personal experiences of studying and working at post-secondary universities in Canada. It thus seems vital to re-evaluate what constitutes contemporary experiences of education not only in the classroom but in the context of expanding areas of research.

As funding networks are initiated and developed, relations continue to change between universities and students, academics and business communities. How and why particular networks are encouraged requires sustained investigation that goes beyond the scope of this essay. Readings argues that "the ideology of autonomy" underlying the conventional image of the academic must be challenged and that pedagogies emphasizing "the production of sovereign subjects" be re-envisioned (154). Imagining "the scene of teaching" (154) as "a *relation, a network of obligation*" (155), he provokes thought about how to envision the scene of research in a similar way.

Readings' conception of a radically dialogic interaction between educators and students demands resistance to closure (155); nonetheless, academic accountability to funding institutions often entails the provision of documentation to substantiate the progress or successful results of research. In short, this method of accountability emphasizes the practical use value of research to a service-based society and downplays the significance of critical thinking. It is in this context that Readings' educational theory sheds light on a too narrowly conceived notion of accountability that forecloses possibilities of cultivating organic networks and innovative scenes of research.

Humanities academics—at various stages of their careers—face ongoing pressure to publish research that meets the demands of a university culture industry, and yet they remain dependent upon the approval of external funding institutions. In Readings' view, "the governmental structure of the nation-state is no longer the organizing center of the common existence of peoples across the planet, and the University of Excellence serves nothing other than itself, another corporation in a world of transnationally exchanged capital" (43). While the changing role of the university in a global market economy has elicited a lot of debates, humanities researchers in Canada continue to rely on the federal government as a primary source of funding. This reality raises questions about the culture of the humanities as researchers adapt to political and economic change.

The federal budget released in January 2009 by Stephen Harper's Conservative government stated that business-oriented research would receive increased financial support through SSHRC. This incentive was met with notable criticism. NDP Member of Parliament Niki Ashton (Churchill, Manitoba) presented a petition signed by more than 17,000 "students, researchers, academics and concerned individuals, people from coast to coast and around the world" to the House of Commons in June 2009 (nikishton, *Niki Ashton presents*). The petition begins by identifying SSHRC's long-standing tradition of "promoting and supporting university-based research and training in the humanities and social sciences" but claims that "the Federal Budget presented on January 27th contains a 20% funding increase for this program [SSHRC], with a caveat that has the potential to halt this kind of research: 'Scholarships granted by the Social Sciences and Humanities Research Council will be focused on business-related degrees'" (Ashton, *Petition*). The petition not only demands that the preceding sentence be removed from the document, it also asks the federal government to "ensure that SSHRC funding not be allocated to one specific discipline but to the range of studies in the social sciences and humanities" (Ashton).

In her presentation, Ashton warned that the funding initiative reflected "the government's attack on the social sciences and humanities and, fundamentally, the attack on academic freedom" (nikishton, *Niki Ashton presents*). On behalf of petitioners, she noted the relevance of such research to "social justice, civic and economic empowerment" and argued that "this government is stunting our research community and turning it back." In a follow-up email sent to petitioners, Ashton offered encouragement but no resolution:

> We must continue to work together. The battle continues in the face of ongoing actions and interference of the Minister of Science and Technology, Gary Goodyear. In advance of the next budget, we will continue to make it clear that not only is discipline-related earmarking unacceptable but that social sciences and humanities research in Canada is vital. The contributions made by students, researchers, academics and people working in the social sciences and humanities are integral to moving our country forward. (Assistant 2, "Thank you!")

The 2009 federal budget intervention represents *new* funding for business-related research; thus, the 20 per cent increase does not replace or reduce existing funds for standard research. Nonetheless, the incentive references the economic contingencies of knowledge production and raises questions about the changing role of social sciences and humanities research in contemporary Canada. In this case, business-related research receives not only an explicit economic incentive from SSHRC, but, implicitly, it acquires social, cultural, and political capital with the help of the Conservative government.

It is at the intersection of culture and economy that testimonial scholarship becomes increasingly valuable as a means to assess the various ways that budgets restructure research in the humanities and elsewhere. My argument for testimony does not support an antagonistic opposition between politics and theory, experience and discourse. One of the values of combining testimonial scholarship with institutional critique resides in its potential to theorize the politics of experience and to politicize theories of discourse within and outside the university. Institutional critique must confront the life of, within, and beyond the university; in doing so, it can challenge the structural privileges and abuses of power enabled not only by institutions but also by individuals.

In her recent study of the 1990s academic memoir boom in the United States, Cynthia G. Franklin reminds her reader that "feelings and affect... comprise socially constructed forms of knowledge, or ideologies, that are all the more powerful for passing as natural" (15). Following this claim, my argument thus does not endorse solipsistic manipulations of experience as the unquestionable evidence of critique; rather, I make the case for the political and theoretical research of academics persistently engaged in the assessment of their roles in the management of resources and distribution of finances that expand or limit areas of research and contexts for educational experience.

Academic testimony supplements administrative records of professional practice with personal experience, but its reception varies among audiences. Previous resistance to academic testimony has often been the result of limited readings based on a discourse of identity politics, whereby a person or group asserts their specific identity against the assumptions of a homogenizing, dominant elite. In other contexts, academics have been criticized for masking their own privileges within the academy as they adopt auto/biographical modes to discuss the politics of marginalization (Franklin 1–24). In my view, it is more productive to expand our understanding of the uses of testimony and to make available to scholars a set of critical practices that help them intervene in the ways knowledge and experience are constituted, evaluated, and marketed by both academics and the university. The culture of academic professionalization must find ways to critically re-engage itself with personal experience, for it is often what informs how we think and work ethically. The remainder of this essay suggests how academics have theorized uses of experience in scholarship geared toward institutional critique.

The place of the personal in scholarship has been an extensive, varied, and ongoing debate; the subject was particularly relevant during the 1990s, a period dubbed "the decade of life narratives" (Schaffer and Smith 1) and as a time in which "meta-institutional criticism" proliferated, particularly within "English departments" (Bérubé and Lyon 198).[2] As academics began "to interrogate the institutional status of literary study" by transforming their respective disciplines into "object[s] of study" (198), they frequently adopted self-reflexive modes in scholarship.

Testimonial practices vary among individual authors of institutional critique, but a common goal is to assess how "agency" is constituted "through situations and statuses conferred on them" (J. Scott 34). While academic testimony may share features with auto/biography and academic memoir, it requires distinction, in my view, for the way that it draws on personal memory and institutional history as resources for critical thinking. As a "critical practice" and a species of "life-writing," it can be particularly effective when it "encourages (a) the reader to develop and foster his/her own self-consciousness in order to (b) humanize and make less abstract (which is not to say less mysterious) the self-in-the-writing" (Kadar 12).

Candace Lang provides further insight into life-writing as a critical methodology. She argues that the "self-reflective" is "the most essential component of...theoretical activity" as "the critic attempts to define her own presuppositions, methodological tools, and consequences of those choices" (43). She continues:

> it seems to me that the recent trend toward autobiographical or personal
> criticism is a necessary development in the evolution of critical theory,
> a further elaboration of the self-reflexive moment of theory through a
> move beyond the ostensibly 'rational' determinants of reading, in order to

identify some of the highly specific, localized (both spatially and tempo-rally), empirical factors affecting the critical agent. (43–44)

The experience of performing research is both personal and pro-fessional, yet one's capacity to account for this doubling of conscious identity—or, as Smaro Kamboureli phrases it, "the reciprocity that exists (or ought to exist) between an academic's professional discourse and her daily life" (*Scandalous* ix)—is limited, for such accounts are uneasily as-similated into academic discourse. The mingling of the personal with the professional involves a form of risk management, for when an ostensibly "objective" form of discourse is inflected by the "subjective," then its au-thoritative value becomes susceptible to criticism and doubt. In H. Aram Veeser's estimation, "A critical practice that breaks long-standing rules is bound to encounter resistance" (x); yet, the increasing trend toward aca-demic self-reflexivity or "Confessional criticism," as Veeser calls it, may require the "drafting [of] new rules for judging scholarship, ranking jour-nals, and preserving decorum, etiquette, and style" (xi).

To stimulate new forms of intellectual activity one must "make available for scrutiny the evolution and tentativeness of our thoughts" (Boone 1153), but the extent to which such tentativeness is accepted by academic communities who value knowledge as a commodity remains questionable. Readings calls upon educators to find "a way of developing an accountability that is at odds with accounting" (154) and to displace the "single and authoritative point of view" valorized in the "University of Excellence" (153).[3] He argues that "no judgment is final; there is always another link in the chain. Questions of value are systematically incapable of closure" (132). This dialogic approach to educational experience empha-sizes the processes rather than the products of intellectual development.

The protocols of academic discourse are frequently passed on from teacher to student and may impact generations of research. Marianna Torgovnick endorses experimentation as she considers the long-term ef-fects of traditional academic writing:

When we pass on the academic style to our graduate students or newest colleagues, we train them to stay within the boundaries, both stylistically and conceptually. When we encourage experimental critical writing, we do not always know what we will get, but we stimulate the profession to grow and change. We don't control the future of the profession only when we give grades or make hiring or tenure decisions; we control it at the level of the sentence. (27)

"Writerly writing" can be used to skilfully draw upon insights gained from both personal and professional experience (27). This process is essential, to Torgovnick, for "even if it offers no facts from the writer's life, or offers just a hint of them here and there, it makes the reader know some things about the writer—a fundamental condition, it seems to me, of any real act of communication" (27).

The reader of scholarship is often a student or another academic who is also a participant in the discourse community in which the writer works. If academic discourse has been traditionally conceived of as a form of "systematic exposition" that follows the "law of noncontradiction" (Marius 28), then it is the unsettling of academic voice that we should consider as an intervening research methodology. Testimonial scholarship may elicit confirmation, contestation, or supplementation by other academics. Testimony may critically displace the institutional power and personal authority of individual scholars when it is regarded as a supplement. For Jacques Derrida, the supplement not only "adds itself" as "a surplus" but it "intervenes or insinuates itself *in-the-place-of*" (*Of Grammatology* 144, 145). It does not function to "complement" but to agitate (145), and it marks a form of "substitutive perversion" that simultaneously replenishes and threatens "our constitution" (177). Testimonial supplementation may thus elicit the comparative analysis of experience to cultivate scenes of research where alternative forms of accountability become a shared responsibility.

In Susan David Bernstein's conception of "first-person theorizing" there are multiple strategies for "stag[ing] a challenge to customs of voice in scholarship" (177). She identifies four effects of first-person theorization in academic criticism—de-familiarization, interruption, transgression, and dissension—that, in her view, unsettle the "rhetorical sovereignty of supposed objectivity" (178). Because the "first person subject takes a close-up stance" in discourse (178), Bernstein argues, the convention of "detached distance" in academic writing is contested. In her view, "feminist theory invokes representations of personal experience as a *structure* and *source* of knowledge" (178; my emphasis). An author may use "confession" to more intimately engage his or her audience, but this technique can also cultivate voyeuristic, fetishistic, or exploitative tendencies. As Bernstein suggests, "promiscuous identification" can occur between writers and readers where there is "a desire to domesticate identity difference" (176, 177). Thus, "first-person theorizing" is necessarily "contestatory" when it mediates relations between author and reader, language and experience, *and* interrogates forms of power residing within and between these relations. Bernstein notes the significance of tracing how these effects change over time, however; for when the "first-person" becomes normative in scholarship, the "transformative potential also diminishes" (178).[4]

So as not to completely displace the "transformative potential" of which Bernstein speaks, it is valuable to consider what it means to be critical of our chosen forms of accountability. Smaro Kamboureli pursues this issue in the following way:

> Does self-location, that most frequently recurring and debated issue today, suffice to immunize academic discourse against the perils of representation (speaking for or about others), against the politics of the institutions that we are complicit with—however strong our avowed desire to change them? What cultural and political dynamics does the theatre of the classroom dramatize? How do we as individuals negotiate our political stance vis-à-vis the history both of ideas and of the institutions in whose contexts we teach? In other words, how do we position ourselves in relation to representation? (*Scandalous* 2–3)

The final question she asks is particularly compelling given that academic discourse is a discursive performance in the representation of intellectual and institutional history. Ethical questions persist if we examine our research as a form of representation—and narration—invested with multiple and often contradictory desires.

While the "politics of the institutions" can and should be critiqued, our pedagogical negotiations with them should also be considered. With these issues in mind, I would like to discuss how recent testimonial scholarship, emerging from the field of Canadian auto/biographical studies, effectively scrutinizes uses of the personal in professional discourse as it simultaneously undermines the rhetoric of excellence and methods of accountability that seem dominant in contemporary university culture.

The authors of *Tracing the Autobiographical* signify the trend in auto/biography studies of moving beyond conventions of genre toward questions of critical practice. In their introduction, Jeanne Perreault and Marlene Kadar insist that any historical discourse is an act of communication between readers and writers who share responsibility for its effects (6). While the contributors have a unified vision for the book, they assert themselves as scholars of distinctive research (3). In this study, auto/biographical practices are assessed in a variety of contexts ranging from testimony and propaganda, poetry and theatre, to television and the Internet.

Perreault and Kadar locate themselves, personally and professionally, in their research by acknowledging their limitations but also by striving to articulate ways in which they can be accountable for it. Collectively, the writers identify as "Canadians," "women," "feminists," and "academics" (7). They acknowledge that *"these facts may not cohere* to produce a uniform vision of Canada" but assume the

> *responsibility to listen* for echoes and murmurs, as well as for clear authoritative declarations; to watch for the appearance of auto/biography in unexpected places; to trace patterns from the materials left behind; and to undertake the struggle with words and meanings that will extend our sensitivity to the world we are making and the peoples with whom we share it. (7; emphasis mine)

Both declarative and conditional, the authors reveal the "tentativeness of [their] thoughts" (Boone 1153) and take a scholarly stance that is both collaborative and supplementary. The introduction sets the stage for more specific accounts of experience in the individually-authored chapters.

In her chapter, "Reading the Autobiographical in Personal Home Pages," Linda Warley theorizes how academic personas are constructed online. Auto/biography studies, in her view, have yet to adequately investigate the "models of identity" circulating in "cyber narratives" (25); thus, part of her research intervention is to explore the contingencies of a digital and interactive medium (26–33). Her research also provides critical insight into the politics and culture of academic professionalization as she compares her own web page design with that of another academic.

She recalls the editorial decisions she made with the help of a web designer to publicize her academic credentials online. Although the site itself is intended to "serve a purely professional function" (34), the experience of creating it involves "a complex process of sorting through [her] likes, dislikes, desires, and fears" (34). She explains, "The [web] designer tried to get me to choose one that was 'inviting' and 'friendly.' Apparently professors need to present images that students find inviting and friendly; otherwise we are judged to be too serious, even intimidating. I wonder if this is especially so for female professors" (34). Although she feels the pressures of self-exposure, she insists "the home page is my professional self, not my personal self" (34). Working within "the genre of the home page" (35), she struggles to remain accountable, both to her values concerning privacy and to the institutional demands of publicity.[5]

Warley's investigation into another academic's online persona enables her to achieve critical distance in the assessment of her own. She acknowledges her affiliation with Nick Bontis, for they are both professors working within Canadian universities, but questions how post-secondary institutional culture reproduces gender ideologies that regulate academic performance in particular ways. More specifically, she suggests that professional protocols vary according to gender and according to disciplinary field. Her initial impression is that Dr. Bontis's online persona is an "exaggerated performance," while hers seems full of "silences and omissions" (40). Identifying herself as a female English professor, Warley explains that she is "used to having to account for [her]self in terms of scholarly acts and achievements" and that this process has "shaped [her] sense of what is and what is not appropriate in terms of making a professional home page" (35). Nick Bontis, on the other hand, is a male professor who works within the discipline of business. This biographical information influences her reading of the technological sophistication of the home page that ultimately markets Bontis as an academic (36). That Bontis can be "the professor and the corporate man" (37)—not to mention the family man (38–39)—suggests how gender and profession affect the range of identifications that can be mobilized.

The polarities established by Warley's analysis of English and business, female and male professor, are, to some extent, predictable. As Warley argues, "the model of identity upon which Dr. Bontis draws is familiar: it is based on action, work, and personal achievement. The institutional context of the university reinforces this *masculine model* of the professor" (37; emphasis mine). While the ready association she makes between success and masculinity requires further scrutiny, it returns us to questions of judgement and "intellectual excellence" in the culture and discourse of academic research (Kadar 12). According to Warley, "All academics are required to *sell themselves* in these terms: our CVs, annual performance reports, applications for grants, sabbatical leaves, and tenure all require such shameless self-promotion" (37; emphasis mine).

In this context, how does "self-promotion" as institutional protocol function in relation to accountability? Academics who participate in institutional critique should testify, at least in part, to their own complicity in the reproduction of ideologies in academic discourse. Self-reflexivity need not be an occasion for "shameless self-promotion" (Warley 37); rather, it can be a form of theorization used to foreground the contradictions—and hypocrisies—that persist in the idea of the university and the identity of the professor. Warley's major criticism of Bontis's online persona is that it "lack[s] irony and self-scrutiny" (39). She finds him obligated to address the "powerful ideology of masculinity" that circulates on his web page and persists in our culture "despite the insights generated by several decades of theoretical work in gender studies" (39).

While Warley argues that Bontis's adoption of the "third-person narrative voice" allows him to mobilize different versions of himself on a single home page, she also recognizes how this multiplicity "suggest[s] that no single representation is adequate or complete" (38).[6] In short, she realizes that "the home page is not entirely self-made" (40). His persona has greater complexity than she at first imagines, for while it "conforms to the script of the academic and corporate man," it also reflects a commitment to "family and other communities of belonging" (40). In critiquing her first impression, she realizes that "discursive productions," more generally, are "complex, contradictory processes" (J. Scott 34).

Warley's research is derivative but does not lack innovation; she sustains interest and credibility by allowing testimonial supplements to agitate her initial hypothesis. The comparative analysis of two academic home pages enables her to generate a more complicated meditation on the institutional pressures to conform to an exclusive standard of professional excellence that does not account for the variety of life situations experienced by professors, male or female. Her inconclusive analysis displaces her authority as a critic and creator of life narratives without undermining it. Such research thus implies how corporate ideologies of excellence profile academics and affect self-perception in the experience of academic success and failure.

To conclude, I would like to offer suggestions about why terms such as *excellence* and *accountability* have been politicized within the field of auto/biography studies. Liz Stanley reminds us that auto/biographical criticism has changed over the last two decades in response to the scholarly emergence of women's studies, a field that not only recovers the life histories of women but also studies the effects of a variety of institutions on the private lives of individuals (42). In her view, "feminist auto/biographical analysis" must continue to develop critical methods to better investigate how "the dynamics of work" affect personal identity and our own role(s) in the production of public personas—what she calls our "audit-selves"—within the university and beyond (58). The increasingly interdisciplinary approach to auto/biographical criticism is significant not only because it raises the potential for methodological innovation in the culture of research but also because it complicates questions of accountability as they circulate in critiques of the post-secondary institution.

In his critique of higher education, Richard Malin Ohmann argues that "accountability has been and is a contested field of meaning and a terrain of conflict" (144).[7] He aligns the emergence of accountability as an institutional discourse with "the right's project of containing sixties movements" to suggest that it is "about capital's project of recomposing itself internationally, marketizing whatever areas of life had previously eluded that process, and dominating workers of all sorts in ways more pervasive but less confrontational than those that marked Fordism" (144). Accountability, in research, often involves a series of calculations. Some of them may function to strategically market and promote our work while others serve to credit colleagues, funding institutions, and significant others who helped us realize our projects.[8] Research might thus be conceived not only as a commodity for capitalist consumption but also as a resource to be exchanged by various communities.[9]

Ohmann argues that academic responsibility in research extends beyond the employment contract of the university to engage with concerns of the larger society: "we earn our privileges not just by guarding and augmenting our special bodies of knowledge but by undertaking to put those knowledges to work for the good of all" (136). Thus, his suggestion that "accountability" induces practices of "self-policing" (136–37) to displace socio-political questions of experience, in addition to "free inquiry, critical thinking, socially beneficial knowledge, and other such ideals, however wide their appeal to the public" (138), is significant, particularly as new research areas develop in response to issues of public concern.

In *Personally Speaking: Experience as Evidence in Academic Discourse*, Candace Spigelman argues for "the intellectual integrity of experiential discourse," stating that "in addition to its appeals to emotion and identification, personal experience can make logical appeals, which can be evaluated as evidence in academic writing" (107). She extends the relevance of this "new configuration of academic prose that blends personal experience and academic argument" to suggest how it "has a more significant impact in the public space beyond the classroom" (130–31). She describes new uses of the personal where collaborative work can occur: "students learn public forms of writing by way of community outreach, public service projects, Internet chat rooms and Web writing, cross-institutional paired writing assignments, oral history collections and adult literacy programs" (131). This interactive approach suggests that "understanding comes by way of participating in, as well as interrogating, public contexts" (131).[10]

While I have argued for the intersection between academic testimony and institutional critique, I also note that testimonial modes currently pervade popular forms of entertainment. It thus remains unclear how to sustain what Spigelman calls "the intellectual integrity of experiential discourse" (107), for some of her examples of experience-based education seem to favour a society where training in practical skills and services emphasizes value. Readings argues that "the question of the University cannot be answered by a program of reform that either produces knowledge more efficiently or produces more efficient knowledge" (163). Knowledge, in this context, must thus be re-evaluated in relation to "production, distribution, and consumption" to assess "the extent to which the University *as an institution* participates in the capitalist-bureaucratic system" (163).

Intellectual excellence, in the epigraph that begins this essay, remains a term worthy of interrogation, particularly since we, as academics, are disciplinary subjects who, in following the institutional protocols of our professional culture, participate in the reproduction of dominant ideologies. The emergence of new disciplines and methodologies can, in some cases, be historically situated in relation to the institutional changes that have necessarily occurred in response to political activism and civil rights movements, but this does not mean that such events are relegated to the past. Testimonial practices in academic scholarship represent just one way of reconfiguring and reinvigorating our conceptions of knowledge, truth, and experience for a range of audiences. This discussion is not intended to privilege testimonial practices in scholarship as the most "excellent" example of an intervening research methodology, but I hope it stimulates thought for future directions in academic research.

The practice of academic reflexivity raises many questions that I cannot adequately address here. For instance, I wonder how the disciplinary protocols and expectations vary, not only on the basis of important factors such as gender, race, nationality, age, and so on, but also on the basis of educational experience, employment status, or research publication.

Cynthia G. Franklin's research suggests that "most [U.S.-based] academics in the 1990s wrote their memoirs at around the age of fifty, after they became full professors and established a national reputation" (4). While her analysis differentiates memoir from other forms of academic life-writing, it provokes questions concerning the privilege that enables discursive performances of radicalism within the academy. In what locations do emerging forms of critical practice and experimentation gain acceptance? In what locations are they marginalized, and why? Is "critical" reading necessarily "political"? How does our critical reading of the author who produces a life narrative serve to reposition us as figures of power who assume the right to speak for, and pass judgement upon, others?[11] Finally, can we—and should we—ever be secure with accountability as an *incomplete* theory and practice, knowing that there are conditions, personal and professional, that limit our ability to respond?

Given the recent concerns over the disciplinary earmarking of funding through SSHRC, we should become better prepared to formulate a response to the following assertion: "We need to think about a community in which communication is not transparent, a community in which the possibility of communication is not grounded upon or reinforced by a common cultural identity" (Readings 185).

NOTES

1. Institutional critique and first-person scholarship are not synonymous practices; institutional critique does not always adopt the personal mode, and the personal is invoked in scholarship in a variety of ways that I do not address. See critics such as Cary Nelson, *Manifesto*, Stanley Aronowitz, Bill Readings, and Henry Giroux, "Introduction," for varied examples of institutional critique. For elaborated discussions of testimony and witnessing, particularly as they pertain to traumatic historical events, see Shoshana Felman and Dori Laub, as well as Cathy Caruth.

2. See the Guest Column and Forum of Letters in the October 1996 issue of *PMLA* 111.5 for a sketch of debates surrounding the use of the personal in academic discourse (1146). Susan David Bernstein cites this debate to suggest how the personal mode is disciplined through "its regularized and predictable appearances in academic

writing" (173). Also see *Confessions of the Critics* for an essay collection of debates surrounding academic-reflexivity during the 1990s. Notably, the publication dates for this book and the PMLA issue coincide with that of *The University in Ruins*.

3.   The binarism Readings establishes between "accounting" and "accountability" is oversimplified. For critical responses to his methodology see, for example, Dominick LaCapra, Nicholas Royle, Asha Varadharajan, and Shirley Neuman. Also see the 1995 commemorative issue of *The Oxford Literary Review* 17, entitled "The University in Ruins," for an international response to Bill Readings and his work in the wake of his untimely death.

4.   Bernstein originally wrote this article in the early 1990s; she provides an updated preface to her article, reproduced in an anthology in 1999, to acknowledge the extensive critical conversation regarding first-person scholarship developed by academics in the interim. She does not indicate, however, whether or not she believes that the now pervasive use of first-person has, in fact, resulted in political inefficacy.

5.   Warley invokes the term *genre* but implies the difficulty of reading for convention or standardized practice in the "professional home page" (35). Some home page information—such as teaching and publication history—resembles that which appears in other professional contexts; however, the extent to which authors combine personal and professional "selves" varies (35). The particularities of individual home page aesthetics, multimedia, and hyperlink technologies, she argues, affect the reception of academic narrative as personal and, or, professional in complex ways that require continued study.

6.   Warley cites these three versions as "Professor Bontis," "Dr. Bontis," and "Nick" and explains that they appear in sections in his page entitled "Teaching," "Businesses," and "Family," respectively (37–38).

7.   Ohmann cites the 1970s as a "pivotal" period during which the term *accountability* was used in book publications "with reference to teaching" (142). He explains, "A keyword search at the library I use (University of Massachusetts, Amherst) turned up 585 book titles, only 6 of them predating 1970, and none of those 6 about education" (142).

8.   Jane Gallop argues that "literary scholarship has always been replete with personal narratives" (1149). She identifies evidence of the personal "in prefaces, acknowledgements, dedications, footnotes," as well as "in arguments, examples, paraphrases, juxtapositions, interpretations, and evaluations" (1149–50).

9.   Ruth Perry draws attention to the relation between the corporate privatization of the university and the resistance of academic discourse to uses of the "personal." While she argues that we use "our personal voices to describe the loss and to reconstitute a noncommercial sense of public," she urges us to be strategic: "Let us

reconstruct our attenuated civic sphere as public intellectuals rather than further commodify the personal. We can afford the privatization of criticism no more than we can afford the privatization of any other resource" (1167).

10. Spigelman has influenced my critical approach, for she also invokes Derrida's theory of the supplement as a method of reading experience in academic discourse, though not with the same emphasis on testimonial practice.

11. See Smaro Kamboureli's "Critical Correspondences: The Diasporic Critic's (Self-)Location," in her book *Scandalous Bodies: Diasporic Literature in English Canada,* for an extended discussion of academic "self-location," particularly as it relates to the culture of discipline within the university. She pursues ethical questions regarding one's right and capacity to speak for others and explores the "incommensurability of identity" (5) experienced by the "diasporic critic" (21). As Kamboureli asks, "What determines the role of the diasporic critic? How does she move inside the cultural and political syntax of the communities in which she participates? And what is her intellectual task?" (21).

NINE

Don't Mind the Gap

EVOLVING DIGITAL MODES OF
SCHOLARLY PRODUCTION ACROSS
THE DIGITAL-HUMANITIES
DIVIDE

Susan Brown

THE HUMANITIES ARE BEING SWIFTLY retooled by digital media and methods. More and more material from the past is being digitized, and the record of our current culture is increasingly "born digital," whether we are talking about politics, media and communications, fine arts and letters, or the scholarly record. Some gets printed; much does not. The amount of digital material in existence in 2006 was estimated to total 161 exabytes, or 161 billion gigabytes, which amounts to "about 3 million times the information in all the books ever written" (Gantz, "Expanding" 1). This quantity is slated to increase tenfold by 2011 (Gantz, "Diverse" 1). If one of the primary aims of the humanities is to make sense of the human record and human experience, the rapid shift to digital media for recording, interpreting, preserving, and engaging in human activity is of profound significance. Furthermore, access to digital primary sources as the basis of future humanities scholarship will depend as much on how material is digitized and archived, and by whom, and its ability to be sorted, searched, and to interact with other materials, as it will on what is being digitized. The tools developed for archiving, teaching, research, communication, and dissemination will transform the humanities beyond what we can imagine.

The digital-humanities divide must therefore be crossed in pursuit of what has been characterized as "the most important humanistic project of our time" (J. Drucker, "Review" 7). Of course, in a literal sense that divide doesn't really exist; virtually all scholars now working in the humanities in Canada are academic cyborgs: computers are integrated into research methods, teaching practices, and institutional lives. Nevertheless, there exists a gap between "digital humanists" and scholars who suppose that new-technologies work is remote from their own concerns. For many, the humanities should focus on critically assessing the impact of the digital turn and preserving the cultural heritage and literacy apparently threatened by it. Digital humanists seem a breed apart, often based within traditional humanities units but apparently removed from usual research practices, and sometimes engaged in projects that seem alien to their supposed disciplinary base ("Summit" 4). Humanities conferences feature papers on digital undertakings or resources but focus on content rather than method. Debates over digital methods remain confined to the still small group who attend interdisciplinary digital humanities conferences where the particularities of research problems take a back seat to technical concerns, since few beyond the presenter will know the knowledge domain involved in a presentation.

My title thus refers to the divide between the digital and the humanities as categories, and also between generations of digital resources. It invokes the iconic phrase "Mind the Gap" that originated in that slightly ominous Big-Brother-like announcement repeatedly intoned on some London Underground platforms, warning travellers to step carefully between the platform and the carriage in cases where the fit between them is poor. Unevenness developed from having to make a new technology fit the old, as when early rail lines had to curve to follow the existing public roadways above them (Mole). The phrase is now familiar from other cities, including Toronto, but the story of its advent in 1968 has a particular resonance. Here is the Wikipedia[1] version:

> The Underground management chose what was then a new technology, digital recording, in order to be able to save the announcement using solid state equipment that would have no moving parts. As storage capacity

was highly expensive, the phrase had to be relatively short. A short warning would also be easier to fit in writing on the platform.

The recording equipment was supplied by AEG Telefunken. According to the *Independent on Sunday*, sound engineer Peter Lodge (who owned a company called Redan Recorders in Bayswater), working with a Scottish Telefunken engineer, initially recorded a professional actor reading "Mind the gap" and "Please stand clear of the doors," but the actor insisted on performance royalties and the phrases had to be re-recorded. In the event, Lodge read the phrases to line up the recording equipment for level [that is, to adjust the volume] and those recordings were chosen for use. ("Mind the Gap")

Incommensurate infrastructure and technologies throw up problems for users—in the words of Michael Palin, "It's an acknowledgement that the thing doesn't quite work" (iii). These problems plus the pressure for economic "efficiency" spur further innovation to make redundant the human personnel who for years did the job of warning passengers to watch their step. Adopting a pioneering technology has in its turn a profound impact on form and content, throws up intellectual property issues, and blurs the line between expert and technician, content-provider and publisher. The result has reproduced itself virally with greater persistence than anyone could have foreseen, in this case in everything from a plethora of "Mind the Gap" merchandise to book titles, popular songs, films, and videogames. Incorporated into the trans-national vocabulary of the well-travelled, "Mind the Gap" gestures at the anxieties associated with navigating a complex network. To me, it speaks strongly to the gap between intention and result in the implementation of new technologies, their diverse impacts on the people whose lives they mediate, and the richly creative response of human culture to such impacts. This resonance is no doubt increased by my strong awareness, arising from feminist critique, that gaps, omissions, and silences should be interrogated for the meaning that may inhabit them as indices of the organization of power, knowledge, and discourse.

I invoke the gap to acknowledge these continuities with our present situation while insisting that it is imperative that humanities scholars not be put off by the digital-humanities divide. The broader scholarly community must address it by engaging with the development of digital tools and methods for teaching, conducting research, and disseminating its results, despite the advertised risks. As the examples of the Underground announcement and the QWERTY keyboard illustrate, apparently provisional or trivial technological innovations may persist and have broad and unforeseeable impacts.[2] From the insight that humans and artifacts are mutually constituted, we must recognize that work underway now in information and communication technologies will reshape incalculably how work in the humanities will be conducted, indeed how it will be accessed and understood, through much of this century. Although contingency and chaos theory would stress that the outcome cannot be determined, the more those in the humanities assert agency in this process, the more likely that those reshapings will be desirable.[3]

My own experience of this gap emerges from a decade spent developing with colleagues a major digital resource in literary history, *Orlando: Women's Writing in the British Isles from the Beginnings to the Present* (Brown, Clements, and Grundy 2006).[4] Insofar as *Orlando* emerged from the desire to devise new ways to do literary history, this work meant constantly negotiating that gap between the platform of "traditional" research practices and a moving vehicle: the development of second-generation computing tools to support humanities research ("Summit" 4). Bringing my initial interests in Victorian literature, feminist critique, and literary history into dialogue with that swiftly expanding area now called the digital humanities[5] transformed my research agenda and expanded my sense of the horizon of humanities research. I here survey some key transformative impacts of the digital turn on core activities in the humanities as a basis for arguing that working at the interface between the digital humanities and humanities research must now be understood as one of the most pressing, if also among the most daunting, imperatives on the humanities research agenda.

Suspicion in the humanities of digital technologies is overdetermined by numerous factors. The involvement of the military industrial complex in the development of the Internet in the 1960s—epitomized by the concept, presented by Paul Baran of RAND Corporation, of a decentralized network and automated packet switching (the method by which the Internet moves information about) to ensure communication and information resilience in the event of a nuclear war—has been succeeded by the increasing use of electronic information gathering, tracking, and surveillance in the "war on terror" post 9/11 (Abbate 7–42; Ross 4; Latham). The commerce-driven hype associated with digital culture has met with skepticism within an institutional environment that, in and beyond Canada, conceives of itself as resistant to corporatization. Critiques of capitalism and globalization can crystallize into a healthy skepticism of what Daniel Dinello calls "technologism," "a harmful system of propaganda that serves to support military and corporate demand for unbridled and autonomous expansion of dangerous technologies without questions or moral concerns" (275). Yet, as Dinello argues, discerning such a hegemonic discourse does not excuse technophobia, any more than it leads most of us to eschew technologies such as the World Wide Web, which Thomas Swiss and Andrew Herman remind us is both "an instrument and an activity through which self and world are cast into sense" (2).

Profound regard for print and the forms of knowledge print culture has fostered, as well as a focus on the past, are further reasons why scholars may consider technological issues inimical to their values: the projected "end of the book" and the culture it represents are laid at the feet of the computer (Birkerts). Longstanding investments in imaginaries of the "human" that go back at least as far as the Romantics fuel hostility to technologically oriented work (Keep). However, as strong as their hold is, even on many who have shed the epistemologies of "humanism," Andrew Ross reminds us of their cost: "A humanism that wants to police its borders with the technosphere carries with it an ugly record of policing the ecosphere. As for its global dimensions, a broader social overview of the humanist project further exposes the degree to which its historical claims have been and still are waged in the interests of white masculine power" (165). Engagement with new technologies opens up, in the words of Lucy Suchman, the "exciting prospect of alternate conceptualizations of what it means to be human...not an autonomous, rational actor but an unfolding, shifting biography of culturally and materially specific experiences, relations, and possibilities inflected by each next encounter" (281).

Yet, recognition of such possibilities is difficult within an institutional context in which the techno-science-driven research funding model has choked funding for the humanities, social sciences, and basic or "pure" sciences, making work that involves technology seem inimical to the interests of the humanities (CFHSS report as referred to in Marjorie Stone's essay in this volume). New information and communication technologies are also implicated in the workload increases, speed-up, and organizational restructuring that have resulted from the underfunding of Canadian universities since the mid-1970s (Menzies and Newson), with the result that engaging with such innovations may feel like abetting the very forces that are eroding the professoriate's labour conditions. Beyond the academy, digital technologies have also exacerbated economic and social inequalities, both globally and within technologized nations (Dean et al., "Symposium"). Thus Donna Haraway's meditation on the technological turn through the figure of the cyborg spans Silicon Valley workers and academics. These and many other aspects of digital culture cry out for assessment by the humanities. A strong sense of the liminality of our era, Vincent Mosco argues, makes us susceptible to mythologies that "stitch together, however strangely and for however brief a time, those powerful, potentially disabling contradictions in life" and shape not only individual lives but whole societies (53). As one of these, the mythology of "the digital sublime" demands rigorous analysis and critique.

But critique is not enough, if it means detachment or evasion. Technologies, broadly defined as the use of tools or machines to interact with or modify the world, have a pervasive and global impact on landscapes, weather, food, and bodies as well as more obvious activities in "high-tech" societies. Notwithstanding the continuing legacy of romanticism's construction of "nature" as beyond technologies, there is no space in the contemporary world—intellectually, institutionally, or materially—free of the impact of technologies. Thus, even resistance to new technologies requires coming to terms with their seductions and should be tempered by recognition of their potential to be other than they are. Although, as Andrew Feenberg has argued, computer systems are hardly neutral and have often strengthened existing patterns of domination and inequity, they are versatile machines that can be put to diverse purposes (15). Indeed, historian Janet Abbate attributes the Internet's success not to its later commercialization but to the "community's decentralized authority, its inclusive process for developing technical standards, and its tradition of user activism" (182). World Wide Web inventor Tim Berners-Lee designed it to foster democracy, individual agency, and social transformation (206; see also Schuler, Turner). The academy can harness such aspects of digital technologies to desirable ends. Indeed it has, for instance, in circumventing through open-access initiatives the ravenous acquisition of scholarly journals by large commercial publishing firms. Although stemming from the sciences, where journals costs were reaching obscene levels, such initiatives are proving of major benefit to the humanities. They have permitted the founding of online digital journals in new areas despite continuing library cutbacks and the crisis in scholarly publishing; they have made available out-of-print or rare publications; they are making research results more accessible than ever before. This is merely one example of how the academy can foster technological applications that work against the grain of these technologies to create what has been characterized as a "cultural insurrection" (Downes).

The central involvement of university libraries in providing infrastructure for open-access archives, as well as the investment of considerable monies to develop and support tools, demonstrates the institutional flexibility and initiative required to leverage the power of the computer in innovative ways.[6] But equally important are the cultural shifts and support systems that enable such initiatives to thrive and establish user communities. As John Seely Brown and Paul Duguid have shown, digital technologies are caught up in powerful social networks, communities, and institutions that have a profound impact on whether a new technology is adopted. What in a digital resource is readable, knowable, and learnable by whom depends on larger cultural factors ranging from accessibility (a spectrum of concerns including both machine availability—the "digital divide"—and the ability to receive what the machines communicate, which may depend on such factors as language, sightedness, literacy, and education level) through support (from training and IT help to informal social networks) to factors such as age, ethnicity, geography, gender, and divisions of labour (DiMaggio et al.; Gajjala; Harcourt; Kolko et al.; Leung; Selfe and Hawisher; Spender; Star, ed.). Because technologies are embedded in human culture, change happens not just in initial stages of "invention" or "design" but through the iterative processes of human adoption and adaptation of technologies, and the creation of cultures that support them.

Among those aligned with the humanities, creative arts practitioners are trailblazers in the development of new media applications. So are those interested in new pedagogies, whose embrace of new technologies should not be dismissed as driven by top-down pressure for efficiencies (although that is in the mix), but as an attempt to keep up with the changing needs and literacies of students, the vast majority of whom—now—were born after the advent of the personal computer. Humanities scholars in general need to learn from such groups how to foster communities of engagement with digital culture. Only thus will the humanities provide analysis and leadership for the remaking of civil society in a digitized world.

LITERACIES

Critical thinking and literacy are widely held to be crucial to civil society. Reading and thinking are being transformed by the digitization of communications, education, and the public sphere. The ease and cheapness with which digital technologies can produce and disseminate images as well as text are producing a shift from textuality to visuality. Voice and sound technologies such as podcasting are shifting dissemination toward orality, and even much electronic text is perhaps best understood in relation to the oral (Ferris). Stuart Moulthrop draws on Espen Aarseth's work on open and dynamic textualities to characterize the electronic archive as a site for continuously evolving literacies. Contending that it works against "textual fundamentalism" and in favour of "discursive alternatives," he embraces the notion of "a general literacy of pathwork" among alternative possibilities (229, 230).

If the humanities are to contribute to these evolving literacies, if we want to foster active engagement with new technologies rather than passive consumption of them, then scholars in the humanities must energetically engage with new media and technologies (diSessa 27–28; Jones; Selfe). Fostering new literacies does not mean abandoning old ones. At the very least, older literacies need to be preserved as points of access to the past; they will remain crucial to historical interpretative work so that, for instance, it remains possible to read a nineteenth century novel. But such literacies, as advocates for the humanities have long argued, are broadly applicable and immensely versatile. The humanities have developed enriching literacies involving complex framing and historicizing, which digital environments desperately need to realize their potential. As Shlomo Argamon and Mark Olsen point out, although the Web is a vast set of interlinked materials, its knowledge structure remains largely implicit: genuine "knowledge browsers" will need to leverage precisely the kind of contextualizing, or making explicit the important connections between disparate phenomena, that are the purview of the humanities (34). Now that huge quantities of existing books and periodicals are being put online, the digital archive presents myriad challenges for contextualization, navigation, and searching. The humanities are best equipped to ensure that the digital universe "enriches everyone's meaningful experience with information, rather than dehumanizes it by possibly omitting its context" (Argamon and Olsen 35).

Even within the academy, we need to invent new literacies and new textualities to foster critical thinking through digital media. Although the codex seems unlikely to die anytime soon, scholarly print publication is in a bad way (Alonso et al.). Within this context, scholars working in the humanities need to consider seriously the claim that "scholarly argument is...fundamentally rooted in print" (Ingraham). The digital era opens up the prospect of unharnessing intellectual inquiry from methods and modes of representation that developed symbiotically with the establishment of print culture.

ARCHIVES

The digital turn presents major challenges for documenting culture and cultural transformation. The archive, the raw data of much activity in the humanities, has been fundamentally altered. The immateriality of digital media increases the danger of loss: for instance, informal electronic media such as emails are crucial to future studies in such areas as language, discourse, and history. The flexibility of the medium is also its curse. Electronic publications are far more ephemeral than print, some being updated or replaced daily, and quick changes to technology increase the possibility of obsolescence: even if preserved, electronic data can become inaccessible if the systems for which it was created disappear. Humanities scholars are being asked to participate in the archival project, but few, for instance, archive digital research materials collected with funding from SSHRC.[7]

Libraries are perforce remaking themselves, and we vitally need leadership, co-ordination, and widespread participation in infrastructure development to establish standards to enable archiving, ensure resources for large archiving initiatives, and integrate digital resources with library tools and collections (Humanities). The shift toward electronic scholarly journals concurrent with a model of electronic licensing (usually involving access to a remote server rather than local retention) endangers the ability of libraries to preserve the scholarly record.[8] Maintaining electronic archives poses very different challenges from those associated with print, and providing the resources to establish an infrastructure of archives should be a primary goal of universities, funding agencies, and governments (American Council of Learned Societies).

If scholars of the future are to have access to the primary materials for knowing and analyzing culture, we need robust, sophisticated, and well-supported archives. We require a national solution for this problem, given that many major archives and other opportunities for off-site archiving are based in the United States, and hence subject to the USA PATRIOT Act with its sweeping provisions for undisclosed search and surveillance of records, including library records, by law enforcement and intelligence agencies. A further challenge associated with electronic archives, and a far greater one from a technical perspective, is the fact that, in order to engage effectively with their contents, scholars will require new means of sorting and winnowing the mountains of digital materials that are amassing daily, not to mention new modes of analysis, representation, and publication, which is to say, tools for scholarly production and dissemination.

TOOLS

Increasingly, humanities scholars will use electronic methods not just as hyped-up versions of older technologies and tools—the word processor for the typewriter, the online catalogue for the card catalogue—but as integral to scholarly undertakings in ways that will transform their research activities. That is why we must shape them to our purposes. This is a formidable undertaking, not least because humanities scholars often resist methodological formalization, and because many of our methods rely on close contact with our materials. But that is why we will be poorly served by others' methods and tools, and why what we make will be innovative. Computers have been of great assistance in adapting tools associated with print technologies, but as we strive to forge truly new methods to deal with a previously unimaginable—and certainly unreadable—volume of digital sources, we stand to make immense gains by demanding that computers help us to sift, structure, relate, and analyze cultural material. We want to be able to ask big, complex questions while remaining grounded in particularities, and we want new ways of representing answers to those questions. To do so requires new tools for the production of scholarly research from inception to publication. The results will offer new ways of accessing, investigating, and telling the human story.

Just as print publications are highly naturalized technologies for the dissemination of scholarly materials, the tools of humanities research are so naturalized and the language of tools so foreign that we don't tend to consider that part of our job is tool assessment, although we engage in it all the time. Digital research methods pose greater challenges to assessment than more naturalized tools and are equally crucial to research methodology. A familiar example of why such assessment matters is that web search engines operate on different bodies of material and produce relevance rankings according to various criteria, from the revenue considerations that cause some engines to prioritize particular links to the attempt in Google™ Scholar, working on a subset of what is online, "to sort articles the way researchers do, weighing the full text of each article, the author, the publication in which the article appears, and how often the piece has been cited in other scholarly literature" ("About Google™ Scholar"). Critical awareness of our tools requires that we be able to discern how they work.

Such transparency will become exponentially important as we rely increasingly on finding, collecting, and sorting analytic aids. We will come to depend on tools to provide mediated views of archives and bodies of research. Humanities scholars, particularly those whose work centres on texts, have been slow to adopt tools that distance us from our sources, but visualization and other types of mediation are likely to develop as means of interacting with vast sets of digital materials (Moretti; MacDonald and Black). But how well they serve the humanities will correlate with their legibility as systems, and with how involved humanities scholars are in their development. The Extensible Markup Language (XML) markup schema is one good example of a quite transparent digital methodology; when properly documented, text marked up with XML makes explicit the "knowledge representation" that governs how a text operates in a digital environment (Sowa), so that queries can be shaped with great precision. The Text Encoding Initiative (TEI) has developed a set of guidelines to assist in the use of XML to produce archival-quality scholarly editions. *Orlando* employs XML to mediate and provide several modes of access to roughly fifty volumes worth of scholarly prose that no one is likely to read in full (Susan Brown et al., "SGML").

The Networked Interface for Nineteenth-Century Scholarship (NINES) is an experiment in mediation designed to foster new scholarly uses of a thematic digital research collection. Individual researchers can, on the Web, use NINES tools to compile their own mini-collections within a large body of primary and secondary materials located at other sites. Its system allows researchers to exploit both structured markup and social networking features such as a folksonomy that will evolve as researchers apply "tags" to organize their collections (Hammond et al.). NINES enables users to order and annotate their collections, providing the means to create online "exhibitions" in which sources are placed in direct dialogue with commentary or argument ("About NINES"). The NINES peer-review criteria address both the scholarly content and the technical features of materials submitted to the federated collection, institutionalizing best practices that support archiving, repurposing, and linking within a federated collection. An important feature of NINES, in fact, is a series of workshops to actively train and mentor humanities scholars so the collection will grow. As a review remarks, such projects move away from traditional tools to imagine how new kinds of research might take place; as such sites develop more organic interfaces and offer access to expansive thematic collections, they seem "likely to entice very traditional scholars to engage in more robust online research activities" (Knight).

DISSEMINATION

Initiatives such as NINES, the TEI, and *Orlando* respond to the challenges and possibilities that digital media offer to humanities scholarship from its earliest stages through to its publication. They ask what it means to pursue scholarly thought in a different medium, to trouble the distinctions between "primary" and "secondary" sources, among text, markup, and metadata, or writing, reading, interpreting, and arguing. Consider what Jerome McGann has to say about linear historical argumentation:

> Every so-called fact or event in history is imbedded in an indeterminate set of multiple and overlapping networks. The typical procedure in works of history is to choose one or more points in those networks from which to construct an explanatory order for the materials. Furthermore, works of history commonly cast the explanatory order in a linear form, a sequential order of causes and consequences. These procedures are of course perfectly legitimate heuristic methodologies for studying human events, but they foster the illusion that eventual relations are and must be continuous, and that facts and events are determinate and determinable in their structure. ("History" 197)

Similar arguments can be adduced about the explication of any complex phenomenon: the multi-valence and social embeddedness of most objects of study in the humanities make their analysis ill-suited to linear exposition, adept as writers of scholarly text have become at using print to invoke multiple perspectives, frameworks, and modes of inquiry that work against simplification, and ironic as this characterization of text may seem to scholars who read far fewer books cover-to-cover than we would like. Perhaps precisely because print textuality is so complex and is itself bound up with technologies that it can be fairly characterized as "cybertextuality," linear print remains the primary tool for modelling the knowledge produced in the humanities (Lancashire).

Online publishing forces the issue, given the reliance of the architecture of the World Wide Web on hyperlinking. Michael Grossberg notes that "electronic publishing—with its propensity for hypertext links and multiple layers of argument and evidence—seems hostile to...linear argumentation and explicit interpretive narratives." Information technologies offer unprecedented flexibility, asking us to rethink our models of analysis and argumentation. But while computer simulation and modelling have revolutionized the sciences (Bement), the humanities have been slow to take up such possibilities (Beynon et al.). This is despite early digital visionary Vannevar Bush's belief that the proper end of technology—indeed the only way to avert war and human self-destruction—lay in the pursuit of wisdom through the human record.

Devising new modes of argument may mean devising new technologies if those available do not serve the ends of the humanities, for as scholars from Marshall McLuhan to Andrew Feenberg have insisted, technologies carry meaning, are cultural products, and have profound shaping effects on the worlds in which we live. Critical investigation may reveal startling intersections between certain cultural moments and the architecture of both software and hardware. For instance, Alan Liu has remarked on the congruence between, on the one hand, the refusal by a high cultural criticism invested in "detailism" and "localism" to provide "an orderly discourse of knowledge based on a set of operations for transforming discrete perceptions into cognition" (81) and, on the other, the type of reading associated with the Web, in which readers flit from "fragment to fragment in a hallucinatory blur of strangely discontinuous discontinuity" (78). Different epistemes may lend themselves to different representational forms and demand different interfaces, software, or perhaps finally even platforms to produce them.[9] But even if we view electronic textualities as more continuous with print textualities than the early hype surrounding hypertext let on, the question of how the electronic environment can best serve the purposes of scholarly argument and dissemination is wide open.

Associative and relational discourse, narrative, and argument are key modes of humanities discourse that are largely opaque to free text searching or mechanistic indexing. This makes tools like Google™ ill-suited to real knowledge work in the humanities, where few terms are unambiguous enough to yield good results when divorced from context. As Jeffrey Garrett has argued, noting that Foucault's *The Order of Things* seldom names the French Revolution as such, "the relevance algorithms most commonly used in...online libraries for full-text searching are based on a blind count of mechanically harvested keywords." This is in contrast to the advanced intellectual undertaking of indexing or cataloguing, in which a human agent often moves beyond the words in a text. Given the dependence of words upon context for meaning, the gap between signifier and signified, and the associative operations of the human mind, such search engines become very blunt tools for the discovery of materials. Garrett argues, "By relying on machine concordances and full-text searching, we are staking much of the future of textual analysis on the results of a relentless, almost instantaneous, but ultimately dumb process performed by machines." Much productive thinking has emerged from engagements with textuality in the context of digital humanities work, but it will be a major and crucial undertaking to imbue technical systems for the humanities with sensitivity to the complexities of language and discourse, an undertaking in which humanists need to be involved.

RESEARCH ACROSS THE DIVIDE

Since digital modes of scholarly production are highly experimental, working at the interface of the digital-humanities divide constitutes, in itself, research, provided that the two aspects of the research seriously engage with one another. This includes archival development, creating generalized digital tools for access or analysis, or developing new pedagogies or critical literacies. In this essay, however, I hope to bring home particularly the importance of the pursuit and address of "core" humanities research activities, linked to specific disciplines or knowledge domains, by digital means. Such research is needed to move digital humanities work forward, to ensure it serves the humanities at large, and to counter the pressure created by larger trends or technical advances.

Working at the gap between humanities research questions and digital humanities development allows digital tools and research results to emerge from a dialectical relationship, allowing the research processes to change in concert with the production of new modes of engaging in research. Scholars must make explicit the priorities and categories that inform their work, and what they "mean"—at least for what they want a computer to be able to process—in new and challenging ways. Such self-consciousness can work as an extension of much recent theoretically and politically informed work in the humanities, and importantly brings digital methods and tools under scrutiny as well.

Digital humanities work needs researchers who are simultaneously "in" and "out." They must be technologically proficient enough to be visionary about methods and tools but driven by agendas other than technological ones, so that their doubled vision provides a basis for different ideas and perspectives than would otherwise arise in a field that seems curiously insulated from the political engagement that has shaken up other areas of the humanities. Feminist critique draws its power from the same kind of simultaneity of insider and outsider status. Marginality, liminality, and hybridity—all of which concern gaps and unstable affiliations with identities and communities—provide valuable vantage points for engagement with shifting technologies (Star, "Power" 50–53). The border position of humanities researchers who are willing to edge up to the gap combines expertise in the evidence and methodologies associated with particular domains of knowledge with an openness to, but not a complete immersion in, technological concerns. Such scholars must be full participants in the digital aspects of the research, not least because, as Joanna Drucker has argued, "the cultural authority of the computer derives from its relation to symbolic logic at the expense of those inventions and sensibilities that characterize imaginative thought." She advocates instead "speculative approaches [that] seek to create parameter-shifting, open-ended, inventive capabilities—humanistic and imaginative by nature and disposition" (440).

The ability to provide digital materials for analysis by traditional methods is important, but as Willard McCarty has argued, "as far as the humanities are concerned, all meaningful uses of computing are heuristic" (6). Humanities scholars need to overcome the conviction that using computers to do research is a reductive activity, in order for that assumption to become less and less true. Systematic knowledge representation is a facet of digital humanities that grows naturally out of the methods and emphases of computational science, and it has served some areas of the humanities, such as the editing community, quite well, but it is not the be all of digital method for the humanities. As Drucker and Bethany Nowviskie have argued, "The computational processes that serve speculative inquiry must be dynamic and constitutive in their operation, not merely procedural and mechanistic" (431). The Web 2.0 movement, in which user participation feeds back into and modifies the system with which users have been interacting, provides one model for such research (Miller). Experimental digital humanities work that emerges from putting theory into dialogue with practice is crucial to providing diverse, competing models for conducting and disseminating humanities scholarship digitally.

Such dialogue leads to an interrogation of the fundamental activities, outcomes, and uses of humanities scholarship. Orlando Project founders Patricia Clements, Isobel Grundy, and I were initially lured toward computers by the expansiveness of digital media, but our understanding of what could be gained developed only gradually as we began to figure out how to undertake the project digitally. Paradoxically, it seems crucial that we weren't fully conversant with the state of humanities computing at the outset and hence were not in the grip of the paradigms of the field. At that time, the major projects were engaged with textual editing, developing the theory and practice to support the rigorous development of online editions based on existing texts. Within the humanities, in 1995, no one was undertaking the production of what we now call "born digital" scholarly materials that weren't tied to a core set of primary texts. *Orlando* was in its conception a maverick project. We got excellent advice on methods from computing humanist Susan Hockey, who joined the team, and we began to educate ourselves in this new field. But the concurrence of this process with the development of the project opened up real methodological dialogue. *Orlando* became a major experiment in what has been described as a new paradigm within theories of text markup, that of "performative" markup (Flanders; see also McGann, *Radiant* 206).

The methodological dialogue went in both directions: *Orlando* is indelibly impressed by the digital, and the form of the digital was designed to serve its contents. The systems we created impacted everything from the conceptual organization of the materials to the form of our prose, and they dictate what you can do with it. They emerged from the pull between our conceptions and what we could realize practically, and necessitated constant reflection on priorities and methods as we engaged in the exhilarating and infuriating attempt to make technical systems reflect intellectual aims. As the introduction to the project insists, *Orlando* is "literary history—with a difference," and that difference is the extent to which digital methods permeated the design and production of the scholarship and "allowed the history's underlying principles and priorities to be embodied in the textbase" (Brown, Clements, and Grundy, "Scholarly Introduction").

Building *Orlando* was a practical response to the question of how to enact digital historiography. What, for instance, constitutes a "narrative" in a hyperlinked textual environment? Can a set of search results, produced by a user's interaction with a set of texts structured on common intellectual principles, be understood as a new kind of literary-historical narrative? For instance, searching on the Destruction of Work tag through the entire *Orlando* corpus produces a set of micro-narratives, collaboratively written by various project participants, in which the predominance of the destruction of early women writers' works by others reverses over time to a pattern of women destroying their own writings. Can such results be understood, particularly insofar as the embedded structure or tagging is itself making certain claims about the material— that is to say, it is heuristic—as a new kind of scholarly argument, though it is not "authored" by a particular individual? Alternatively, requesting occurrences of the words "Jew OR Jewish" in Cultural Formation discussions, and revealing the tagging context, reveals an overwhelming pattern of representing these terms within the tagging as either a religious denomination or an ethnicity. The two exceptions to these are in the case of mid-Victorian Grace Aguilar, in the context of ideas of nationalism that contributed to Zionism, and Eva Figes, whose Jewishness is represented as race or colour in the context of its reception in the era of Nazism and English racism. The markup here suggests an argument about changing discursive and ideological frames for Jewishness in Britain, one that emerges from the collective tagging of the concept across the history of British women writers. This example reveals the symbiotic relationship between the prose "content" of the project and its digital "structure" within a complex representational system: the intellectual work weaves its way through both. For these and other reasons, we contend that *Orlando*, despite its surface resemblance to a standard electronic reference work, is a new kind of literary history.

Working in digital technologies led Orlandians to important methodological self-scrutiny regarding numerous aspects of historiography, including causality, chronology, context, coverage, and evidence. It led us to consider the multiple functions of scholarly works, and to try to aim at a broad range of users and uses, from the expert scholar to a student or a general reader. Divorcing the delivery or interface work from the scholarly process would have been impoverishing if not absolutely impossible: interface went to the heart of the research. And our conviction as scholars that this resource was greatly needed fuelled the difficult push from prototype to completion. This matters, since projects brought to fruition become much more useful testbeds for everything from usability research to experimental publishing and sustainability models, to further technical or content development. They also stand a much better chance than prototypes of convincing more people of the value of digital humanities work.

INTERFACE

Precisely because how we conduct our work is increasingly bound up with how we publish our work, we need widespread involvement in both tool and interface development from humanities scholars in the course of their research. Experimentation in new modes of delivery, the experimental dissemination of scholarly results, should be a major priority. Willard McCarty regards the term *delivery* as metaphorically freighted with connotations of knowledge commodification and mug-and-jug pedagogy (6). However, I would argue that we should mobilize the less stable connotations of *delivery* as "being delivered of, or act of bringing forth, offspring," which offers a model open to a range of agents and participants, in which the process and mode of delivery have a profound impact on what is delivered. And without getting evangelical, surely too we can revive that earlier sense of "setting free; release, rescue, deliverance" (*Oxford English Dictionary*), in that delivery at this point is in many respects about overcoming the obstacles of rudimentary forms of digital representation and navigation. In this period of transformation, the scholarly interface requires not only experimentation but also careful assessment to see what works to make digital materials amenable to use by those in the humanities.

For that reason, research across the digital-humanist divide must include serious usability work on ourselves as a user population—investigating carefully our habits and needs, and how well particular tools and the interfaces that mediate them suit what we do.[10] This is crucial to prevent interfaces being developed out of an understanding of web habits based on commercial culture, since human-computer interaction work, methodologies, and central tenets about user interest are overwhelmingly driven by corporate interests. Simply porting over the results of studies based on web marketing and other commercial contexts into the development of digital tools for the humanities could warp our approaches. On the other hand, developers of academic sites, often scholars themselves, often proceed with a disregard for usability and design that may mean that the results of their labour go completely unused by others (Warwick et al., 2008). What we need is to distinguish our particular user communities and test the tenets of usability studies to figure out how to design systems that will really work for and with us.

FUNDING AND INSTITUTIONS

I have been arguing that our need in Canada to work toward a research climate that acknowledges serious engagement in humanities research with digital methods, dissemination, and interfaces constitutes a pressing priority. Responding to the digital turn pushes research toward transformation, innovation, and risk in ways that will benefit both researchers and the profession as a whole as it moves inexorably toward new ways of doing and publishing its work. We need enough highly experimental and groundbreaking work at the digital-humanities divide that we can learn from failures as well as successes (Unsworth). How that climate is supported institutionally, in our national research infrastructure, and in our funding programs, will have an enormous impact on our rapidly changing modes of scholarship. This research environment must be fostered in the face of an awareness that technology adoption is being propelled by a conviction of its economic value and its suitability as a vehicle for a free market capitalism that is largely hostile to the structure of Canadian public education and libraries, the values that Robert Fulford has identified, one hopes misleadingly, with "The Ideology of the Book."

Electronic publishing offers the opportunity to disseminate alternatives to and critiques of market values rather than scholarly affirmations of them. This means, among other things, challenging the ideology and commodification of "information." The representation of humanities content on the Web notably tends toward conservative and unreflective knowledge representation: in the context of literary sites, for instance, static biographical entries on singular authors or topics abound. The "information" age values ungrounded information rather than critical thinking, "just the facts" being the implied methodology of conventional organization into received categories (e.g., in literary studies, via authors and titles). Perhaps the single greatest challenge facing the digital humanities is to develop interfaces that implement, in the words of McGann, "the full dynamic—and decentering—capabilities" of the "radiant textualities" afforded by electronic text (*Radiant* 74).

To meet that challenge, we must recognize experimental interface development and electronic publication as in themselves crucial modes of scholarly inquiry. They need to be understood—and funded—as real research. For electronic publication's much-vaunted cheapness is only true in a limited way: new media can only be "free" if underpinned by some kind of infrastructure for production, sustainability, and archiving. Development costs for producing methodologically innovative scholarship in new media are substantial: its experimentality makes it economically inefficient. Nor should this surprise. Only a few information services such as telephony have demonstrably increased productivity, despite the fact that, as William F. Birdsall has observed, the ideology of information technology rests on the assumption that IT drives a free market economy.

So we need vibrant, adequately funded centres to support electronic resource production—for these are the trailblazers among the electronic publishers—and we must as a community undertake to develop and assess methods of digital publication. We need multiple, competing models with sufficient scholarly content and usability to enable testing of their results on a real user population over a period of time. So, for instance, given the embrace by the young of Web 2.0 social networking systems, we need to investigate how such models might be employed in humanities research and dissemination. But given the skepticism about the cultural impact of Web 2.0 (Keen), along with the uncertain evolution of the Internet economy of trust and authority (Bilder), we also need to test the extent to which more structured expert-applied indexing of the sort that has traditionally been relied upon in scholarly publishing and libraries can add value to electronic systems. Evaluating competing systems rigorously, so that their success or failure is not a result of promotion or the decisions of non-specialists, will depend upon an informed pool of scholars in the humanities to assess digital initiatives and publications.

The large-scale funding I'm advocating here might seem to pull scarce money away from "core" endeavours in the humanities disciplines under the SSHRC umbrella. In addition, the advance of the digital humanities research and infrastructure in Canada has been indebted to policy-oriented funding programs and agencies, such as the CFI, that stand apart from the traditional research councils and their assessment processes. The efficacy of "bigger" science models right across the academy in Canada requires careful assessment (Atkinson-Grosjean). However, while such patterns exist, they are further reason for yoking humanities computing work to research undertakings within and across disciplines, since such integrated work extends research monies, which might otherwise go to applied or technological projects in other fields, more broadly through the humanities. Initiatives that combine pressing humanities research with more broadly applicable work on information technologies will be positioned to meet the demand by funding councils for transferability or applicability. Such projects offer the possibility to experiment with how "bigger" science models might be re-imagined to support humanities scholarship.

Funding digital humanities work is a multi-faceted challenge in Canada. Despite the perception that we are ahead of the United States in terms of per capita investment in cyberinfrastructure, digital humanities work needs more dedicated funding (American Council of Learned Societies 25). The SSHRC Strategic Plan rightly stresses the need to support the development of "specialized, high-tech tools" (*Knowledge Council* 10). The existing Image, Text, Sound and Technology program is laudable in its desire to increase "researchers' familiarity with, and effective use of, these new tools" (SSHRC "Image"). However, this program provides modest, short-term grants that cannot support major initiatives and hence are unlikely to have the kind of transformative impact on researchers that I have described. The program situates the technically oriented work it supports in silos, away from broader undertakings. Considerable lobbying pushed the CFI toward funding digital humanities infrastructure projects, but funded projects make up a tiny proportion of the overall budget. It is therefore crucial that SSHRC put major resources behind its commitment to "research tools for the 21st century," which it associates with "deeper understanding" (*Knowledge Council* 13), as well as pursuing partnerships with other agencies such as the CFI for funding the various facets of digital projects.

A substantial portion of this funding should be directed, I am arguing, for hybrid projects that combine tool and interface development with major research endeavours. This grant program will need to be carefully designed, and it may require a different assessment process and particularly flexible program criteria. When large multidisciplinary projects have a substantial digital component, they can get caught in assessment by traditional humanist assessors who do not understand or are actively hostile to the digital component. The higher costs associated with digital humanities work also work to the disadvantage of junior or even mid-career scholars. If the practice of awarding large collaborative grants in the humanities almost exclusively to full professors persists, paradigm shifts may register more slowly in large-scale research undertakings, a particular concern when digital humanities work is transforming so rapidly.

Collaboration and interdisciplinarity are virtually inevitable in digital humanities work. Such collaborative work can feel foreign to humanities scholars in its resemblance to a science or social science model with a lab, multiple graduate students, and post-docs. Yet this mode of research is rewarding, particularly insofar as it involves graduate students in research beyond activities associated with preliminary or wrap-up phases of projects, integrating them into the research and dissemination activities themselves and providing them with a broader experience. The big research model has significant costs, however, in other ways. For instance, we need to recognize institutionally and in project design that management, direction, grant-writing, and other administrative activities take substantial effort and time. Collaboration often also means collaboration between institutions: it requires good will and innovation at all levels of the university system to foster work across traditional boundaries and create new kinds of relationships. Collaboration among researchers from diverse disciplinary backgrounds and institutions to tackle real research problems in new ways can only emerge from well-funded and institutionally vigorous research environments, so that researchers are not simply forced to fall back on existing models, work with models developed to serve other needs, or abandon projects at the prototype phase.

Interdisciplinarity in practice often means multidisciplinarity, with people who mediate between diverse disciplinary languages and interests: such key roles are often filled by digital humanities scholars. For the kind of research I am describing here to flourish, institutions must make digital humanities more than a desirable add-on in hiring priorities and create dedicated positions. The number of Canadian sites at which the integration of humanities and digital research is fostered by research centres with permanent academic and technical staff must be expanded. Humanities programs must also revise their curricula both to train future digital humanists and to produce cohorts of students who are digital adepts. The humanities will have broad social impacts if their graduates boast digital literacies that encompass training in critique, research, and expression, along with the ability to historicize and situate phenomena within complex frameworks. We too will gain from such literacies as we rely on our peers and institutions to assess digital publications for both method and content (Raben paragraph 5; Siemens et al.). This will be all the more pressing as the scholarly print monograph disappears, as it is almost sure to do, as the primary basis for awarding tenure or promotion.[11]

New media and digital technologies offer immense possibilities. This massive shift in signifying practices and the distribution of information is transforming our world and with it the profession of the humanities. It is critical that we engage with this process, with the gap between where we are now and where we need to get to. We need to move toward conducting research with digital tools and publishing in new media, not because we inhabit a society that does not consider the heritage of the past worth material shelf space or scholarly publications worth the paper they were once printed on, but because the digital turn offers genuine opportunities for intellectual engagement and methodological innovation. Although tools and publishing have been regarded as ancillary to the real business of doing research, they are hardly so now. Research engaged with electronic modes of scholarly production will have an incalculable impact on the shape of humanities research far into the future.

The future of digital humanities in Canada depends on many factors including institutional support, granting council policies and programs, and the development of various infrastructures. But it depends first and foremost on achieving widespread participation from scholars throughout the humanities in digital initiatives as an integral part of our research. If we do not as a community achieve a broad understanding of the implications of digital methods and practices, and fail to develop modes of research and publication that emerge from our intellectual activities and needs, we will find ourselves working with tools created for other interests, and for other ends. That would be a major opportunity lost in retooling the humanities. We should not mind the digital-humanities gap, in the sense of being put off by it; instead, we should mine it: recognize it as an abundant site for innovative research endeavours, and make it our own. We will then as a community become active and informed allies in the creation of digital archives and resources that will serve the needs of the humanities and society at large into the future. We will create digital tools, interfaces, and literacies that enable ourselves and our students to take on key cultural roles as the rhetoricians of what Richard Lanham describes as the "attention economy." And we will take our research and the communication of it in unforeseen and transformative directions.

AUTHOR'S NOTE

This essay is dedicated to the memory of Norman Feltes, who asked us in his published work and his insistent professional presence to think seriously about the technological, ideological, and economic forces underlying major changes in the production and dissemination of texts. I want to thank audiences who heard and responded to portions of this essay at the Colloquium on Scholarly Publishing, Congress of the CFHSS, Université Laval, Québec, May 2001, and the inaugural Symposium on Digital Humanities: Practice, Methodology, Pedagogy at the Centre for Studies in Print and Media Cultures, Simon Fraser University, May 2007, as well as participants in the Retooling the Humanities symposium at the University of Guelph in October 2006. Many thanks to Isobel Grundy for detailed comments on an earlier draft of this essay.

NOTES

1. I cite the open and collaborative Wikipedia site as a provocation. As it happened, being familiar with the London Underground announcements and mulling over the possibility of using this phrase in my title, I turned to Google™ to try to discover its provenance. The Wikipedia site was first among the results. I found it a well-sourced article that confirmed the claim that Wikipedia is a good resource for general knowledge, particularly on topics related to technology. But whereas the usual impulse might have been (Warwick "Whose Funeral?"; Sukovic "Scholarly") to obscure my use of electronic resources by citing only the sources to which Wikipedia led me, I decided to cite Wikipedia itself as a nod to the ways that research practices are changing, as well as an acknowledgement of the debate over the value of Wikipedia as a resource for teaching and scholarship (see "Wikipedia"; Davidson). Although the article may be changed at any time by anyone with web access, pages are monitored by the community and most vandalism is corrected rapidly. Wikipedia preserves all previous versions of an article, so by accessing the article's history readers of this essay can view "Mind the gap" as it was when I accessed it on 27 February 2007.

2. Whether or not one accepts the disputed view that the QWERTY key layout was designed to slow down typing, it was certainly devised to avoid the jamming of the type bars on mechanical typewriters by separating commonly used letters. The QWERTY keyboard prevails despite the obsolescence of the technology that prompted it (Liebowitz and Margolis 7).

3. My thinking here is influenced by Lucy Suchman's approach to agency in relation to technologies, which is grounded in feminist theory and a recognition of the particularities of cultural-historical practices (285 and *passim*).

4. See the Scholarly Introduction at <http://orlando.cambridge.org/protected/ svDocumentation?formname=t&d_id=ABOUTTHEPROJECT> for an overview of this literary historical textbase.

5. This field, concerned, in the language of the newly founded *Digital Humanities Quarterly*, with "the practice of humanities research in and through information technology, and the exploration of how the humanities may evolve through their engagement with technology, media, and computational methods," covers the expanding terrain of new media, hypertext, text corpora, text encoding and analysis, computational linguistics, statistical models, knowledge representation, visual communication design, game theory, and digital-oriented issues of textuality, interfaces, information browsing and retrieval, and tool development as they affect the humanities ("About DHQ"). For an overview see Schreibman et al.

6. The Open Journal Systems developed by the Public Knowledge Project at Simon Fraser University is an excellent instance of a well-conceived and supported open-access tool. On the wide-ranging challenges of the digital archive see Martin and Coleman.

7. The Council's definition of what scholars are required to archive is broadly inclusive: "Research data includes quantitative social, political and economic data sets; qualitative information in digital format; experimental research data; still and moving image and sound data bases; and other digital objects used for analytical purposes." See <http://www.sshrc-crsh.gc.ca/site/apply-demande/ policies-politiques/edata-donnees_electroniques-eng.aspx>.

8. See "Urgent Action Needed to Preserve Scholarly Electronic Journals," edited by Daniel J. Waters. This statement has been endorsed by the Canadian Association of Research Libraries, the (U.S.) Association of Research Libraries, the (U.S.) Association of College and Research Libraries, and other similar organizations.

9. The nascent field of "platform studies," heralded by a series from MIT Press (platformstudies.com), probes the impacts of the material features and capacities of computer systems.

10. Usability studies are an important area of human-computer interaction research that investigate the factors involved in whether, or how, someone can learn a computer system (ranging from hardware to software or a website) and use it successfully. Mainstream usability experts argue that web users won't scroll, read lengthy texts, or engage in sustained thinking or analysis, as indicated by the title of usability guru Jakob Nielsen's book *Designing Web Usability: The Practice of Simplicity*, and his guidelines to "be succinct," "write for scannability,"

and "split up long information" (Nielsen 101). Pronouncements on usability for higher education purposes echo mainstream usability principles, pushing toward short and simple content and navigation, and stressing the Web as a source of information rather than knowledge (e.g., Shiratuddin et al.). See Susan Brown et al., "Between Markup and Delivery."

11. The Modern Language Association's 2002 report on "The Future of Scholarly Publishing" lamented the narrowing of criteria for tenure to the "holy grail" of the scholarly monograph, with the accompanying devaluation of other forms of scholarly publication, in the context of the decreasing opportunities for monograph publication (177). Given these findings about the strain the rapid changes in scholarly publishing were creating in the tenure system, and the explicit recommendation that departments develop guidelines for evaluating electronic publications, the MLA "Report on Evaluating Scholarship for Tenure and Promotion" reports disturbingly on the "state of evaluation for digital scholarship, now an extensively used resource for scholars across the humanities: 40.8% of departments in doctorate-granting institutions report no experience evaluating refereed articles in electronic format, and 65.7% report no experience evaluating monographs in electronic format" (Modern Language Association).

TEN

Do the Humanities Need a New Humanism?

Diana Brydon

The question of our relation to regimes of value is not a personal but an institutional question. A key condition of any institutional politics, however, is that intellectuals do not denigrate their own status as possessors of cultural capital; that they accept and struggle with the contradictions that this entails; and that their cultural politics, right across the spectrum of cultural texts, should be openly and without embarrassment presented as their politics, not someone else's.

—*Frow*, Cultural 169

INTRODUCTION: THE CONTEXT TODAY

DO THE HUMANITIES NEED a new humanism? I think so, and I see a consensus emerging to this effect, although many of the details still need to be worked out across a range of positions (Kristeva; Mbembe and Posel; Said, *Humanism*; D. Scott; Spivak, *Death*). In essence, many agree with Edward Said that "it is possible to be critical of humanism in the name of humanism" (*Humanism* 10), "situating critique at the very heart of humanism" (47) and recognizing that such critique carries practical consequences for the work that we do in the humanities. In his influential *Keywords*, under the entry on "Humanity," Raymond Williams discusses the new nineteenth-century use of humanism "to represent the developed sense of **humanist** and the **humanities:** a particular kind of learning associated with particular attitudes to CULTURE (q.v.) and **human** development or perfection" (bold font in original 123). This learning and these attitudes now seem to be changing once again.

Grant Farred summarizes the situation as follows: "The needs, ethical justifications, epistemic imperatives, and very possibilities and historical conditions for knowledge production are at stake" (50). Xiaoying Wang agrees: "The Kantian notion of the autonomy of reason—one of the most powerful expressions of the ideal of free intellectual inquiry, not least in the Humanities—is no longer acceptable in the commercialized world of advanced capitalism, and knowledge becomes something that needs to prove its worth by market or marketlike standards" (525). Geoffrey Galt Harpham notes a related dimension of this problem, suggesting that, according to *The Humanities in American Life*, "[The humanities] show how the individual is autonomous and at the same time bound...," concluding "that humanities are inconceivable without some idea of the human" (26). In response to Harpham, Jonathan Culler concludes that "the term humanities seems to have tied a set of academic disciplines to a particular ideology of the human" (40). In such a context, Maureen McNeil, in *New Keywords*, working with the keyword "Human," provides a different orientation to her definition than did Williams: "**Humanist** may be a synonym for humanitarian, although it may also refer to someone who is a student of human affairs or who pursues the studies of the **humanities**" (bold font in original 165). These various meanings beg the question of what the humanities mean today. They have lost their anchoring in that "particular kind of learning" identified by Williams but have not yet found "the new humanism we need" (Kristeva 14).

While neither humanism nor the humanities rate discussion in Bill Ashcroft, Gareth Griffith, and Helen Tiffin's *Key Concepts in Post-Colonial Studies*, a succinct definition of humanism is provided in the glossary at the end of Peter Childs and R.J. Patrick Williams's *Introduction to Post-Colonial Theory*. Here they note that the universal "man" implied in humanism "masks the oppressive minority (in the numerical sense) interest of the white, middle-class, heterosexual European male" (231). Such an insight may generate the "sobering argument" put forward by Pheng Cheah in *Inhuman Conditions*, which identifies "the constitutive marking of the inhuman within the human" to suggest that "since we have never known a human condition that has been purged of the inhuman, instead of seeing the inhuman as a fall from an ideal humanity, we should ask: How does the inhuman force field sustaining global capital induce effects of humanity, and how are these effects contaminated?" (232). Such reversing of the assumptions that ground the beginning of analysis can take different forms. Attending to the co-constitution of inhumanity and humanity at a philosophical level can be complemented by renewed attention to the relation between the universal and the particular within material relations. As Anna Lowenhaupt Tsing notes, while post-colonial theory has renewed attention to the particular over the past few decades, "There has been much less attention to the history of the universal, as it, too, has been produced in the colonial encounter." She argues that "post-colonial theory challenges scholars to position our work between the traps of the universal and the culturally specific. Both conceits have been ploys of colonial knowledge, that is, knowledge that legitimates the superiority of the West as defined against its Others" (1). As this system of knowledge comes under question, so too do the kinds of particularisms and universalisms that it once seemed to legitimate. This is the territory that I negotiate here in the hope of broadening current discussions about "retooling the humanities" beyond the limited terrain through which they are currently defining themselves.

I have kept the epigraph from John Frow's *Cultural Studies and Cultural Value* at the top of my page while working on this essay because it reminds me of what I think is at stake in this book's deliberations: as humanists, we are institutionally positioned in ways that accord us privilege, even when we feel under threat, and it is our responsibility to recognize that privilege and use it, not to hide behind the mask of interpretation but to recognize openly that all interpretations we offer will arise in relation to our situation and our investments. That does not mean that as academics we are not dedicated to a search for truth.[1] It merely means that we recognize the fallibilistic nature of human understandings of the true; that is, that it is "open to revision on the basis of new or relevant information" (Moya 13).[2] This is one of the foundations of academic research that the humanities share with the other sciences. What might such a position mean for retooling the humanities in the research contexts that this book discusses? Should we be framing our research questions and our projects differently? Could we explain our projects in more satisfying ways to a larger public without sacrificing what is most important about them? If the mission of the humanities is changing in response to globalizing pressures, how may we articulate that mission today? As part of that larger project, how may we situate the national in global and international contexts in ways that ensure our continuing agency?

Behind these questions lie others. How are we to understand the relations across the humanities, humanism, and humanitarianism, and those between the particular and the universal that these relations have charted? What is the mission of research in the human sciences today, and how well is it responding to the changes being brought about by globalizing processes (Appadurai "Grassroots," "Right"; Davidson and Goldberg)? If we recognize, with Asha Varadharajan, that "the articulation of crisis itself functions as a species of crisis management" (621), then how do we move beyond the rhetoric of crisis to more productive understandings of our current moment? As Linda Hutcheon notes in the special millennial issue of PMLA, "our ongoing sense of embattlement as a profession" has been a constant of the twentieth century for this organization (1726).[3] Yet to note continuities in this history is not necessarily to deny the present moment its own specificity.

For some, the problem is merely that the humanities have a public relations problem in conveying the value of the work that they have always done. Others, particularly in the United States, blame the postmodern and cultural turns in which the humanities turned their backs on traditional humanism and/or old left politics (McCann and Szalay; Sanbonmatsu). As Eric Lott notes, "By now, blaming the counterculture for the 'cultural turn' in left political theory so as to indict both is a pretty tired act" (471). Yet such arguments continue to be made and rewarded, and that is because at their best they raise genuine questions about the malaise of the humanities today. At the same time, however, this malaise needs to be placed in the wider context of the contemporary university and all its forms of knowledge construction (Hohendahl), while recognizing the different national and regional contexts in which this situation plays out somewhat differently (Farred; Morris; Parker; Therborn).[4]

The decline in cultural capital of humanities research, as opposed to the rise in prestige of a few elite universities (see Donoghue, "Prestige"), is in many ways mirrored by what is happening in the sciences. The corporatization of the university is leading to greater public distrust of all forms of knowledge production. The disinterested pursuit of truth is questioned when private partners provide research funding and claim the right to control the dissemination of research findings. The religious right is challenging scientific conclusions. The justification for knowledge production has become its ability to serve short-term economistic ends rather than to advance understanding in its broadest sense. In short, the current malaise of the humanities is both particular to the humanities as currently practised and defended *and* part of a larger problem. Furthermore, this problem is to some extent exactly the kind of problem that the forms of analysis developed in the humanities are in theory well-suited to solve: we pride ourselves on our attention to complexity and contextualization, our ability to negotiate conflicting interpretations, and even our ability to "use words in defense of human life" (Ngugi 36). However, too many of our own justifications have tried to work either within the narrow framework of the marketplace or in the kind of highly theoretical formulation that leads Gayatri Spivak to describe the arena of the humanities as "the uncoercive rearrangement of desire" (*Death* 101). These extremes demarcate the current territory of the debate. Will it be possible to find a middle ground between them, or should the humanities community seek a more complete re-charting of the terms under which these debates take place? I remain open to persuasion but lean toward seeking fresh ways of conceptualizing these debates.

In an effort to re-chart the terms of the debate, the first section of this essay attends more closely to the current demand for "retooling" the human sciences and the various responses developed within my discipline, English studies, and my country, Canada, to this demand. My final three sections specifically address humanities research, in part because, as Peter Hohendahl notes, "the defense of the humanities has been made first and foremost in the context of the undergraduate college" (3–4). As such, it has not always been effective in addressing questions relating to research. The second section addresses the work of the now defunct LCC in partnering in the creation of public interest research. In many ways, the LCC, as an independent policy-oriented public body, responsible to Parliament but with the authority to initiate research as well as respond to specific requests from the Justice Minister, modelled an ideal mode of collaboration linking the general public, academic research, and the policy community. Its demise weakens these links at a time when they seem to be needed more than ever. I draw an analogy between the ways in which the LCC worked and one of the directions in which the new humanities might move. The third section charts a complementary direction, looking briefly at my own post-colonial work toward developing a new humanism as one example of how humanities research is reconfiguring itself in response to changing needs and public dynamics, especially globalization. The fourth considers humanities participation as I have experienced it within a large-scale interdisciplinary research project. I conclude that researchers in the humanities need to continue to investigate ways of connecting our work to that of our colleagues within our own and other disciplines and the public. We should not wait for specific attacks on our work to craft a response but rather attempt to change the thinking of circulating discourses at every level on which they operate.

THE CASE FOR CHANGE

According to recent documents published by SSHRC, Canada's national funding agency for work in these fields, the humanities need to change. The only question is how to manage it. This demand for change, many think, implies pressure for the humanities to become more instrumentalist, more like those social sciences that are oriented toward policy formation or more like those techno-sciences aimed toward patenting new technologies. Those pressures exist, and while there is consensus that they need to be resisted, how to frame dissent and design alternatives remains under debate. In response, some seek to defend the status quo and others to return to the traditions of earlier times. Still others respond with cynicism about the ways in which the commodification of knowledge and careerism now seem unavoidable. Still others imply that the humanities, far from being irrelevant, continue to influence contemporary civil society. The 2003 *English Studies in Canada* (ESC) "Readers' Forum: What's Left of English Studies?" introduces a range of positions historicizing and analyzing possibilities, many of which require further attention. In what follows, I focus on this Canadian example rather than the many U.S.-based special journal issues devoted to this topic because, despite globalizing pressures, nation-based institutions and their funding systems still make a difference.[5]

Several of the articles in ESC address my own sense of the particular urgency and nature of the problems that Canadian humanities practitioners currently face. Christopher Keep names one of the issues that I wish to pursue here: "if we accept the proposition that the cultural authority of the humanities is in decline," he argues, the cause may be "our lingering devotion to an idea of the 'human' that is increasingly anachronistic" (59). He concludes that "we need to resist the romantic myth of man's fall into the mechanical and to consider alternative models of the human other than that offered by the idealist tradition" (65). While Keep deplores the desire for "some pure, unsullied space exterior to the machinic order" (65), my own perspective coming from post-colonial studies leads me to place my emphasis on the full implications of such a desire for some "pure, unsullied space," rather than on the machinic specifically as one source of the problem.[6] Nicholas Brown and Imre Szeman find the governing difficulty in "the conditions of and for thinking today" in Capital (17). These conditions are evolving as I write. What can be done with such an insight? My interest falls on how Capital's system continues to renew its legitimacy through managing and directing such desires: that is, not just the desire for purity but also the corresponding desire to sully or defy it, what we might call, in general terms, the post-modern dynamic. This dynamic takes shape at broad theoretical levels, such as the conditions for thinking humanism, and at very particular levels, three of which I am raising here: the phenomenological experience of being human as invoked through poetry; the work of independent advisory bodies to the government, LCC (funding for which was cut to zero by the Stephen Harper government the very day the first version of this essay was due, 28 September 2006); and the research conducted within the SSHRC-funded MCRI on "Globalization and Autonomy," led by political scientist William D. Coleman, in which I have participated.

I continue to believe that we need to attend to the contradictions of humanism, its current vulnerability and its potential for transformation, so that the opening of the "imagination to hope" (46), lauded by Daniel Heath Justice in his contribution to the ESC Forum, may be realized and transformed into action for achieving the social justice that he desires. Heath Justice finds "the human connection" (47) alive in English studies today and "still a site where progressive change can occur, where a passionate investment in transformation and challenging intellectualism can save lives and enrich our reality" (53). Many of us may share the experience he describes on a personal level, especially in relation to the dynamics of the classroom, without finding it sufficient to the institutional challenges and structural changes underway in the current moment. It is not enough to argue that our teaching translates our scholarship into the broader public sphere through the face-to-face engagements with students we all treasure, nor does it seem convincing to suggest that the kinds of pressures identified in the SSHRC discussion document are not present elsewhere, as Patricia Badr and Sandra Tomc argue in their contribution to the ESC forum.

Identifying SSHRC's discussion document, Badr and Tomc assert that "such legislative pressure is not part of the elite U.S. university system, where the assumption is that experts should be allowed to do their jobs as they see fit" (15). I think this misunderstands the SSHRC initiative, which is not about legislative pressure but community debate and renewal, and shows naiveté about the current U.S. system. Given what we know about the various forms of political, financial, and peer pressures on U.S.-based academics, and pressures subtle and not-so-subtle toward self-censorship going back most memorably to the McCarthy era and revived during the current "war on terror," their claim that the elite U.S. university system is a pure space not subject to populist pressures seems a surprising claim. The various U.S.-based special issues of academic journals devoted to the crisis in the humanities cited in this article present a different picture. Institutional pressures to conform do vary from one system to the next, and more often operate, when this is feasible, through subtle means of rewards and disincentives, often linked to a combination of sanctioned ignorance and the sheer unthinkability of alternatives rather than through direct political interference. Nonetheless, enough evidence exists of how such pressures work within every system to make such a claim unconvincing.[7]

At the same time, I also question their implied approbation for a system in which experts are not subject to outside scrutiny and accountability beyond their own circle. University research requires the protections of academic freedom, but this does not mean that ideas should not be subject to academic standards and questioning, both within and beyond the academy. Political interference to punish the holders of unpopular research positions, whether they are taken by Philippe Rushton[8] or Ward Churchill,[9] would destroy the integrity of the system. The right of researchers to explore unpopular ideas must be defended. At the same time, however, such positions must be assessed for the quality of their evidence and argumentation. The Rushton and Rushdie[10] affairs blew up at roughly the same time. Without addressing the nature of their very different unpopular interventions into the public sphere, I argue that then–Ontario Liberal Premier David Peterson's call for Rushton to be fired was as misguided as the Ayatollah's fatwa against Rushdie. The unpopularity of certain ideas with vocal sectors of the public cannot be the criterion for their rejection but, in the case of research, the research itself must be refuted or maintained by the best and most carefully observed academic standards if respect for research is to be maintained.[11]

As the chart Badr and Tomc employ to open their article indicates, serious attention to the questions that matter can easily be swamped by faddishness, in academia as elsewhere. Indeed, if they are correct in arguing that "the humanities have, in large measure, already shaped contemporary civil society" (14), then in my view the humanities certainly do have a lot to answer for. Contemporary civil society shows little regard for serious scholarship and little respect for the disinterested search for truth. By casting the SSHRC discussion document in terms of a style makeover, through the image of a "frumpy" humanities in need of "a drastic makeover" (8), and then arguing that the discipline really is just fine because what motivates it is a "shared commitment to creative momentum" (15), they sidestep the opportunity here for radical re-thinking of goals and achievements. If they are right in finding that "the students educated in humanities programs in the 1980s and 1990s now run Hollywood, run CNN, run *Time* and *Vogue*, run the History Channel, HBO, and the CBC" (14), then what they find laudable, I find damning. These media seem complicit with dominant orthodoxies in ways that ignore the growing gaps between rich and poor, promoting instead the revival of colonialist modes of representing the world. They promote what Henry Giroux terms a "politics of disposability" through advocating the nihilistic view that "truth-telling as such is impossible" (qtd. in Sanbonmatsu 197; see also Wang). While Sanbonmatsu's critique of post-modern orthodoxy is far too sweeping, lumping together, by his own admission, "two dozen different disciplines, subfields, and areas of study, including Cultural Studies, Postcolonial Studies, Rhetoric and Composition, English Literature" and a range of other humanities disciplines, and "even" some of the social sciences (199), as dangerous carriers of what he calls the postmodern virus (198), his article exemplifies the fact that there are rewards to be found not just in promoting but also in attacking post-modern research initiatives. I find Badr and Tomc's breezy defence of the postmodern as ineffective as his thunderous denunciation.

There are contradictions, then, in what is being said about the impact of humanities research. On the one hand, it is defended for upholding traditional values and, on the other, for forming the avant-garde. On the one hand, it continues to be attacked (from the left as well as from the right) as dangerously subversive of the fabric of society and, on the other, as increasingly irrelevant. These various assessments of societal impact do not necessarily rule each other out. They often blur in SSHRC's expression of the desire for greater collaboration with a wider range of partners and stakeholders and broader dissemination of research findings. These are key components of SSHRC's new strategic plan emerging out of the transformation consultations of 2004. Without denying the societal shift toward demanding greater accountability from public institutions, I believe that the concern about societal impact comes—at least in part—from the humanities community itself. This shift in focus is to some extent recommended by the earlier report of the Working Group on the Future of the Humanities: *Alternative Wor(l)ds*. The new SSHRC strategic plan, called the *Knowledge Council*, argues that current activities "don't go far enough in getting research knowledge to Canadians—they do not give us systematic interaction between the research community and the rest of the society that will guarantee excellent research knowledge reaches the people who need it" (12).

In this essay, I ask whether such systematic interaction is desirable and, if it is worth pursuing, what conditions might make it possible. First, I wish to question the assumptions implied by the language used by SSHRC in this instance. It is too crudely utilitarian to convey the value of the full range of humanities research, and it may not even fully suffice to meet the needs of policy communities. The rhetoric of *Alternative Wor(l)ds* is ambiguous. "The people who need it" is a vague phrase that suggests decision-makers more than the general public: it could be read to exclude more than include. The report of the commission of inquiry into the Maher Arar case, for example, suggests that the RCMP believed that even the politicians responsible for this jurisdiction did not need full disclosure, let alone the general public. Surely the general public in a functioning democracy are the people who need it, yet the trend today, as I will outline below in my discussion of the LCC, is toward limiting information to elites.

Other questions arise around the nature of "systematic interaction" and "excellent research knowledge." I would argue that policy-making communities do not need academics to prescribe specific policy options. Like the broader public, policy makers need academics to provide them with a full picture of the situation under investigation, the range of possible policy options to which it gives rise, and some sense of the strengths and weaknesses of each. In other words, they need information and open-ended analysis that benefits from a richly contextualized sense of the situation, the historical record, knowledge of what has happened and is happening in comparative contexts, and some understanding of the positions of those involved. These, academic research can provide. Such provision, however, works best on an ongoing basis so that the depth of understanding required will be there when urgent demands unexpectedly emerge. Rather than attempt to justify humanities research by calculating indirect financial benefits, lauding the desirability of "creative communities" for promoting a climate of "innovation," and celebrating national sentiment through telling the nation's story, humanities researchers might concentrate on sharing the actual results of our research with an audience broader than simply our peers.

In the May 2006 PMLA, Wendy Hesford argues that "the Bush administration's encroachment on civil liberties, unlawful surveillance and detentions, silencing of minority voices, feeding of global anxieties, and crushing of dissent remind us of the urgency and critical work of the humanities" (795). This statement invokes McNeil's linking of the humanitarian and the humanities, making a standard rhetorical gesture toward what now seems an insufficiently examined case for the current role of the humanities. The Canadian government is enacting its own variation on such "security" themes, and even provincial governments, on the urging of the UN Security Council, have the power to enact regulations (rather than laws) with profound implications for the conduct of daily life, which could easily pass beneath the radar of most of us (LCC, *Crossing Borders*). It is not easy to see what Canadian scholars of the humanities will do—or could do—about the abolishment of many social justice–related programs made by the minority Conservative government during its term of office. Les Whittington and Bruce Campion-Smith list "Jobless youths, volunteers, aboriginals, the illiterate and many others" as among those hardest hit (Whittington). The Court Challenges Program and the LCC were also cut at that time. It is not clear to me that the critical work of the humanities, my own included, is responding adequately to such changes nor that it is necessarily well designed to do so. The following section considers the work of the LCC as a model for the kind of humanities-based interdisciplinary collaboration that could provide the new humanism that we need.

THE LAW COMMISSION OF CANADA

Established by the *Law Commission of Canada Act* in 1996,[12] the LCC was mandated to "adopt a multidisciplinary approach to its work that views the law and the legal system in a broad social and economic context" (*Law Commission of Canada Act*). The Commission's *2006 Annual Report* states that "the mission of the Law Commission of Canada is to engage Canadians in the renewal of the law to ensure that it is relevant, responsive, effective, equally accessible to all, and just" (I). In the report, the "President's Message" elaborates several principles: "To strive for relevant law, one has to first accept that society is much more dynamic than law"; "Adopting new concepts and approaches to law is one of the means that society relies on to respond to change"; "The relevance of the law cannot be determined solely through legal analysis. It is one of the hallmarks of modern society that new knowledge emerges from a multitude of disciplines"; and "As an independent federal entity, the Law Commission is committed to engaging Canadians in a non-partisan dialogue on the nature of required changes to the law" (I). These propositions are rooted in the mandate of the Act. At the time the Commission's funding was cut, it was working on the following issues: "the increasing number of vulnerable workers, the growing space that private security services occupy, the advent of globalization, and the strong affirmation of indigenous legal traditions by many aboriginal peoples" (I).

On 26 September 2006, the minority Conservative government of Canada announced that it was cutting funding to the LCC to zero (see Ibbitson for details). On their website, the Commission notes that they were informed of this decision on September 25. It states: "Over the past nine years, the Commission engaged Canadians in the process of law reform through the forging of productive networks among academic and other communities while consulting the public through various innovative means." Their follow-up press release stressed "the character-istics that set Law reform agencies apart from other mechanisms." These include its "unique multidisciplinary approach to law reform," its "in-dependence," "transparency," and ability to consult "with experts and Canadians from all walks of life." Of particular value is the "ability of law reform bodies to examine both the legal and social implications of re-form, to take a long-term view, to openly consult with the public and to bring politically difficult topics into the open for debate."[13] In contrast, the apparent rationale for cutting the program reveals an impoverished understanding of the needs of an advanced democratic society in a glo-balizing world (see Archer; Russell). The Justice Minister at the time, Vic Toews, is quoted as saying, "The Law Commission provided government with advice that we found that we could receive through other mecha-nisms at our disposal" (Archer). He lists his own government department, the legal community at large, and the Canadian Bar Association as alter-native sources of advice.

This logic is refuted by many. Lorne Sossin in the same article is cited as suggesting that to properly assess the work of the LCC, "It's not a bot-tom line that's going to see a payoff in increased productivity or a tangible gain in a particular year....It's about creating networks and relationships that will have much greater and deeper payoffs down the road" (Archer). This is why the LCC's partnerships, drawing on the research of experts from many disciplines, including "jurists, philosophers, criminologists, sociologists, economists, etc." (Le Bouthillier) and involving the wider public, remains so important both nationally and internationally. Le Bouthillier points out that "the impact of this decision is that Canada is distancing itself from the model adopted by other countries such as the United Kingdom, Australia, New Zealand, Ireland and some thirty others with which we share an important part of our legal heritage." This claim is reinforced by Mark Perry's account of the international conference sponsored by the LCC, building on several years of research "on the com-plicated relationship between public police forces and private security agencies" (242). Perry notes the strong degree of interest, both interna-tionally and across a broad spectrum of participants and the breadth of topics covered, which nonetheless reinforced the overall focus "on the transformation of policing and the growth in demand for such services" (243). He also remarks that "the views from around the world showed coherence that I would not have predicted" (242). Canadians are part of a global system and we need national research bodies, such as the LCC, to enable us to put changes occurring here in broader contexts if we are to devise effective means for dealing with them.

In cancelling funding, such arguments for a broadly based view of the societal changes that the law must address are rejected, as is an interdisciplinary and broadly consultative approach to legal reform. For the government to cut LCC funding at a time when it had a financial surplus, in order to pay for more tax cuts, indicates a short-sighted view of the relation between law and society and possibly even, as some have suggested, an aversion to research that calls into question their beliefs (see Russell). The government substitutes a narrowly instrumentalist and reactive view of the law for the forward-looking mandate originally given the Commission. The analogy with shifts in attitudes to higher education is clear. Jeffrey Geiger notes that "Britain is moving away from a publicly funded higher education system, and the accompanying ideal of a university education as one of the social benefits of taxation—knowledge funded out of public resources for the public good—seems to be fading" (63). Similar shifts are happening in Canada.

Even a response somewhat critical of an LCC publication, such as Margaret Hall's review of *Restoring Dignity: Responding to Child Abuse in Canadian Institutions,* concludes that "the Report is a tremendous resource for individuals and organisations with an interest in institutional child abuse" (299). Hall's review is especially interesting for at least two reasons. She argues that the LCC may not have been sufficiently at arm's-length from a government agenda in this case, and that "the Report spreads itself too thin" (295–96). While she finds the report valuable in creating a profile of the "dangerous institution," that is, the type of institution in which children are likely to be at risk (296), and in evaluating various forms of redress, in identifying "eight criteria which the ideal process of redress would incorporate" (296), and in making "six general recommendations and 47 specific recommendations" (298), she argues that "what is needed is an evaluation of how the approaches discussed in the Report could fit together to address the range of needs and interests arising from institutional abuse" (300). In other words, the integrating function that only such work can provide needs to be strengthened rather than broken down into its component parts and addressed in a piecemeal fashion. Her critique centres on the LCC's decision to recommend an overall "'best' response, and its failure to then confront the inherent contradiction of that model" (301). Basically, she values the depth and breadth of the research but believes that in this case the LCC rushed too quickly to a policy recommendation that did not suit all cases. With the abolishment of the LCC, such wide-ranging research and consultation will have to be sacrificed in favour of the focussed policy recommendation designed to suit whatever problem seems most pressing at the moment. In my view, the reactive model is never as useful, in the end, as the proactive model that the LCC embraced.

In his presentation to the Standing Committee on Justice and Human Rights, on 1 November 2006, on the effects of the abolition of the Commission, Yves Le Bouthillier makes several important points to this effect. "Perhaps most importantly," he suggests, "the elimination of the Law Commission removes an important neutral voice from a highly politically charged debate." While he is referring to work on Indigenous law in this instance, the same is surely true of ongoing work on policing, globalization, vulnerable workers, and other projects now cut short before completion.

As the open letter to the Minister of Justice protesting this cut observes, the LCC was "uniquely positioned" to explore a range of "complicated questions that go to the heart of justice in this country." Whereas "Parliament and the ministry of justice develop policy and make laws[, t]he law commission does neither. Instead, it gathers the best expertise and sponsors comprehensive research on the toughest questions. Most important, it engages Canadians directly in deliberating upon how law and the legal system can best serve their communities." These are functions that cannot be replaced by the organizations cited by Toews. They are also dimensions of the Law Commission's work that I had noted in its regular participation in the yearly Congress of the Humanities and Social Sciences run by CFHSS and in its partnership with the SSHRC-funded

MCRI on "Globalization and Autonomy," with which I have been involved since 2001.

One initiative that I had taken to advance the critical work of the humanities in relation to broader societal concerns was to arrange an interdisciplinary workshop discussion of the LCC's discussion paper *Crossing Borders: Law in a Globalized World* at the University of Manitoba in October 2006.[14] In the first version of my present essay, this section on the LCC was designed as a good-news story on potential best practices, modelling ways in which humanities researchers and independent public bodies might collaborate. The workshop brought together colleagues from a range of disciplines to educate ourselves about the ways in which globalization is affecting law-making and enforcement in Canada and internationally and to brainstorm among ourselves about how such issues might best be addressed. Our initial plan was to provide feedback to the Commission. Now that the Commission's funding has been completely cut, we will need to find other venues for discussing these questions, most likely in a more piecemeal way.

Crossing Borders provides a range of case studies and a series of questions on which the Commission sought public input as it prepared to advise the federal government about the implications of globalization for law reform in Canada. This strikes me as a good example of the ways in which our independent research might be pooled from time to time in response to new problems requiring fuller contextualization before fully workable solutions could be defined. I found that many of the people across campus who work on various aspects of the law in its social and historical contexts had not always met one another due to the compartmentalized nature of our daily work. The provision of a discussion paper such as this, the result of a collaboration of a legal scholar and a political scientist, both Scholars in Residence at the Commission for a year, is exactly the kind of research collaboration that might productively translate specialized scholarship into a mode that is more accessible across the broader public sphere. The document cites school children who were involved in earlier consultations along with legal experts, and the issues raised carry profound implications for the character of our democracy and the quality of our lives.

It shows why a view of knowledge premised only on short-term "need" is limited. Persuading readers that they need such information is one thing, but the current legal situation extends far beyond perceptions of need. Current debates about what rules should govern globalization (including those provided by international agreements and resolutions of all kinds, treaties, and provisions for international monitoring and accountability), who should make these rules, and in what contexts (through international bodies such as the United Nations, nation-to-nation agreements, public-private arrangements, or private organizations) are clearly as much about democracy and values as they are about need. They raise questions about legitimacy and accountability, sovereignty and justice, which are not easily resolved. These larger contexts of value and desire constitute part of the territory of the humanities, yet those of us working in the humanities are not always able to see the contributions our work might make to such discussions. Humanities scholars note that the humanities prefer critique, problematization, and the raising of questions to presenting solutions or packaging knowledge as product, as if these disqualify us from policy debates. Yet these skills can be helpful in such a context. We like to show how complicated an issue may be. The challenge is to distinguish our talent for complexity from what Len Findlay terms the urge to embrace opacity. Insofar as our research can illuminate complexities, this too is a strength many policymakers are learning to appreciate. Rather than accept a given frame of reference, we may prefer to recontextualize an issue, to demonstrate how its reframing may lead to new questions as well as different solutions. Such an approach may take more time to develop, but it can sometimes save time in the long run. Just as the world is learning to appreciate the wisdom of the "slow food" movement, there is now a climate of thinking in which our ability to take the long-range view and the circuitous route may be redefined as a strength rather than a weakness. We are more likely to have a future playing devil's advocate than technical advisor. Our role may lie more in correcting tendencies toward ideological oversimplifications of the past and present than toward prescribing precise futures. We may excel in demonstrating the multiple ways in which an issue may be couched rather than selecting one straight route forward.

In many of these ways, our modes of working are sometimes at odds with those selected by our colleagues in the social sciences. The CFHSS report "Large-Scale Research Projects and the Humanities" (2006) makes these points well. It reflects my own experience working in interdisciplinary contexts. Humanities researchers often work and publish alone, but this does not mean that we do not collaborate. Our forms of collaboration may operate at a more informal level and may be acknowledged differently, in notes, prefaces, and acknowledgements. Our writing styles often differ, with humanists privileging process over conclusions, so that the meaning emerges out of the entire fabric of an argument whereas social scientists tend to signal the development of an argument broken down into its constituent parts and leading to a clearly articulated set of conclusions. If such is the case, then how do we bring understanding of the value of our methods and modes to larger constituencies, especially those confronting serious problems that seem to demand the kind of immediate solutions that our methods do not offer readily?

I have no immediate answers to these questions. They continue to challenge me. This is not the first time that the mission and conduct of the humanities has been questioned. The contemporary moment, however, offers a particular challenge and an opportunity for serious self-examination. This is a time when scholarship across the board is being questioned and when its cultural capital is diminishing (see Mooney). It also seems to be a time when we need to combine expertise if we are to address problems of global magnitude: cultural, environmental, social, and political. Colleagues in the sciences are reorganizing to change the way they conduct, publish, and vet their work and how they communicate its value to a wider society. Those of us working in the humanities also need to move beyond temptations toward defensiveness or flippancy to consider our mission in light of the challenges represented by our changing times.

Of particular interest to me is the way in which understandings of culture are changing perceptions of the disciplines. Although many in the humanities cling to the notion that culture is our province of expertise, in fact responsibility for culture as currently understood has largely migrated into anthropology, communications, film, sociology, area studies, and even business schools. Mathew Arnold's notion of literature as "modernity's moral anchor" (Viswanathan 137) is rightly questioned on many fronts. While the critical literacies taught within some forms of humanities study are more urgently needed now than ever, other forms of literacy once associated with careful, close reading of canonical texts seem to be yielding their centrality to newer forms of digital, visual, and multimedia literacies. Some within the discipline even question the applicability of the concept of "research" to the kind of largely interpretive work that most people still conduct within literature departments. I think that such a position is mistaken, but it indicates the lack of consensus about the most basic terms of the debates that this book is designed to address.

John Sanbonmatsu may be the latest young polemicist to launch his career through attacking the cultural turn, the humanities, and Humanities Institutes. He blames postmodernism for ineffectuality in the face of contemporary challenges, while dismissing far too quickly the problems inherent in traditional humanism. He writes:

> Prior to about 1970, higher education in the West had been legitimated ideologically in terms of the university's role in fulfilling traditional humanistic ideals—increasing the storehouse of human knowledge, shaping individual character, creating an informed national citizenry, and so on. The fact that this mission was largely a fiction, or that these lofty ideals worked hand in glove to promote the interest of capital and the state, is not the point. (201)

It is not the point for him, but it is for me. He sees this mission as not only preferable to what has replaced it, but precisely valuable for its messianic qualities. His desire to return to what he terms "holism in theory and practice" (221) blinds him to the value of critiques of traditional humanism and to the many modes in which humanism is being reinvented to provide a more capacious understanding of the human and our place within a globalized planet. His critique of post-colonial thinking, based mainly on the early work of Homi Bhabha, ignores (among other things) the theories of transplanetarity advanced by Paul Gilroy and Gayatri

Spivak and the advocacy of a new form of humanism put forward by thinkers such as Aimé Césaire, Frantz Fanon, Edward Said, David Scott, and Sylvia Wynter. These are not identical projects, but they work in parallel fashion and sometimes intersect. To what extent might such work redirect contemporary inquiry in the humanities beyond its current impasse? Are there implications within such planetary and new humanist thinking for how to reorganize academic work in the humanities and reconnect it to the world?

"A HUMANISM MADE TO THE MEASURE OF THE WORLD"[15]

What David Scott terms "the connection between humanism and dehumanization" (119) may have been the major dilemma of the twentieth century, sharpened for many who found colonization troubling, and even for many who did not, by the events of the Holocaust. While postcolonial scholarship notes that "humanism and colonialism inhabit the same cognitive-political universe inasmuch as Europe's discovery of its Self is simultaneous with its discovery of its Others" (Scott 120), neither Aimé Césaire, Frantz Fanon, nor Edward Said wishes to abandon humanism entirely. Instead, they want to reform it to make its achievements more closely match its declared aspirations. The Caribbean scholar Sylvia Wynter follows in their footsteps, aspiring, as David Scott puts it, "to a certain ideal of humanism—a dissonant, a non-identitarian, but nonetheless a comprehensive and planetary humanism" (121). While Sanbonmatsu argues that collective action for change cannot be realized without repudiating poststructuralist theories, these thinkers, based on their own experiences of racism and colonialism, argue on the contrary that only such a rethinking of foundations and *working through* the legacies of history can lead to progressive social change. Wynter's work, as explained by Scott, "is concerned to anchor the human and its projects in its material (social and bodily) conditions" and "to track the 'codes' and 'genres' in terms of which the understanding (including self-understanding) is constituted" (121). Such work challenges the codes through which the white middle class establishes its hegemony and notes how these codes are changing in response to globalizing pressures. In her interview with Scott, Wynter suggests that "the new code is now that of eugenic/dysgenic, selected/dyselected, in place of the earlier rational/irrational as well as of that of the spirit/flesh" (182). If this is so, then understanding how the new codes operate may require alliances with disciplines, particularly in the sciences, whose work we have not generally considered, certainly not in full interdisciplinary partnerships, before. At the same time, we will need to consider how the residual codes continue to operate today.

Dionne Brand's poetry and fiction demonstrate how the kind of creative work studied in the humanities may contribute to re-theorizing community and global citizenship today, within a reconfigured humanist structure.[16] I argue that Brand's poetry has always been political in ways that challenge Habermasian notions of the public sphere as a place of purely rational deliberation *and* theories that pit the global against the local. Reading backwards from *Inventory* to her earlier works, it is possible to identify how she develops a practice of affective citizenship beginning from the emotional register in which injustice lodges itself in the very body of the poet as a special kind of witness, one who declares: "there are atomic openings in my chest/to hold the wounded" (*Inventory* 100). To reconcile the Shelleyian task of the poet as legislator for the world with her own notions of democracy and equity, she must first describe accurately what is at stake in conflicts now, presented not as information nor analysis but through poetry and story as intimate inventory in an inspired revision of the Gramscian sense of this term.[17] The inventories of *Inventory* provide a different kind of truth, extending beyond the reach of the news as currently mediatized and now distrusted by many. Brand develops an affective citizenship capable of challenging dominant imaginaries on a terrain that they have successfully claimed as their own: the emotional registers of the political. She reclaims citizenship from the claims of ownership asserted by bodies such as the National Citizens Coalition and the National Taxpayers Association, relocating citizenship within the lived experience of a redefined humanity.[18] Brand's poetry, and the modes of interpretation developed within the humanities to analyze poetry's complexities, remind those of us working in the humanities that we have work of value to contribute to contemporary discussions of citizenship, community, and democracy.

COLLABORATIVE, INTERDISCIPLINARY WORK

"Transdisciplinarity does not in itself suffice to reconstruct the new humanism we need."[19]

To bring this kind of interpretive work into effective dialogue with other interpretative communities—the social sciences, policy circles, and the public—will not be easy. The translation challenges, as I have suggested, are different. My interest here is in extending the dialogue across research communities. To work across disciplines, it seems that literary study will need to complement its almost exclusive focus on the particular (the phenomenological and performative intimacies made so urgent in Brand's work) with the insights of disciplines that consider phenomena on a larger scale. Their perspectives can provide greater distance from our tendency to valorize the specific in order to consider how the larger picture coheres. During a meeting of the Globalization and Autonomy research group, a fellow literary scholar addressed the social scientists among us to the effect that she was used to working on one author, possibly one work by one author, and found herself taken aback by the scale at which the social scientists worked, which was usually the scale of the nation-state. While she was exaggerating a little, the point seems to hold. When our project was first conceived, the social scientists assumed that "autonomy" referred to state autonomy almost exclusively. Until the humanists raised the issue, they had not thought of autonomy in personal terms, nor in philosophical rather than purely political terms. Our project, then, has benefitted from such simple exchanges, enabling us to appreciate more fully just what is meant when globalization theorists speak of how interscalar relations have become a distinguishing feature of globalization today. Such work can take place in disciplinary, multidisciplinary, and interdisciplinary contexts. The point, I think, is that researchers need always to be aware of our different audiences in such contexts and be willing to make concessions to get our points across. There is often, as Anna Tsing notes, "a cross-disciplinary misunderstanding of terms" at play in such situations (4).

In her introduction to *Friction*, Tsing characterizes tendencies within the humanities and social sciences very differently than my colleague had, writing that

> Humanities scholars and social scientists tend toward opposite poles. Where the former often find the universalizing quality of capitalism its most important trait (e.g., Jameson 2002), the latter look for unevenness and specificity within the cultural production of capitalism (e.g., Yanagisako 2002; Mitchell 2002). Where the former imagine mobilization of the universal as key to effective opposition to exploitation (e.g., Hardt and Negri 2000), the latter look for resistance in place-based struggles (Massey 1995) and unexpected linkages (Gibson-Graham 1996). (4)

Here specificity is claimed as the province of the social sciences and universalism as the terrain of the humanities. What are we to make of such inconsistent assessments? Such mutual misunderstandings can only become productive if fully engaged. Humanities fields are internally so heterogeneous that it is difficult to select a single theorist as typical of the group. For every Jameson, Hardt, and Negri, we could substitute a scholar of the particular. Yet to a humanist such as me, what seems striking is how often humanities scholarship on a particular question seems almost entirely inconsequential to transdisciplinary elaborations of that question.

When I began work on the volume now titled *Renegotiating Community: Interdisciplinary Perspectives, Global Contexts* as part of the MCRI "Globalization and Autonomy" project, I was struck by the way in which Gerard Delanty's book on *Community* in Routledge's Key Ideas series surveyed a range of disciplinary engagements with the concept without ever considering the discipline of English and work by F.R. Leavis or Raymond Williams. The revival of attention to community has occurred simultaneously within humanities and social sciences disciplines, yet there has been little interaction across the divisions separating the social sciences from the humanities. Where there is interaction, it often seems, from my perspective, to be the humanists working with social science research, but this observation may only reflect my own situatedness as a humanist currently working within predominantly social science–dominated teams. In my work on autonomy, I have observed a similar lack of dialogue across disciplinary divisions. There seems to be little interaction between the work on autonomy within analytic philosophy and that conducted within political science or continental philosophy or feminism.

Our MCRI enabled us to cross some of these disciplinary divides in ways that have been productive for our thinking and our research results. Nonetheless, translating our research into a format suitable for Aid to Scholarly Publications (ASPP) peer review was challenging.[20] If a peer reviewer has not experienced the kind of transformative dialogues in which we have participated over the last four years, he or she may judge our work according to his or her own disciplinary imperatives and find it lacking. Adjusting interdisciplinary work to speak to several disciplines simultaneously, while also addressing a wider interdisciplinary community, is a challenge we continue to negotiate. The more we engage in explaining the often invisible assumptions and protocols that guide our work to others whose training puts them outside our circle, the more adept we will become at thinking about how to communicate our work beyond the classroom and the specialist academic journal. These are new skills for which there are currently few rewards beyond those intrinsic to the work itself. Collaboration, especially across disciplines, is time-consuming.

If we wish to encourage SSHRC to pursue this path, then the academic rewards system will need to be restructured, the time allowed for such work adjusted, and the funding supplied most likely increased. SSHRC is recognizing some of these necessities through the MCRI program and the new Strategic Clusters. These programs will train a new generation more attentive to the demands of communicating across disciplinary and knowledge-community differences. I see hope for reconnecting with a broader public in the kind of training that such initiatives provide, especially for a newer generation of scholars. It will be important, however, for researchers in the humanities to continue to investigate ways of connecting our work to that of our colleagues and the broader public. Current budget cuts reinforce the point that we should not wait for specific attacks on our work to craft a response but rather attempt to change the thinking of circulating discourses at every level on which they operate.

My argument in this essay has been that the new humanism that we need must be capacious enough to encompass interpreting a poem such as Brand's as well as responding to a discussion document issued by a public body such as the now-defunct LCC. What unites these parts of my argument is the insistence on the need for a broadly contextualized understanding of humanities research as dedicated to understanding the complex linkages and disjunctures that form the context for any policy decision. As the Law Commission itself demonstrated in framing its investigation of policing, *In Search of Security*, in such a way as to embrace both public and private policing functions, resetting the terms of discussion can be as important as designing solutions to pre-defined problems. In redefining policing to conform to its contemporary transformation into a mix of public police and private security, the report demonstrates the need for continual creative thinking in the service of the public good. The humanities, too, carry the potential for this kind of imaginative renewal, but it will require a collective commitment.

AUTHOR'S NOTE

I wish to thank Daniel Coleman and Smaro Kamboureli for the invitation to develop my thinking on this question in the workshop that they organized on "The Culture of Research: Retooling the Humanities," held at the University of Guelph in October 2006. My thanks also go to them and the other participants in the workshop for focussed discussion and advice for revision. I am grateful as well to the CRC program, which has enabled my research on humanities community and which helped to fund my research and my participation in this project. The research for this essay first developed out of my ongoing research with the SSHRC-funded MCRI on Globalization and Autonomy and my SSHRC-funded research on the ends of post-colonialism.

1. Asha Varadharajan argues that "the conflation of every form of investment with self-interest is a gesture as sentimental as that which separates culture from the barbarism it feeds" (630). And Frederick Cooper recognizes: "Postcolonial studies has a strong stake in not carrying the contextualization of truth claims into a dismissal of truth as just another Western conceit" (414).

2. See also Satya Mohanty's essay "Can Our Values Be Objective? On Ethics, Aesthetics, and Progressive Politics" and the essays responding to his work in the special issue on "Objectivity in Ethics, Politics, and Aesthetics," which comprise the complete issue of *New Literary History* 32.4 (Autumn 2001).

3. Said notes in *Humanism and Democratic Criticism* that "no matter who is writing or speaking, where, when, or to whom, the humanities always seem to be in deep and usually terminal trouble" (31).

4. While Farred addresses Latin America and the United States, Morris considers Hong Kong, Australia, and the United States, Parker works within the context of Europe and the United Kingdom, and Therborn provides a much more wide-ranging, European-based but global narrative of the fortunes of socialism in the postwar period than that offered by McCann and Szalay.

5. Nonetheless, it is alarming how many of these discussions seem to operate with little sense of earlier debates within the discipline. It is surprising how little reference is made, for example, to past issues of two MLA publications, the *ADE Bulletin* and *Profession*. In particular, the *ADE Bulletin* dedicated to "The University of Excellence," 130 (Winter 2002) and issues of *Profession*, with the texts of various Presidential Fora, chart the history of these debates and remain essential reading for scholars attempting to make sense of them.

6. Arjun Appadurai's *Fear of Small Numbers* addresses the genocidal implications of the desire for purity in its contemporary global manifestations.

7. I find Frank Donoghue's argument, in "Prestige," more convincing. He argues that with the rise of for-profit universities, "the prestigious universities and colleges are the last refuge of the humanities; in turn, the humanities have become the curricular vehicle of prestige" (157)—but only for the elite schools. Other universities are trapped between "the prestige model and the market model" (158) in a system that is "bad news for the humanities" (160).

8. Philippe Rushton is a psychology professor at the University of Western Ontario who was accused of racism for his work on genetics after he sent out a 1989 summary version of research he conducted on the science of race in a mass mailing to professors across the North America. For an account of the incident see the *UWO Gazette*, vol. 93, issue 68, 1 February 2000.

9. Ward Churchill, a professor at the University of Colorado at Boulder, came to mass media attention in 2005 for an essay published on the World Trade Centre attacks in 2001. His university defended his right to engage in controversial political speech. Later, an investigation was launched into allegations of research misconduct in relation to some of his other publications. The committee investigating these claims concluded that he should be sanctioned for "research misconduct." There is debate about whether or not this investigation was in some way launched in retaliation for his earlier controversial statements about the World Trade Centre attacks. He has since been fired from his tenured post.

10. Salman Rushdie was condemned to death by Ayatollah Ruhollah Khomeini on 14 February 1989 in response to the publication of his novel *The Satanic Verses*.

11. Fiction should not be confused with research. The timing of the two public outcries, however, was so close that students coming late into one of my classes thought we were discussing Rushdie when we were in fact discussing Rushton. This confusion reminded me of how similar the momentum of such public revulsion might be, and of the need to avoid emotional appeals in adjudicating the claims involved.

12. In 1992, a previous government had abolished Canada's first Law Reform Commission. Realizing what it had lost, the federal government established the new commission in 1997.

13. This material, and all reports, publications, and calls, were publicly available on the LCC website until their funding was cut. For several months, I could find no sign of this material on the Web. The site had simply disappeared. Thanks to the efforts of Annette Demers, reference librarian at the University of Windsor's law library, the Commission's records and reports were discovered to be stored with Library and Archives Canada in their Electronic Collection. This news was posted on the news aggregator SLAW on 13 February 2007. See <http://www.slaw.ca/2007/02/13/the-late-law-commission-of-canadas-records/>. The sudden disappearance of the original LCC website and the research reports posted there reinforces my argument that Canadians need open access to such research. By eliminating funding, the government has not only stopped some innovative research in mid-stream, but it also served to close down broad public access to the results of this research. It is not clear how complete the LCC archive is, and it is not easily found (if found at all) through a simple Google search.

14. This workshop was arranged through the CFI-funded Research Centre on Globalization and Cultural Studies and the "Law and Society" research cluster at the University of Manitoba. Colleagues from English, history, law, and sociology met to discuss the report. A report on the session may be found at the Centre's website: <http://www.umanitoba.ca/centres/gcs/>.

15. In *Discourse on Colonialism*, Aimé Césaire writes: "At the very time when it most often mouths the word, the West has never been further from being able to live a true humanism—a humanism made to the measure of the world." My epigraph takes the last half of this citation from its use as an epigraph to David Scott's interview with Sylvia Wynter, "The Re-Enchantment of Humanism: An Interview with Sylvia Wynter" (119).

16. This section summarizes part of the argument of my article "Dionne Brand's Global Intimacies: Practising Affective Citizenship," which appeared in the *University of Toronto Quarterly* special issue "The Ethical Turn in Canadian Literature and Criticism," 76.3 (Summer 2007): 990–1006.

17. In the Introduction to *Orientalism*, Edward Said cites Gramsci's *Prison Notebooks*: "The starting-point of critical elaboration is the consciousness of what one really is, and is 'knowing thyself' as a product of the historical process to date, which has deposited in you an infinity of traces, without leaving an inventory." Said adds: "The only available English translation inexplicably leaves Gramsci's comment at that, whereas in fact Gramsci's Italian text concludes by adding, "therefore it is imperative at the outset to compile such an inventory" (25). Brand has told the author that she had Said's citation of Gramsci posted above her desk while she was composing *Inventory*.

18. She does not mention such bodies by name, but the shifting scope of her employment of the pronoun "we" makes it clear that she refuses their narrowly conceived definitions of citizenship and community.

19. This epigraph is taken from Julia Kristeva's "Thinking in Dark Times" (14).

20. The application form, for example, requires us to identify three dominant disciplines for the book from a prescribed list, and of course any assessor must come from a specific field and background.

Coda

RETOOLING THE HUMANITIES

Daniel Coleman &
Smaro Kamboureli

OUR CONTRIBUTORS COLLECTIVELY OFFER a wide-ranging assessment of
the state of the humanities today. Building on their arguments, and
recalling our reference to the double meaning of *retooling*—retooling as
re-equipping and redesigning—we draw attention below, in a condensed
and schematic fashion, to some of the assumptions and conditions that,
in our view, require revisiting and retooling. Far from being exhaustive, we simply want here to gesture toward those critical and practical
aspects of the humanistic profession that may help us, on the one hand,
retain what is valuable about humanities research and, on the other,
address the challenges facing us.

Reflection and contemplation
Central to how knowledge and learning take place—and not just in the
humanities—time-consuming critical reflection and contemplative analysis become all the more essential in our era of shortened attention
spans and sound bite–sized public information. Reflection and collaboration, which have both solitary and collective phases, must be nurtured.

Informed dissent, diversified criticism

In a post-9/11 world, when the "War Against Terror" has rationalized a concerted shrinking of public freedom of speech, thought, and movement, as well as a homogenization of public discourse, we must create space for dialogue between diverse critical traditions and forms of knowledge production.

Solitary work as collaboration

Some of the rhetoric expressed in support of collaborations between the university and industry or of collaborative clusters holds up the solitary scholar as a figure for derision. This short-sighted and anachronistic stereotype fails to acknowledge that what are ostensibly solitary acts, such as reading or study alone in one's office, are in fact processes by which scholars dialogue with and learn from the research of others.

The value of single-authored works

It is important that research agencies and universities value and facilitate as much solitary research time that results in single-authored books as collaborative research that takes the form of volumes edited by two or more scholars. For all the benefits of collaborative research endeavours or of digital technologies for recording and managing data, there is no equivalent to the individual's sustained engagement with an extensive argument that is central to the production of the scholarly monograph. Single-authored works enable a focus and a coherence of expression that are rarely possible in collaborative writing. They require scholars to develop disciplined research and reading habits, to maintain their focus on a topic and thus gain in-depth understanding of its complexity, and to find lucid and effective ways to communicate their findings.

Collaboration as a diverse praxis

Collaboration can yield results that reveal links between or among study areas and disciplines that cannot be otherwise discerned, while at the same time it encourages researchers to express their findings in terms accessible beyond their immediate professional sphere. But teamwork need not take place exclusively in cluster-based projects that involve intricate and labour-intensive grant applications, costly overhead expenses, complex infrastructures, and thus high levels of management that take time away from actual research. Other viable collaborative models—workshops, manuscript development meetings, organizing peer-editing sessions, co-operatively organized conferences, or affiliation with research centres—have long generated productive dialogue that focusses on, rather than distracts from, solitary collaboration—an oxymoron, yes, but one that speaks to some of the enabling aspects of knowledge production in the humanities. Collaboration is always already embedded in humanities research.

Evaluating and facilitating the impact of humanities research
The means through which knowledge mobilization is measured—for example, annual reports for the CFI and the CRC, and increasingly for SSHRC, expect scholars to declare the number of times they have had their research sought out by government, health, business, or non-profit sectors—would suggest that humanities scholarship and patentable or policy-oriented research operate on the same level playing field. Beyond reducing accountability to accounting, this method of determining the impact of knowledge produced by humanists implies that failure to indicate such links is synonymous with the non-relevance of their research. Yet this is not the case; the impact of humanistic research does not lend itself to an exclusively quantifying evaluative approach. In addition to establishing report templates that are more directly applicable to humanistic knowledge, universities and research agencies, in collaboration with humanists, should devise ways that can help bridge the gap between humanities scholarship and non-academic sectors. Such a concerted effort should start with the recognition that the onus of having humanistic knowledge circulate in non-academic venues should not fall squarely on humanists alone. If SSHRC can now support research that concerns management and business, there is no reason it cannot establish a program that can help address the challenges facing humanists—challenges that are at once internal to the university system and external to it—in mobilizing more effectively the knowledge they produce.

Recalibrating assessment systems at universities and research agencies to recognize the consequences of the culture of research and the mobilization of humanistic knowledge

If it is becoming more important that humanities scholars actively engage in shaping public opinion—or to put it more accurately, in shaping a different public—then different kinds of publication, such as popular newspapers and magazines, as well as various web-based venues for public interaction, will need to be fully recognized by university and granting-agency assessment committees as legitimate research and not included, as is presently the case, under the category of "other" contributions. If scholars are to manage large-scale collaborative research institutes, build and maintain websites, organize workshops and conferences, teach, mentor, and train students, and still keep up with their individual writing and research, then the protocols for credit and recognition, and standards for assessing quality (not just quantity) will need review and revision. Moreover, such changes in the tenure, promotion, and annual assessment systems would be effective only if they were to take place across universities.

Time as an infrastructure need for humanities research

The present emphasis on knowledge-as-product often blinds us to the actual processes by which knowledge is generated. Most humanities scholars depend on time more than any other resource to carry out their research, not to mention that there is a direct correlation between time and the quality or significance of knowledge produced. What's more, humanists do not do research and then "write it up" at the end; the act of composition produces knowledge. Research agencies and universities should expand the meaning of infrastructure so that it refers not only to buildings and technical equipment but also to Research Time Stipends and other support systems that can free time.

Recalibrating the relationship between research and teaching to recognize the mentoring and training of students as future professionals

In the humanities, pedagogy—be it classroom teaching or active mentoring and training of students—is an integral element of most humanistic research. As in other disciplines, it is often difficult, if at all possible, to draw a line between where research "ends" and pedagogy "begins"—or vice versa—especially in the cases of scholars working collaboratively with students or in research centres with student assistants. However, because mentoring in the humanities often takes place beyond and above any formal arrangements between scholars and students, this continuum of research-pedagogy in the humanities is not always recognized for what it entails (consider, for example, CFI's rule that the infrastructure it supports not be related to nor benefit pedagogy in any way; or, the fact that, in the humanities, professors do not claim co-authorship in their supervisees' publications, as is commonly the case in laboratory-based disciplines, even if they were produced with funding, lengthy discussions, and rigorous editing provided by the supervisor). Universities should develop means of formally acknowledging the relationship of training and mentoring students to research and teaching, and rewarding those scholars who perform such activities selflessly with dedication and excellent results.

We are aware that this brief outline identifies only a few of the urgent areas to be reviewed and retooled in the Canadian humanities. We hope our highlighting them here will provide stimulus and focus for a wider and ongoing discussion of the future of the humanities.

WORKS CITED

Aarseth, Espen J. *Cybertext: Perspectives on Ergodic Literature*. Baltimore: Johns Hopkins University Press, 1997. Print.

Abbate, Janet. *Inventing the Internet*. Cambridge: MIT Press, 1999. Print.

"About DHQ." *Digital Humanities Quarterly*. DHQ, 24 April 2007. Web. 1 October 2009.

"About Google™Scholar." *Scholar.Google.com*. Google, 2009. Web. 1 October 2009.

"About NINES." *Nineteenth-century Scholarship Online*. NINES, n.d. Web. 29 September 2009.

Abu-Laban, Baha, ed. *University Research and the Future of Canada*. Ottawa: ActeXpress/University of Ottawa Press, 1989. Print.

Adorno, Theodor. "Culture and Administration." *The Culture Industry*. Ed. J.M. Bernstein. London: Routledge, 1991. 107–31. Print.

———. "On the Fetish Character in Music and the Regression of Listening." *The Culture Industry*. Ed. J.M. Bernstein. London: Routledge, 1991. 29–60. Print.

Agamben, Giorgio. *State of Exception*. Trans. Kevin Attell. Chicago: University of Chicago Press, 2005. Print.

Alonso, Carlos J., Cathy N. Davidson, John M. Unsworth, and Lynne Withey. "Crises and Opportunities: The Futures of Scholarly Publishing." *American Council of Learned Societies Occasional Papers* 57 (2004). Web. 1 October 2009.

American Council of Learned Societies Commission on Cyberinfrastructure for the Humanities and Social Sciences. "Our Cultural Commonwealth." *American Council of Learned Societies*. 2006. Web. 1 October 2009.

Andrew, Caroline, Monica Gattinger, M. Sharon Jeannotte, and Will Straw, eds. *Accounting for Culture: Thinking Through Cultural Citizenship*. Ottawa: University of Ottawa Press, 2005. Print.

Anonymous. Unpublished interview. 20 April 2006. Print.

Appadurai, Arjun. *Fear of Small Numbers: An Essay on the Geography of Anger*. Durham: Duke University Press, 2006. Print.

———. "Grassroots Globalization and the Research Imagination." *Public Culture* 12.1 (2000): 1–19. Print.

———. "The Right to Research." *Globalisation, Societies and Education* 4.2 (July 2006): 167–77. Print.

Archer, Bert. "Laying Down the Law." *The Globe and Mail* 30 September 2006: F2. Print.

Argamon, Shlomo, and Mark Olsen. "Toward Meaningful Computing." *Communications of the ACM* 49.4 (April 2006): 33–35. Print.

Aronowitz, Stanley. *The Knowledge Factory: Dismantling the Corporate University and Creating True Higher Learning*. Boston: Beacon Press, 2000. Print.

Ashcroft, Bill, Gareth Griffiths, and Helen Tiffin. *Key Concepts in Post-Colonial Studies*. London: Routledge, 1998. Print.

Ashton, Niki. "Petition in Support of the SSHRC." *ndp.ca*. New Democrat Party, 2009. Web. 13 July 2009.

Assistant 2. "Thank you! SSHRC-Niki Ashton." Message to Melissa Stephens. 13 July 2009. Email.

Atkinson-Grosjean, Janet. "Big Science, Boundary Organizations, and the Academy." *Academic Matters: The Journal of Higher Education* (April 2007): 6–9. Print.

AUCC. "Momentum: The 2008 Report on University Research and Knowledge Mobilization." Association of Universities and Colleges of Canada, 2008. Web. 3 October 2009.

Auden, W.H. "In Memory of W.B. Yeats." *Collected Poems*. Ed. Edward Mendelson. New York: Vintage, 1991. 247–49. Print.

Axelrod, Paul. "Service or Captivity? Business-University Relations in the Twentieth Century." Neilson and Gaffield 45–61.

———. *Values in Conflict: The University, the Marketplace, and the Trials of Liberal Education*. Montreal and Kingston: McGill-Queen's University Press, 2002. Print.

Badr, Patricia, and Sandra Tomc. "The New and the Noteworthy and the Making of a Civil Society." In "Readers' Forum: What's Left of English Studies?" *English Studies in Canada* 29.1–2 (March/June 2003): 7–16. Print.

Baeker, Greg, with John Foote, Sharon Jeannotte, and Marilyn Smith. "'All Talents Count': A Pilot Inventory of National Cultural Policies and Measures Supporting Cultural Diversity: Canadian Country Profile." Strategic Research and Analysis Directorate, Department of Canadian Heritage, June 2001. Web. 3 October 2009.

———. "Cultural Policy and Cultural Diversity in Canada." Prepared for the Council of Europe Study on Cultural Policy and Cultural Diversity. Strategic Research and Analysis Branch, Department of Canadian Heritage, 28 August 2000. Web. 3 October 2009.

Bal, Mieke. "Introduction: Travelling Concepts and Cultural Analysis." *Travelling Concepts: Text, Subjectivity, Hybridity.* Ed. Joyce Goggin and Sonja Neef. Amsterdam: ASCA Press, 2001. 7–42. Print.

Bannerji, Himani. *The Dark Side of the Nation: Essays on Multiculturalism, Nationalism, and Gender.* Toronto: Scholars Press, 2000. Print.

Bartholomew, Amy, and Jennifer Breakspear. "Human rights as Swords of Empire." *The New Imperial Challenge.* Ed. Leo Panitch and Colin Leys. New York: Fernwood, 2003. 125–45. Print.

Bement, Arden L. "Cyberinfrastructure: The Second Revolution." *The Chronicle of Higher Education* 5 January 2007. Web. 3 October 2009.

Benjamin, Walter. "Die Aufgabe des Übersetzers." *Illuminationem: Ausgewählte Schriften.* Ed. Siegfried Unseld. Frankfurt am Main: Suhrkamp, 1961. 56–69. Print.

———. "The Task of the Translator." *Illuminations.* Ed. and intro. Hannah Arendt. Trans. Harry Zohn. London: Collins/Fontana, 1973. 69–82. Print.

Benhabib, Seyla. *The Claims of Culture: Equality and Diversity in the Global Era.* Princeton: Princeton University Press, 2002. Print.

Berland, Jody. "Marginal Notes on Cultural Studies in Canada." *University of Toronto Quarterly* 64.4 (1995): 514–25. Print.

Bermann, Sandra, and Michael Wood, eds. *Nation, Language, and the Ethics of Translation.* Princeton: Princeton University Press, 2005. Print.

Berners-Lee, Tim, with Mark Fischetti. *Weaving the Web: The Original Design and Ultimate Destiny of the World Wide Web.* San Francisco: Harper San Francisco, 1999. Print.

Bernstein, Susan David. "Confessional Feminisms: Rhetorical Dimensions of First-Person Theorizing." *Language and Liberation: Feminism, Philosophy, and Language.* Ed. Christina Hendricks and Kelly Oliver. Albany: SUNY Press, 1999. 173–206. Print.

Bérubé, Michael, and Janet Lyon. "Free Speech and Discipline: The Boundaries of the Multiversity." *The Employment of English: Theory, Jobs, and the Future of Literary Studies*. Ed. Michael Bérubé. New York: New York University Press, 1997. 183–203. Print.

Beynon, Meurig, Steve Russ, and Willard McCarty. "Human Computing—Modelling with Meaning." *Literary and Linguistic Computing* 21 (2006): 141–58. Print.

Bilder, Geoffrey W. "In Google We Trust?" *Journal of Electronic Publishing* 9.1 (Winter 2006). Web. 3 October 2009.

Birdsall, William F. "The Internet and the Ideology of Information Technology." *Isoc.org*. Internet Society, n.d. Web. 3 October 2009.

Birkerts, Sven. *The Gutenberg Elegies: The Fate of Reading in an Electronic Age*. Boston: Faber and Faber, 1994. Print.

Bissoondath, Neil. *Selling Illusions: The Cult of Multiculturalism in Canada*. Toronto: Penguin, 1994. Print.

Bok, Derek. *Universities in the Marketplace: The Commercialization of Higher Education*. Princeton: Princeton University Press, 2003. Print.

Bonner, Kieran, Diana Brydon, Marjorie Stone, and Julia Wright, with a response by Smaro Kamboureli. "Building Research Networks: A Panel." Ed. Jessica Schagerl. *Open Letter* 12th ser. 9 (2006): 83–103. Print.

Boone, Joseph A. "The Inevitability of the Personal." Letter in Forum. *PMLA* 111.5 (1996): 1152–54. Print.

Bourdieu, Pierre. *Homo Academicus*. Trans. Peter Collier. Stanford: Stanford University Press, 1988. Print.

Boyer, Ernest. *Scholarship Reconsidered: Priorities of the Professoriate*. Menlo Park: Carnegie Foundation for the Advancement of Teaching, 1990. Print.

Brand, Dionne. *Inventory*. Toronto: McClelland & Stewart, 2006. Print.

Brassard, Genevieve. "Finally, a Graduate Advisor for the Real (Academic) World." Rev. *Graduate Study for the Twenty-First Century: How to Build an Academic Career in the Humanities*, by Gregory M. Colon Semenza. *Pedagogy: Critical Approaches to Teaching Literature, Language, Composition, and Culture* 6.3 (2006): 567–74. Print.

Brown, John Seely, and Paul Duguid. *The Social Life of Information*. Boston: Harvard Business School Press, 2000. Print.

Brown, Nicholas, and Imre Szeman. "What's Left of the Dialectic? A Polemic." In "Readers' Forum: What's Left of English Studies?" *English Studies in Canada* 29.1–2 (March/June 2003): 17–24. Print.

Brown, Susan, Patricia Clements, Renée Elio, and Isobel Grundy. "Between Markup and Delivery; or, Tomorrow's Electronic Text Today." *Mind Technologies: Humanities Computing and the Canadian Academic Community*. Ed. Raymond Siemens and David Moorman. Calgary: University of Calgary Press, 2006. 15–32. Print.

Brown, Susan, Patricia Clements, and Isobel Grundy, eds. *Orlando: Women's Writing in the British Isles from the Beginnings to the Present*. Cambridge University Press, 2006. Web. 3 October 2009.

———. "Scholarly Introduction: Going Electronic." *Orlando: Women's Writing in the British Isles from the Beginnings to the Present*. Cambridge University Press, 2006. Web. 3 October 2009.

Brown, Susan, Sue Fisher, Patricia Clements, Katherine Binhammer, Terry Butler, Kathryn Carter, Isobel Grundy, and Susan Hockey. "SGML and the Orlando Project: Descriptive Markup for an Electronic History of Women's Writing." *Computers and the Humanities* 31.4 (1997): 271–85. Print.

Brydon, Diana. "Canada and Postcolonialism: Questions, Inventories, and Futures." *Is Canada Postcolonial?: Unsettling Canadian Literature*. Ed. Laura Moss. Waterloo: Wilfrid Laurier University Press, 2003. 49–77. Print.

———. "Cross-Talk, Postcolonial Pedagogy, and Transnational Literacy." *Home-Work: Postcolonialism, Pedagogy, and Canadian Literature*. Ed. Cynthia Sugars. Ottawa: University of Ottawa Press, 2004. 57–74. Print.

———. "Metamorphosis of a Discipline: Rethinking the Canadian Literary Institution." Kamboureli and Miki 1–16.

———, ed. *Postcolonialism: Critical Concepts in Literary and Cultural Studies*. 5 vols. New York: Routledge, 2000. Print.

Brydon, Diana, and William D. Coleman, eds. *Renegotiating Community: Interdisciplinary Perspectives, Global Contexts*. Vancouver: UBC Press, 2008. Print.

Bulletin on the Federal Budget. Canadian Federation for the Humanities and Social Sciences. (Doug Owram, President's Message.) 20 February 2003. Web. 5 May 2010.

Bulletin on the Federal Budget. Canadian Federation for the Humanities and Social Sciences. (Noreen Golman, President's Message.) 19 March 2007. Web. 5 May 2010.

Bush, Vannevar. "As We May Think." *The Atlantic Monthly*. The Atlantic, July 1945. Web. 3 October 2009.

Butling, Pauline, and Susan Rudy. *Writing in Our Time: Canada's Radical Poetries in English (1957–2003)*. Waterloo: Wilfrid Laurier University Press, 2005. Print.

Byers, Michael. *Intent for a Nation: What is Canada for? A Relentlessly Optimistic Manifesto for Canada's Role in the World.* Vancouver: Douglas & McIntyre, 2007. Print.

Calamai, Peter. "Prized but Poorly Paid." *The Toronto Star* 12 December 1998: B1, B4. Print.

Cameron, David M. Rev. *Spending Smarter: Corporate-University Cooperation in Research and Development. Canadian Public Policy* 12.3 (September 1986): 530–31. Print.

Canada. *Royal Commission on National Development in the Arts, Letters and Sciences 1949–1951. Report.* Ottawa: Edmond Cloutier, 1951. *Collections Canada.* Web. 3 October 2009.

Canada Council for the Arts. "Introduction: Making the Case for Arts and Culture." Canada Council for the Arts, 2004. Web. 3 October 2009.

Canada Research Chairs Program Guide. Ottawa: Tri-Council and CFI Secretariat, April 2000. Print.

Canadian Association of University Teachers. "Alternative Fifth Year Review of the Canada Research Chairs Program." *CAUT.ca.* CAUT, November 2005. Web. 3 October 2009.

———. "CAUT Almanac of Post-Secondary Education in Canada, 2007." *CAUT.ca.* CAUT, 2007. Web. 3 October 2009.

———. "CAUT Almanac of Post-Secondary Education in Canada, 2008–2009." *CAUT. ca.* CAUT, 2009. Web. 3 October 2009.

———. "Changes in Spending on Academic Rank Salaries as Opposed to Total University Expenditures, Canada." *CAUT.ca.* CAUT, 2006. Web. 27 June 2008.

———. "Government Funding and Tuition as a Share of University Operating Revenue, Canada." *CAUT.ca.* CAUT, 2006. Web. 27 June 2008.

Canadian Corporate-Higher Education Forum. "P003—Corporate-Higher Education Forum fonds—1984–1994." *Private Fonds and Collections from the Holdings of Concordia University Archives.* Concordia University, 2003. Web. 5 December 2007.

Canadian Federation for the Humanities and Social Sciences. "Feminist & Equity Audits 2006: Selected Indicators for Canadian Universities." *fedcan.virtuo.ca.* CFHSS, n.d. Web. 27 June 2008.

———. "Federation Applauds Appointment of New SSHRC President." 28 September 2006. Online posting. CFHSS Discussion Group. Web. 28 September 2006.

———. "Large-Scale Research Projects and the Humanities." *fedcan.ca.* CFHSS, June 2006. Web. 4 October 2009.

———. "Notes on the 'Next Generation: Mentoring in Universities' Workshop." *old.fedcan.ca*. CFHSS, 27 November 2005. Web. 14 February 2007.

———. "Postsecondary Pyramid: Equity Audit 2007." *fedcan.ca*. CFHSS, 2007. Web. 4 October 2009.

Caruth, Cathy. *Unclaimed Experience: Trauma, Narrative, and History*. Baltimore: Johns Hopkins University Press, 1996. Print.

Cavell, Richard. "World Famous Across Canada, or TransNational Localities." Kamboureli and Miki 85–92.

Chan, Adrienne S., and Donald Fisher, eds. *The Exchange University: Corporatization of Academic Culture*. Vancouver: UBC Press, 2008. Print.

Chapman, Helen C. "Becoming Academics, Challenging the Disciplinarians: A Philosophical Case Study." *Breaking the Disciplines: Reconceptions in Knowledge, Art and Culture*. Ed. Martin L. Davies and Marsha Meskimmon. London: I.B. Tauris & Co., 2003. 35–58. Print.

Chartrand, Harry Hillman. "Subjectivity in an Era of Scientific Imperialism: Shadows in an Age of Reason." Abu-Laban 183–211.

Cheah, Pheng. *Inhuman Conditions: On Cosmopolitanism and Human Rights*. Cambridge: Harvard University Press, 2006. Print.

Childs, Peter, and R.J. Patrick Williams. *An Introduction to Post-Colonial Theory*. London: Prentice-Hall/Harvester Wheatsheaf, 1997. Print.

Chow, Rey. "'An Addiction from Which We Never Get Free.'" *New Literary History* 36.1 (2005): 47–55. Print.

Cochrane, William A. "Society's Expectations: Staying Near the Customer." Neilson and Gaffield 29–43.

Collini, Stefan. *Absent Minds: Intellectuals in Britain*. Oxford: Oxford University Press, 2006. Print.

Cooper, Frederick. "Postcolonial Studies and the Study of History." *Postcolonial Studies and Beyond*. Ed. Ania Loomba, Suvir Kaul, Matti Bunzl, Antoinette Burton, and Jed Esty. Durham: Duke University Press, 2005. 401–22. Print.

Côté, James E., and Anton L. Allahar. *Ivory Tower Blues: A University System in Crisis*. Toronto: University of Toronto Press, 2007. Print.

Cowen, Tyler. *Good & Plenty: The Creative Successes of American Arts Funding*. Princeton: Princeton University Press, 2006. Print.

Creighton-Kelly, Chris. "Bleeding the Memory Membrane: Arts Activism and Cultural Institutions." *Questions of Community: Artists, Audiences, Coalitions*. Ed. Daina Augaitis, Lorne Falk, Sylvie Gilbert, and Mary Anne Moser. Banff: Walter Phillips Gallery, 1995. 91–113. Print.

Culler, Jonathan. "In Need of a Name? A Response to Geoffrey Harpham." *New Literary History* 36 (2000): 37–42. Print.

Curtis, Liane, Dipti Gupta, and Will Straw. "Culture and Identity: Ideas and Overviews." *Metropolis*. Metropolis, 2001. Web. 4 October 2009.

Cyr, Raymond J.V. *Spending Smarter: Corporate-University Cooperation in Research and Development*. Montreal: Corporate-Higher Education Forum, 1985. Print.

Davidson, Cathy N. "We Can't Ignore the Influence of Digital Technologies." *Chronicle of Higher Education* 23 March 2007. Web. 4 October 2009.

Davidson, Cathy N., and David Theo Goldberg. "Engaging the Humanities." *Profession* (2004): 42–62. Print.

Dean, Jodi, Jon W. Anderson, and Geert Lovink. "Introduction." *Reformatting Politics: Information Technology and Global Civil Society*. Ed. Jodi Dean, Jon W. Anderson, and Geert Lovink. With a Foreword by Saskia Sassen. London: Routledge, 2006. xv–xxix. Print.

Dean, Jodi, Lee Quinby, and Christina Elizabeth Sharpe. "Symposium: Virtually Regulated: New Technologies and Social Control." *Signs* 24 (1999): 1067–96. Print.

Dean, Mitchell. *Governmentality: Power and Rule in Modern Society*. London: Sage, 1999. Print.

Delanty, Gerard. *Citizenship in a Global Age: Society, Culture, Politics*. Buckingham: Open University Press, 2000. Print.

———. *Community*. London: Routledge, 2003. Print.

Derrida, Jacques. *Of Grammatology*. Trans. Gayatri Chakravorty Spivak. Baltimore: Johns Hopkins University Press, 1997. Print.

———. *Without Alibi*. Trans. Peggy Kamuf. Stanford: Stanford University Press, 2002. Print.

Di Leo, Jeffrey R. "Understanding Affiliation." *Affiliations*. Lincoln: University of Nebraska Press, 2003. 1–16. Print.

DiMaggio, Paul, Eszter Hargittai, W. Russell Neuman, and John P. Robinson. "Social Implications of the Internet." *Annual Review of Sociology* 27 (2001): 307–36. Print.

Diamond, Sara. "President's Interim Report to the OCAD Community." *OCAD*. Ontario College of Art & Design, April 2006. Web. September 2006.

Dickens, Charles. *Little Dorrit*. 1887. Oxford: Oxford University Press, 1982. Print.

Dinello, Daniel. *Technophobia!: Science Fiction Visions of Posthuman Technology*. Austin: University of Texas Press, 2005. Print.

diSessa, Andrea A. *Changing Minds: Computers, Learning, and Literacy*. Cambridge: MIT Press, 2000. Print.

Donoghue, Frank. *The Last Professors: The Corporate University and the Fate of the Humanities*. New York: Fordham University Press, 2008. Print.

———. "Prestige." *Profession* (2006): 155–62. Print.

Dorland, Michael, and Maurice Charland. *Law, Rhetoric, and Irony in the Formation of Canadian Civil Culture*. Toronto: University of Toronto Press, 2002. Print.

Douglass, John Aubrey. *The Conditions for Admission: Access, Equity, and the Social Contract of Public Universities*. Stanford: Stanford University Press, 2007. Print.

Downes, Daniel M. "New Media Economy: Intellectual Property and Cultural Insurrection." *Journal of Electronic Publishing* 9.1 (Winter 2006). Web. 3 October 2009.

Drucker, Johanna. "Rev. of *Humanities Computing*, by Willard McCarty." *Digital Humanities Quarterly* 1.1 (Spring 2007). Web. 3 October 2009.

Drucker, Johanna, and Bethany Nowviskie. "Speculative Computing: Aesthetic Provocations in Humanities Computing." *A Companion to Digital Humanities*. Ed. Susan Schreibman, Ray Siemens, and John Unsworth. Oxford: Blackwell, 2004. Web. 3 October 2009.

Drucker, Peter F. *The Age of Discontinuity: Guidelines to Our Changing Society*. With a New Introduction by the Author. 1968. New Brunswick, NJ: Transaction, 1992. Print.

Dubrow, Heather. "Collegiality: Introduction." *Profession* (2006): 48–59. Print.

Eisenhower, Dwight D. "Farewell Address to the American People, January 17, 1961." *The Eisenhower Presidential Library and Museum Homepage*. Eisenhower Presidential Library and Museum Homepage, n.d. Web. 25 June 2008.

Farred, Grant. "Dossier: Reconfiguring the Humanities and the Social Sciences in the Age of the Global University: Introduction." *Nepantla: View from South* 4.1 (2003): 41–50. Print.

Fatona, Andrea. "Interview." Fung and Gagnon 36–41.

Feenberg, Andrew. *Transforming Technology: A Critical Theory Revisited*. Oxford: Oxford University Press, 2002. Print.

Felman, Shoshana, and Dori Laub. *Testimony: Crises of Witnessing in Literature, Psychoanalysis, and History*. New York: Routledge, 1992. Print.

Fernandez, Melanie. "Reflections of a Former Community Arts Officer." *Fuse Magazine* 28.3 (September 2005): 9–14. Print.

Fernandez, Sharon. "Interview." Fung and Gagnon 73–76.

Ferris, Sharmilla Pixy. "Writing Electronically: The Effects of Computers on Traditional Writing." *Journal of Electronic Publishing* 8.1 (August 2002). Web. 3 October 2009.

Findlay, Isobel. "Working for Postcolonial Legal Studies: Working with the Indigenous Humanities." *Law, Social Justice and Global Development* 1 (2003). Web. 3 October 2009.

Findlay, L.M. "A Way Ahead for the Human Sciences: Paul Ricoeur's *Lectures on Ideology and Utopia*." *Constructive Criticism: The Human Sciences in the Age of Theory*. Ed. Martin Kreiswirth and Thomas Carmichael. Toronto: University of Toronto Press, 1995. 190–200. Print.

———. "'Speaking Truth to Power?': American Usage, Canadian Literary Studies, and Policies for the Public Good in Canada." *English Studies in Canada* 26.3 (2000): 279–307. Print.

Flanders, Julia. "The Rhetoric of Performative Markup." Digital Humanities Conference 2006 Abstracts, 248–49. Web. 7 July 2006.

Foucault, Michel. *Fearless Speech*. Ed. Joseph Pearson. Los Angeles: Semiotexte, 2001. Print.

Franklin, Cynthia G. *Academic Lives: Memoir, Cultural Theory, and the University Today*. Athens: The University of Georgia Press, 2009. Print.

Frow, John. *Cultural Studies and Cultural Value*. Oxford: Clarendon, 1995. Print.

Fulford, Robert. "The Ideology of the Book." *Queen's Quarterly* 3 (Winter 1994): 801–11. Print.

Fulton, E. Margaret. "Historical Commitments in New Times: The Restructuring and Reorientation of Teaching and Research." Neilson and Gaffield 231–49.

Fung, Richard, and Monika Kin Gagnon, eds. *13 Conversations about Art and Cultural Race Politics*. Montreal: Artextes, 2002. Print.

Gaffield, Chad. "Embracing the New Metaphor for 21st Century Universities." Award Acceptance Speech, Distinguished Academic Award 2007. CAUT Bulletin Special Supplement, October 2007. Print.

Gajjala, Radhika. *Cyber Selves: Feminist Ethnographies of South Asian Women*. Walnut Creek: AltaMira Press, 2004. Print.

Gallop, Jane. Letter in Forum. "The Inevitability of the Personal." *PMLA* 111.5 (1996): 1149–50. Print.

Galloway, Gloria. "PM puts spotlight on overlooked funds for science." *The Globe and Mail* 18 May 2007: A9. Print.

Gantz, John F., et al. "The Diverse and Exploding Digital Universe: An Updated Forecast of Worldwide Information Growth by 2011." *emc.com*. IDC, March 2008. Web. 3 October 2009.

———. "The Expanding Digital Universe: A Forecast of Worldwide Information Growth Through 2010." *emc.com*. IDC, 2007. Web. 3 October 2009.

Garrett, Jeffrey. "KWIC and Dirty? Human Cognition and the Claims of Full-Text Searching." *Journal of Electronic Publishing* 9.1 (Winter 2006). Web. 3 October 2009.

Geiger, Jeffrey. "Special Relationships: British Higher Education and the Global Marketplace." *PMLA* 119.1 (January 2004): 58–68. Print.

Gill, Lesley. *The School of the Americas: Military Training and Political Violence in the Americas*. Durham: Duke University Press, 2004. Print.

Gilman, Sander L. "Collaboration, the Economy, and the Future of the Humanities." *Critical Inquiry* 30 (Winter 2004): 384–90. Print.

———. *The Fortunes of the Humanities: Thoughts for After the Year 2000*. Stanford: Stanford University Press, 2000. Print.

Giroux, Henry A. "Introduction: Literacy and the Pedagogy of Political Empowerment." *Literacy: Reading the Word and the World*. By Paulo Freire and Donaldo Macedo. Westport CT: Bergin & Garvey, 1987. 1–27. Print.

———. "Youth, Higher Education, and the Crisis of Public Time: Educated Hope and the Possibility of a Democratic Future." *Social Identities* 9.2 (2003): 141–68. Print.

Giroux, Henry A., and Susan Searls Giroux. *Take Back Higher Education: Race, Youth, and the Crisis of Democracy in the Post-Civil Rights Era*. New York: Palgrave Macmillan, 2004. Print.

Golfman, Noreen. *Submission to the House of Commons Standing Committee on Industry, Science and Technology: Regarding Mobilizing Science and Technology to Canada's Advantage*. Ottawa: CFHSS, 2008. Print.

Graff, Gerald. *Beyond the Culture Wars: How Teaching the Conflicts Can Revitalize American Education*. New York: Norton, 1992. Print.

Granqvist, Raoul J., ed. *Writing Back in/and Translation*. Frankfurt am Main: Peter Lang, 2006. Print.

Grey, Stephen. *Ghost Plane: The Inside Story of the CIA's Secret Rendition Programme*. London: C. Hurst, 2006. Print.

Grossberg, Michael. "Devising an Online Future for Journals of History." *The Chronicle of Higher Education* 21 April 2000. Web. 3 October 2009.

Guy, Alex. "The Crisis in University Research Funding." Abu-Laban 80–85.

Hall, Margaret. "Book Review." Rev. *Restoring Dignity: Responding to Child Abuse in Canadian Institutions*, Law Commission of Canada. *The International Journal of Children's Rights* 10 (2002): 295–302. Print.

Hammond, Tony, Timo Hannay, Ben Lund, and Joanna Scott. "Social Bookmarking Tools (I): A General Review." *D-Lib Magazine* 11.4 (April 2005). Web. 3 October 2009.

Haque, Eva. "Multiculturalism within a Bilingual Framework: 'Incorporealizing' the Multicultural Other into the Nation." TransCanada: Literature, Institutions, Citizenship. Vancouver: Simon Fraser University, 23–26 June 2005. Conference presentation.

Haraway, Donna. "A Cyborg Manifesto: Science, Technology, and Socialist-Feminism in the Late Twentieth Century." *Simians, Cyborgs and Women: The Reinvention of Nature*. New York: Routledge, 1991. 149–81. Print.

Harcourt, Wendy. *Women@Internet: Creating New Cultures in Cyberspace*. London: Zed Books, 1999. Print.

Harpham, Geoffrey Galt. "Beneath and Beyond the 'Crisis in the Humanities.'" *New Literary History* 36 (2005): 21–36. Print.

Hassan, Robert. "Chapter 6: The University in Western Societies." *The Chronoscopic Society: Globalization, Time and Knowledge in the Network Economy*. New York: Peter Lang, 2003. 69–90. Print.

Hawisher, Gail E., and Cynthia L. Selfe, eds. *Global Literacies and the World-Wide Web*. London: Routledge, 2000. Print.

Heald, Susan. "Women's Studies, Who Is She? The Discipline According to SSHRC." *Atlantis* 25.2 (Spring/Summer 2001): 87–91. Print.

Heath, Joseph, and Andrew Potter. *The Rebel Sell: Why the Culture Can't Be Jammed*. Toronto: Harper Collins, 2004. Print.

Henderson, James Youngblood (Sákéj). *First Nations Jurisprudence and Aboriginal Rights: Defining the Just Society*. Saskatoon: Native Law Centre, University of Saskatchewan, 2006. Print.

———. "The Indigenous Humanities." "Humanities Futures" panel, University of Saskatchewan, Saskatoon, 31 March 2008. Conference presentation.

Hesford, Wendy S. "Global Turns and Cautions in Rhetoric and Composition Studies." *PMLA* 121.3 (May 2006): 787–801. Print.

Hildyard, Angela. "Subject: CUPE Local 3902 Unit 3 Negotiations." Memo to PDAD&C, University of Toronto, Toronto, 12 October 2006. *CUPE3902*. Web. 8 February 2007.

Hohendahl, Peter Uwe. "The Future of the Research University and the Fate of the Humanities." *Cultural Critique* 61 (Fall 2005): 1–21. Print.

hooks, bell. *Teaching Community: A Pedagogy of Hope*. New York: Routledge, 2003. Print.

Horowitz, Meyer. "Foreword." Abu-Laban xvii–xix.

Hudnall, Amy C. "Modeling Feminist Mentoring: Introduction." *NWSA Journal* 15.2 (2003): 220. Print.

Humanities Advanced Technology and Information Institute, University of Glasgow, and the National Initiative for a Networked Cultural Heritage. "The NINCH Guide to Good Practice in the Digital Representation and Management of Cultural Heritage Materials." *New York University*, 2002. Web. 3 October 2009.

Huntington, Samuel P. *Who are We? The Challenges to America's National Identity*. New York: Simon & Schuster, 2004. Print.

Hutcheon, Linda. "Introduction: *Plus ça change...*" *PMLA* 115.7 (2000): 1719–27. Print.

Hutcheon, Linda, and Marion Richmond, eds. *Other Solitudes: Canadian Multicultural Fictions*. Toronto: Oxford University Press, 1990. Print.

Ibbitson, John. "Fatal Cuts to Law Panel Deeply Ideological." *The Globe and Mail* 28 September 2006: A4. Print.

Ingraham, Bruce Douglas. "Scholarly Rhetoric in Digital Media." *Journal of Interactive Media in Education* (2000). *JIME*. Web. 9 August 2006.

"Information Awareness Office." *Wikipedia*, n.d. Web. 13 August 2010.

Itter, Carole. "A Celebration of Roy Kiyooka." *Brick: A Literary Journal* 48 (Spring 1994): 27. Print.

Jefferson, Anne L. "Accountability of Canadian Universities." *Education* 115.3 (March 1995): 349–50. Print.

Johnson, Kristine. "The Millennial Teacher: Metaphors for a New Generation." *Pedagogy* 6.1 (2006): 7–24. Print.

Jones, Donald C. "Thinking Critically about Digital Literacy: A Learning Sequence on Pens, Pages, and Pixels." *Pedagogy* 7.2 (2007): 207–21. Print.

Justice, Daniel Heath. "Renewing the Fire: Notes toward the Liberation of English Studies." In "Readers' Forum: What's Left of English Studies?" *English Studies in Canada* 29.1–2 (March/June 2003): 45–54. Print.

Kadar, Marlene. "Coming to Terms: Life Writing—From Genre to Critical Practice." *Essays on Life Writing: From Genre to Critical Practice.* Ed. Marlene Kadar. Toronto: University of Toronto Press, 1992. 3–16. Print.

Kadar, Marlene, Linda Warley, Jeanne Perreault, and Susanna Eagan, eds. *Tracing the Autobiographical.* Waterloo: Wilfrid Laurier University Press, 2005. Print.

Kamboureli, Smaro. "For What It's Worth." Afterword. *Pacific Rim Letters.* By Roy Kiyooka. Ed. Smaro Kamboureli. Edmonton: NeWest Press, 2005. 330–46. Print.

———. *Scandalous Bodies: Diasporic Literature in English Canada.* Toronto: Oxford University Press, 2000. Print.

Kamboureli, Smaro, and Roy Miki, eds. *Trans.Can.Lit.: Resituating the Study of Canadian Literature.* Waterloo: Wilfrid Laurier University Press, 2007. Print.

Kamuf, Peggy. *The Division of Literature: Or the University in Deconstruction.* Chicago: University of Chicago Press, 1997. Print.

Katz, Michael B. "The Moral Crisis of the University, or, the Tension between Marketplace and Community in Higher Learning." Neilson and Gaffield 3–27.

Keen, Andrew. *The Cult of the Amateur: How Today's Internet is Killing Our Culture.* New York: Doubleday, 2007. Print.

Keep, Christopher. "Of Writing Machines and Scholar-Gypsies." In "Readers' Forum: What's Left of English Studies?" *English Studies in Canada* 29.1–2 (March/June 2003): 55–66. Print.

Kenney-Wallace, Geraldine A. "The Role of Research in Modern Society." Abu-Laban 18–41.

King, Russell, John Connell, and Paul White, eds. *Writing Across Worlds: Literature and Migration.* London: Routledge, 1995. Print.

Kiyooka, Roy. "Dear Lucy Fumi." *Brick: A Literary Journal* 48 (Spring 1994): 22. Print.

———. *Pacific Rim Letters.* Ed. Smaro Kamboureli. Edmonton: NeWest Press, 2005. Print.

———. *Transcanada Letters.* Ed. Smaro Kamboureli. Edmonton: NeWest Press, 2005. Print.

Klein, Naomi. *The Shock Doctrine: The Rise of Disaster Capitalism.* Toronto: Alfred A. Knopf, 2007. Print.

Knight, Kim. "Collex: Research Report." *Transliteracies Project: Research in the Technological, Social, and Cultural Practices of Online Reading.* Santa Barbara: University of California at Santa Barbara, 2006. Web. 3 October 2009.

Kolko, Beth E., Lisa Nakamura, and Gilbert B. Rodman. *Race in Cyberspace.* New York: Routledge, 2000. Print.

Kramarae, Cheris, ed. *Technology and Women's Voices*. New York: Routledge and Kegan Paul, 1988. Print.

Kristeva, Julia. "Thinking in Dark Times." *Profession* (2006): 13–21. Print.

Kristmannson, Gauti. *Literary Diplomacy. I: The Role of Translation in the Construction of National Literatures in Britain and Germany 1750–1830. II: Translation Without an Original*. Frankfurt am Main: Peter Lang, 2005. Print.

LaCapra, Dominick. "The University in Ruins?" *Critical Inquiry* 25 (Autumn 1998): 32–55. Print.

———. "Yes, Yes, Yes, Yes...Well, Maybe: Response to Nicholas Royle." *Critical Inquiry* 26 (Autumn 1999): 154–58. Print.

Lancashire, Ian. "Cybertextuality." *Text Technology* 13.2 (2004): 1–18. Print.

Lang, Candace. "Autocritique." Veeser 40–54.

Lanham, Richard. *The Economics of Attention*. Chicago: University of Chicago Press, 2006. Print.

Latham, Robert, ed. *Bombs and Bandwidth: The Emerging Relationship between Information Technology and Security*. New York: New Press, 2003. Print.

Law Commission of Canada. *2006 Annual Report*. Ottawa: Law Commission of Canada, 2005/2006. Print.

———. *Crossing Borders: Law in a Globalized World*. Ottawa: Minister of Public Works and Government Services, 2006. Print.

———. *In Search of Security: The Future of Policing in Canada*. Ottawa: Minister of Public Works and Government Services, 2006. Print.

———. "Law Commission of Canada Responds to the Federal Government's Decision to Eliminate Funding." *Library and Archives Canada Electronic Collection*. Web. 13 February 2007.

"Law Commission of Canada Act." *Department of Justice, Canada*: 1996. Web. 2 April 2007.

Le Bouthillier, Yves. "Study of the Effects of the Abolition of the Law Commission of Canada." 1 November 2006. *Library and Archives Canada Electronic Collection*. Web. 13 February 2007.

"Leading in the Age of Imagination: A Strategic Plan for the Ontario College of Art and Design 2006–2012." *OCAD.ca*. OCAD, 4 December 2006. Web. 15 July 2008.

Leung, Linda. *Virtual Ethnicity: Race, Resistance, and the World Wide Web*. Aldershot: Ashgate, 2005. Print.

Lewkowicz, Antoni, and Paul Schellenberg. *Research Chairs: A Systematic Change in Ontario's Universities.* Working Paper. Council of Ontario Universities, May 2006. Print.

Lewis, Philip. "From the Institutional Text to Bicollegiality." *Profession* (2006): 75–86. Print.

Leyerle, John. "The Social Science and Humanities Research Council and University-Based Research." Abu-Laban 523–28.

Li, David Leiwei, ed. *Globalization and the Humanities.* Ed. David Leiwei Li. Hong Kong: Hong Kong University Press, 2004. Print.

———. "Introduction: Globalization and the Humanities." Li 1–18.

Liebowitz, S.J., and Stephen E. Margolis. "The Fable of the Keys." *Journal of Law and Economics* 33.1 (April 1990): 1–25. Print.

Liu, Alan. "Local Transcendence: Cultural Criticism, Postmodernism, and the Romanticism of Detail." *Representations* 32 (1990): 75–113. Print.

Lott, Eric. "Chants Demagogic." *The Yale Journal of Criticism* 18.2 (2005): 471–72. Print.

Lowry, Glen. "'Now the unravellings begun': Re:reading *Transcanada Letters.*" Afterword. *Transcanada Letters.* By Roy Kiyooka. Ed. Smaro Kamboureli. Edmonton: NeWest, 2005. 370–77. Print.

MacDonald, Bertrum H., and Fiona A. Black. "Using GIS for Spatial and Temporal Analyses in Print Culture Studies: Some Opportunities and Challenges." *Social Science History* 24.3 (Fall 2000): 505–36. Print.

Machlup, Fritz. *Production and Distribution of Knowledge in the United States.* Princeton: Princeton University Press, 1962. Print.

Marius, Michael. "On Academic Discourse." *Profession* 90 (1990): 28–31. Print.

Marlatt, Daphne. "A Celebration of Roy Kiyooka." *Brick: A Literary Journal* 48 (Spring 1994): 14. Print.

Marshall, Victor W., and Barry D. McPherson. *Aging: Canadian Perspectives.* Peterborough: Broadview, 1994. Print.

Martel, Yann. "What is Stephen Harper Reading?" *The Globe and Mail* 14 April 2007. Available at *whatisstephenharperreading.ca.* Web. 30 April 2010.

Martin, Andrew. "Notes from the Underground: Filling in the Gap." *The Independent on Sunday* 28 December 2003. *findarticles.com.* Web. 3 October 2009.

Martin, Julia, and David Coleman. "Change the Metaphor: The Archive as an Ecosystem." *Journal of Electronic Publishing* 7.3 (April 2002). Web. 3 October 2009.

Maruca, Lisa. "The SCE and Me: Personal Reflections on Two (Interdisciplinary) Projects." *The Society for Critical Exchange*, 2006. Web. 1 February 2007.

Marx, Karl. *Capital*. Vol 1. Trans. Ben Fowkes. London: Penguin, 1976. Print.

———. "The Eighteenth Brumaire of Louis Bonaparte." *Later Political Writings*. Ed. and trans. T. Carver. Cambridge: Cambridge University Press, 1996. 31–127. Print.

Mbembe, Achille, and Deborah Posel. "Editorial: A Critical Humanism." *Interventions* 7.3 (2005): 283–86. Print.

McCann, Sean, and Michael Szalay. "Do You Believe in Magic? Literary Thinking after the New Left." *The Yale Journal of Criticism* 18.2 (2005): 435–68. Print.

McCarty, Willard. *Humanities Computing*. London: Palgrave Macmillan, 2005. Print.

McGann, Jerome. *Radiant Textuality: Literature after the World Wide Web*. New York: Palgrave, 2001. Print.

———. "History, Herstory, Theirstory, Ourstory." *Theoretical Issues in Literary History*. Ed. David Perkins. Cambridge: Harvard University Press, 1991. 196–205. Print.

McLuhan, Marshall. *Understanding Media*. New York: New American Library, 1964. Print.

McNeil, Maureen. "Human." *New Keywords: A Revised Vocabulary of Culture and Society*. Ed. Tony Bennett, Lawrence Grossberg, and Meaghan Morris. Oxford: Blackwell, 2005. 164–67. Print.

"Mentor." *The Oxford English Dictionary Online*, n.d. Web. 14 February 2007.

Menzies, Heather, and Janice Newson. "No Time to Think: Academics' Life in the Globally Wired University." *Time & Society* 16.1 (2007): 83–98. Print.

Metropolis Project. "About Us." canada.metropolis.net. Web. 30 April 2010.

Michael, Donald A. "The University as a Learning System." Neilson and Gaffield 195–213.

Miki, Roy. "'Inside the Black Egg': Cultural Practice, Citizenship, and Belonging in a Globalizing Canadian Nation." *Mosaic* 36 (2005): 1–19. Print.

———. "'What's a racialized text like you doing in a place like this?': Reforming Boundaries, Negotiating Borders in English and CanLit Studies." *Broken Entries: race, subjectivity, writing: essays*. Toronto: Mercury, 1998. 160–80. Print.

Miller, Paul. "Web 2.0: Building the New Library." *Ariadne* 45 (October 2005). Web. 3 October 2009.

"Mind the gap." *Wikipedia*, n.d. Web. 27 February 2007.

Miyoshi, Masao. "Ivory Tower in Escrow." *Learning Places: The Afterlives of Area Studies.* Ed. Masao Miyoshi and H.D. Harootunian. Durham: Duke University Press, 2002. 19–60. Print.

———. "Turn to the Planet: Literary, Diversity, and Totality." Li 19–36.

Modern Language Association. "Report on Evaluating Scholarship for Tenure and Promotion." *MLA.org.* MLA, 2006. Web. 22 July 2008.

Modern Language Association Ad Hoc Committee on the Future of Scholarly Publishing. "The Future of Scholarly Publishing." *Profession* (2002): 172–86. Print.

Modood, Tariq. "Remaking multiculturalism after 7/7." *Open Democracy* 29 September 2005. Web. 3 October 2005.

Mohanty, Satya P. "Can Our Values Be Objective? On Ethics, Aesthetics, and Progressive Politics." *New Literary History* 32 (2001): 803–33. Print.

Mole, The. "Mind the Gap." *h2g2*. British Broadcasting Corporation, n.d. Web. 19 February 2002.

Molloy, Sylvia. "Mock Heroics and Personal Markings." Guest Column: "Four Views on the Place of the Personal in Scholarship." *PMLA* 111.5 (1996): 1072–75. Print.

Monkman, Leslie. "Confronting Change." Session on "Why Do I Have to Write Like That?" ACCUTE, University of Saskatchewan, May 2006. Conference presentation.

Mooers, Colin. "Multiculturalism and Citizenship: Some Theoretical Reflections." *CERIS* Working Paper No. 37, March 2005. Toronto: Joint Centre of Excellence for Research on Immigration and Settlement. Web. 3 October 2009.

Mooney, Chris. "Learning to Speak 'Science.'" *Seed Magazine* 13 February 2006. Web. 22 July 2008.

Moretti, Franco. *Graphs, Maps, Trees: Abstract Models for a Literary History.* London: Verso, 2005. Print.

Morris, Meaghan. "Humanities for Taxpayers: Some Problems." *New Literary History* 36 (2005): 111–29. Print.

Mosco, Vincent. *The Digital Sublime: Myth, Power, and Cyberspace.* Cambridge: MIT Press, 2004. Print.

Moten, Fred, and Stefano Harney. "The University and the Undercommons: Seven Theses." *Social Text* 79.22.2 (Summer 2004): 101–15. Print.

Moulthrop, Stuart. "What the Geeks Know: Hypertext and the Problem of Literacy." *HT'05: Proceedings of the sixteenth ACM conference on Hypertext and hypermedia.* New York: ACM Press, 2005. 227–31. Print.

Moya, Paula. M.L. "Introduction: Reclaiming Identity." *Realist Theory and the Predicament of Postmodernism.* Ed. Paula M.L. Moya and Michael R. Hames-Garcia. Berkeley: University of California Press, 2000. 1–16. Print.

Neilson, William A.W., and Chad Gaffield, eds. *Universities in Crisis: A Mediaeval Institution in the Twenty-First Century.* Montreal: Institute for Research on Public Policy, 1986. Print.

Nelson, Cary. *Manifesto of a Tenured Radical.* New York: New York University Press, 1997. Print.

———. *Office Hours: Activism and Change in the Academy.* New York: Routledge, 2004. Print.

Neuman, Shirley. "Redesigning the Ruins." *University of Toronto Quarterly* 66.4 (Fall 1997): 663–76. Print.

Newson, Janice and Claire Polster, eds. *Academic Callings: The University We Have Had, Now Have, and Could Have.* Toronto: Canadian Scholars' Press, 2010. Print.

Ngugi wa Thiong'o. "For Peace, Justice, and Culture: The Intellectual in the Twenty-First Century." *Profession* (2006): 33–39. Print.

Nielsen, Jakob. *Designing Web Usability: The Practice of Simplicity.* Indianapolis: New Riders, 2000. Print.

nikishton. "Niki Ashton presents SSHRC petition re: earmark." *Youtube.com.* Youtube, 30 June 2009. Web. 13 July 2009.

"Nova Scotia College of Art and Design Employment Equity Policy." NSCAD. NSCAD, 19 September 2006. Web. 3 October 2009.

O'Brian, John, Naomi Sawada, and Scott Watson, eds. *All Amazed for Roy Kiyooka.* Vancouver: Arsenal Pulp, 1999. Print.

Ohmann, Richard Malin. *Politics of Knowledge: The Commercialization of the University, the Professions, & Print Culture.* Middletown: Wesleyan University Press, 2003. Print.

Open Journal Systems. Public Knowledge Project, Simon Fraser University, n.d. Web. 3 October 2009.

"Open Letter to the Minister of Justice." *The Toronto Star* 29 September 2006. Web. 1 October 2006.

Palin, Michael. Foreword. *Mind the Gap.* By Simon James. London: Harper Collins, 2001. ii–iii. Print.

Panagia, Davide. *The Poetics of Political Thinking.* Durham: Duke University Press, 2006. Print.

Parker, Jan. "Future Priorities of the Humanities in Europe: What Have the Humanities to Offer?" *Arts and Humanities in Higher Education* 6.1 (2007): 123–27. Print.

Pennee, Donna Palmateer. "Literary Citizenship: Culture (Un) Bounded, Culture (Re) Distributed." *Home-Work: Postcolonialism, Pedagogy, and Canadian Literature.* Ed. Cynthia Sugars. Ottawa: University of Ottawa Press, 2004. 75–85. Print.

———. "Pedagogies that Challenge the Cult of Speed in Undergraduate Teaching and Learning." 19th Annual Teaching Support Services Conference, University of Guelph, 16 May 2006. Conference presentation.

Pennee, Donna Palmateer, and Malinda Smith. "Statement from a Coalition of Academics of Colour." *fedcan.ca.* CFHSS, 2007. Web. 27 June 2008.

Perkel, Colin. "Women Academics Still Behind Male Counterparts." *canoe.ca.* CNEWS, 28 January 2007. Web. 14 February 2007.

Perreault, Jeanne, and Marlene Kadar. Introduction. "Tracing the Autobiographical: Unlikely Documents, Unexpected Places." Kadar, Warley, Perreault, and Eagan 1–7.

Perry, Mark. "Conference Report: 'In Search of Security: An International Conference on Policing and Security.' February 19–22, 2003, Montréal, Québec Canada." *Computer Law and Security Report* 19.3 (May 2003): 242–43. Print.

Perry, Ruth. Letter in Forum. "Problems with Personal Criticism." *PMLA* 111.5 (1996): 1166–67. Print.

Piper, Martha. "Building a Civil Society: A New Role for the Human Sciences. 2002 Killam Annual Lecture." Trustees of the Killam Trusts, n.d. Web. 24 August 2008.

Pither, Kerry. *Dark Days: The Story of Four Canadians Tortured in the Name of Fighting Terror.* Foreword by Mahar Arar. Toronto: Viking Canada, 2008. Print.

Polster, Claire. "A Break from the Past: Impacts and Implications of the Canada Foundation for Innovation and the Canada Research Chairs Initiatives." *Canadian Review of Sociology and Anthropology* 39.3 (2002): 275–99. Print.

———. "The Nature and Implications of the Growing Importance of Research Grants to Canadian Universities and Academics." *Higher Education* 53.5 (2007): 599–622. Print.

Poovey, Mary. *Uneven Development: The Ideological Work of Gender in Victorian England.* Chicago: University of Chicago Press, 1988. Print.

Powers, Richard. *Plowing the Dark.* New York: Picador, 2000. Print.

Price, David H. "America the Ambivalent: Quietly Selling Anthropology to the CIA." *Anthropology Today* 21.5 (2005): 1–2. Print.

Raben, Joseph. "Tenure, Promotion, and Scholarly Publication." *Digital Humanities Quarterly* 1.1 (Spring 2007). Web. 3 October 2009.

Rabinbach, Anson. *In the Shadow of Catastrophe: German Intellectuals between Apocalypse and Enlightenment.* Berkeley: University of California Press, 1997. Print.

Readings, Bill. *The University in Ruins.* Cambridge: Harvard University Press, 1996. Print.

Reed, Michael I. "New Managerialism, Professional Power, and Organizational Governance in UK Universities: A Review and Assessment." *Governing Higher Education: National Perspectives on Institutional Governance.* Ed. Alberto Amaral, Glen A. Jones, and Berit Kareseth. Dordrecht: Kluwer, 2002. 163–85. Print.

Renaud, Marc. "A Message from SSHRC Council." *From Granting Council to Knowledge Council: Renewing the Social Sciences and Humanities in Canada. Consultation Framework on SSHRC's Transformation.* Vol. 1. January 2004. 2–3. Print.

———. "Open letter to SSHRC grant holders." 27 October 2003. Print.

———. "Personal Revelations." Interview with unidentified questioner. SSHRC *Annual Report,* 2004. 32–33. Web. 2 July 2008.

Rifkin, Jeremy. *The Age of Access: The New Culture of Hypercapitalism, Where All of Life is a Paid-For Experience.* New York: Tarcher/Putnam, 2000. Print.

Robbins, Bruce. *Intellectuals: Aesthetics, Politics, Academics.* Minneapolis: University of Minnesota Press, 1990. Print.

Rorty, Richard. *Achieving Our Country: Leftist Thought in Twentieth-Century America.* Cambridge: Harvard University Press, 1998. Print.

Ross, Andrew. *Strange Weather: Culture, Science, and Technology in the Age of Limits.* London: Verso, 1991. Print.

Royle, Nicholas. "Yes, Yes, the University in Ruins." *Critical Inquiry* 26 (Autumn 1999): 147–53. Print.

Rubin, Michael Rogers, and Mary Taylor Huber, with Elizabeth Lloyd Taylor. *The Knowledge Industry in the United States, 1960–1980.* Princeton: Princeton University Press, 1986. Print.

Russell, Frances. "Cuts targeted to keep the neo-cons on top." *Winnipeg Free Press* 4 October 2006: A13. Print.

Said, Edward. *Humanism and Democratic Criticism.* New York: Columbia University Press, 2004. Print.

———. *Orientalism.* New York: Vintage, 1979. Print.

———. *Representations of the Intellectual.* New York: Vintage, 1996. Print.

————. *The World, the Text and the Critic.* Cambridge: Harvard University Press, 1983. Print.

Sanbonmatsu, John. "Postmodernism and the Corruption of the Academic Intelligentsia." *Socialist Register* (2006): 196–227. Print.

Scarry, Elaine. *On Beauty and Being Just.* Princeton: Princeton University Press, 1999. Print.

Schaffer, Kay, and Sidonie Smith. *Human Rights and Narrated Lives.* New York: Palgrave, 2004. Print.

Schreibman, Susan, Ray Siemens, and John Unsworth. *A Companion to Digital Humanities.* Oxford: Blackwell, 2004. Print.

Schugurensky, Daniel. "The Political Economy of Higher Education in the Time of Global Markets: Whither the Social Responsibility of the University?" *The University, State, and Market: The Political Economy of Globalization in the Americas.* Ed. Robert A. Rhoads and Carlos Alberto Torres. Stanford: Stanford University Press, 2006. 301–20. Print.

Schuler, Douglas. *New Community Networks: Wired for Change.* Reading: Addison-Wesley, 1996. Print.

Scott, David. "The Re-enchantment of Humanism: An Interview with Sylvia Wynter." *Small Axe* (September 2000): 119–207. Print.

Scott, Joan. "Experience." *Feminists Theorize the Political.* Ed. Judith Butler and Joan W. Scott. New York: Routledge, 1992. 22–40. Print.

Selfe, Cynthia. *Technology and Literacy in the Twenty-First Century.* Carbondale: Southern Illinois Press, 1999. Print.

Selfe, Cynthia L., and Gail E. Hawisher. *Literate Lives in the Information Age: Narratives of Literacy from the United States.* Mahwah: Lawrence Erlbaum, 2004. Print.

Serban, Andreea M., and Jing Luan, eds. *Knowledge Management: Building a Competitive Advantage in Higher Education.* New Directions for Institutional Research Series, no. 113. New York: John Wiley & Sons, 2002. Print.

Seto, DeNel Rehberg. "Taking Responsible Risks." *English Studies in Canada* 32.4 (December 2006): 21–24. Print.

Shiratuddin, N., S. Hassan, and M. Landoni. "A Usability Study for Promoting Content in Higher Education." *Educational Technology & Society* 6.4 (2003): 112–24. Print.

Shohat, Ella, and Robert Stam, eds. *Multiculturalism, Postcoloniality, and Transnational Media.* New Brunswick: Rutgers University Press, 2003. Print.

Siemens, Ray, et al. "The Credibility of Electronic Publishing: A Report to the Humanities and Social Sciences Federation of Canada." *Internet Shakespeare Editions.* University of Victoria, n.d. Web. 3 October 2009.

Siemerling, Winfried. *The New North American Studies: Culture, Writing, and the Politics of Re/Cognition.* New York: Routledge, 2005. Print.

———, ed. *Writing Ethnicity: Cross-Cultural Consciousness in Canadian and Québécois Literature.* Toronto: ECW Press, 1996. Print.

Slaughter, Sheila. *The Higher Learning and High Technology: Dynamics of Higher Education Policy Formation.* Albany: SUNY Press, 1990. Print.

Slaughter, Sheila, and Larry L. Leslie. *Academic Capitalism: Politics, Policies, and the Entrepreneurial University.* Baltimore: Johns Hopkins University Press, 1997. Print.

Smith, Linda Tuhiwai. *Decolonizing·Methodologies: Research and Indigenous Peoples.* New York: Zed Books, 2002. Print.

Smith, Stuart. *Report of the Commission of Inquiry on Canadian University Education.* Ottawa: AUCC, 1991. Print.

Social Sciences and Humanities Research Council of Canada. *Alternative Wor(l)ds: The Humanities in 2010. Report of the Working Group on the Future of the Humanities.* Ottawa: SSHRC, March 2001. Print.

———. "Apply for Funding: Definitions." SSHRC, 2007. Web. 18 June 2007.

———. *Cultivating Excellence: A Special Report Celebrating the 30th Anniversary of the Social Sciences and Humanities Research. Globe and Mail* newspaper insert. May 2008. Print.

———. *From Granting Council to Knowledge Council: Renewing the Social Sciences and Humanities in Canada. Consultation Framework on SSHRC's Transformation.* Vol. 1. Ottawa: SSHRC, January 2004. Print.

———. *From Granting Council to Knowledge Council: Renewing the Social Sciences and Humanities in Canada.* Vol. 3. Ottawa: SSHRC, 2005. Print.

———. "Image, Text, Sound and Technology Research Grants." SSHRC, 2009. Web. 3 October 2009.

———. *Knowledge Council: SSHRC, 2006–2011.* Ottawa: SSHRC, August 2005. Web. 3 October 2009.

———. "New SSHRC president's first priority is to demonstrate value of existing investment." Ottawa: SSHRC, October 2006. Web. 20 October 2009.

———. "Research/Creation Grants in Fine Arts." SSHRC, 5 September 2009. Web. 4 October 2009.

Sowa, John F. "Preface." *Knowledge Representation: Logical, Philosophical, and Computational Foundations*. Pacific Grove: Brooks Cole, 2000. Web. 3 October 2009.

Spanos, William V. *The End of Education: Toward Posthumanism*. Minneapolis: University of Minnesota Press, 1993. Print.

Spender, Dale. *Nattering on the Net: Women, Power and Cyberspace*. Toronto: Garamond, 1996. Print.

Spigelman, Candace. *Personally Speaking: Experience as Evidence in Academic Discourse*. Carbondale: Southern Illinois University Press, 2004. Print.

Spivak, Gayatri. *A Critique of Postcolonial Reason: Toward a History of the Vanishing Present*. Cambridge: Harvard University Press, 1999. Print.

———. "Can the Subaltern Speak?" *Marxism and the Interpretation of Culture*. Ed. C. Nelson and L. Grossberg. Urbana: University of Illinois Press, 1988. 271–313. Print.

———. *Death of a Discipline*. New York: Columbia University Press, 2003. Print.

———. "Scattered Speculations on the Question of Value." *Diacritics* 15.4 (Winter 1985): 73–93. Print.

Stanley, Dick. "The Three Faces of Culture: Why Culture is a Strategic Good Requiring Government Policy Attention." Andrew et al. 21–31.

Stanley, Liz. "From 'self-made women' to 'women's made-selves'?: Audit selves, simulation and surveillance in the rise of public women." *Feminism and Autobiography*. Ed. Tess Cosslett, Celia Lury, and Penny Summerfield. Abingdon: Taylor & Francis, 2000. 40–60. Print.

Stanton, Domna C. "A Sense of Activism." MLA *Newsletter* 37.1 (Spring 2005): 3–4. Print.

Statistics Canada. "Ethnic Diversity Survey." Under "Ethnic Diversity and Immigration," "Products" at statcan.gc.ca/start-debut-eng.html. Web. 30 April 2010.

Star, Susan Leigh. "Power, technology, and the phenomenology of conventions: on being allergic to onions." *A Sociology of Monsters: Essays on Power, Technology and Domination*. London: Routledge, 1999. 26–56. Print.

———, ed. *The Cultures of Computing*. Oxford: Blackwell, 1995. Print.

Stoffman, Daniel. "The Illusion of Multiculturalism." Excerpt from "Who Gets In: What's Wrong with Canada's Immigration Program—and How to Fix It." *Multiculturalism and Immigration in Canada: An Introductory Reader*. Ed. Elspeth Cameron. Toronto: Scholars' Press, 2004. 119–50. Print.

Stoler, Laura. "Racial Histories and Their Regimes of Truth." *Race Critical Theories: Text and Context*. Ed. Philomela Essed and David Theo Goldberg. London: Blackwell, 2002. 369–91. Print.

Stone, Marjorie, Diana Brydon, Austin Cooke, Winfried Siemerling, and Christl Verduyn. "Literary Studies and the Metropolis Project: Bridging the Gaps." *Newsletter, Association of Canadian College and University Teachers of English* (June 2002): 33–47. Print.

Stone, Marjorie, Hélène Destrempes, Sharon Jeannotte, and John Foote. "Immigration and Cultural Citizenship: Responsibilities, Rights, and Indicators." *Immigration, Integration, and Citizenship in 21st Century Canada*. Ed. John Biles, Meyer Burstein, and James Fridere. Kingston: Queen's University Press, 2009. 103–35. Print.

Stone, Marjorie, and Judith Thompson. *Literary Couplings: Writing Couples, Collaborators, and the Construction of Authorship*. Madison: Wisconsin University Press, 2006. Print.

Suchman, Lucy A. *Human-Machine Reconfigurations: Plans and Situated Actions*. 2nd ed. Cambridge: Cambridge University Press, 2007. Print.

Sukovic, Suzana. "Scholarly (R)evolution: Roles of E-texts in the Research Process in the Humanities." *Digital Humanities Conference 2007 Abstracts*. Web. 4 October 2009.

"Summit on Digital Tools for the Humanities. Report on Summit Accomplishments." Institute for Advanced Technology in the Humanities, n.d. Web. 4 October 2009.

Swiss, Thomas, and Andrew Herman. "The World Wide Web as Magic, Metaphor, and Power." *The World Wide Web and Contemporary Cultural Theory*. Ed. Thomas Swiss and Andrew Herman. New York: Routledge, 2000. 1–4. Print.

"Systemic Change Initiative (SCI) at the Alberta College of Art + Design." Handout distributed to ACAD community. ACAD. Web. 1 September 2006.

Szeman, Imre. "Culture and/in Globalization." *Concepts of Culture: Art, Politics and Society*. Ed. Adam Muller. Calgary: University of Calgary Press, 2005. 155–80. Print.

Tamburri, Rosanna. "Gaffield named SSHRC president: Well-known social historian to focus on agency's transformation plan." *University Affairs* (November 2006): 31. Print.

Theis, Jeffrey. "Collegiality and the Department Mailbox: Subdivide and Conquer." *Profession* (2006): 87–94. Print.

Therborn, Goran. "After Dialectics: Radical Social Theory in a Post-Communist World." *New Left Review* 43 (January/February 2007): 63–114. Print.

Thompson, Jon and Patricia Baird and Jocelyn Downie. *The Olivieri Report*. Toronto: James Lorimer & Company, 2002. Print.

Torgovnick, Marianna. "Experimental Critical Writing." *Profession* (1990): 25–27. Print.

"Total Information Awareness." *Wikipedia*, n.d. Web. 4 October 2009.

Toth, Emily. *Ms. Mentor's Impeccable Advice for Women in Academia*. Philadelphia: University of Pennsylvania Press, 1997. Print.

———. "They Will Not Comfort You." *The Chronicle of Higher Education* 7 November 2006. Web. 3 October 2009.

Tsang, Henry. "Art Calling Fool Scold: The Discursive Pedagogy of Roy Kiyooka." *All Amazed For Roy Kiyooka*. Ed. John O'Brien, Naomi Sawada, and Scott Watson. Vancouver: Arsenal Pulp, 1999. 84–93. Print.

Tseghay, Daniel. "Oh, The Humanities! Studying Humankind For the Benefit of Humanity? What Good will that Do?" *Planet S: Saskatoon's City Magazine* 24 May 2007: 18. Print.

Tsing, Anna Lowenhaupt. *Friction: An Ethnography of Global Connection*. Princeton: Princeton University Press, 2005. Print.

Tumbleson, Raymond D. "A Confluence of Crises: Tenure and Jobs." *Profession* (2005): 59–63. Print.

Turner, Fred. *From Counterculture to Cyberculture: Stewart Brand, the Whole Earth Network, and the Rise of Digital Utopianism*. Chicago: University of Chicago Press, 2006. Print.

Unsworth, John. "Documenting the Reinvention of Text: The Importance of Failure." *Journal of Electronic Publishing* 3.2 (1997). Web. 22 July 2008.

"Update! Victory...U of T Sessionals (contract faculty) Denied Research Grants." *tao.ca*. tao, 28 November 2006. Web. 8 February 2007.

Varadharajan, Asha. "Dissolution, Dissensus, and the Possibility of Community." *University of Toronto Quarterly* 66.4 (Fall 1997): 621–33. Print.

Varughese, Anil. "Sessionals Denied Research Support." *The Guardian* Vol. v, no. 2 (November 2006): 1. Print.

Veeser, H. Aram, ed. *Confessions of the Critics*. New York: Routledge, 1996. Print.

———. "Introduction: The Case for Confessional Criticism." Veeser xi–xxvii.

Vida, Sandra. "Roy Kiyooka and the Ardour of Displacement." *Backflash* 23.1 (2005): 6–13. Print.

Viswanathan, Gauri. "Spectrality's Secret Sharers: Occultism as (Post)colonial Affect." *Beyond the Black Atlantic: Relocating Modernization and Technology.* Ed. Walter Goebel and Saskia Schabio. London: Routledge, 2006. 135–45. Print.

Wang, Xiaoying. "Farewell to the Humanities." *Rethinking Marxism.* 17.4 (October 2005): 525–38. Print.

Warley, Linda. "Reading the Autobiographical in Personal Home Pages." Kadar, Warley, Perreault, Egan 25–42.

Warwick, Claire. "Whose funeral? A case study of computational methods and reasons for their use or neglect in English literature." CASTA 2004—The Face of Text. McMaster University. 19–21 November 2004. Conference presentation.

Warwick, Claire, Melissa Terras, Paul Huntington, and Nikoleta Pappa. "If You Build It Will They Come? The LAIRAH Study: Quantifying the Use of Online Resources in the Arts and Humanities through Statistical Analysis of User Log Data." *Literary and Linguistic Computing* 23.1 (2008): 85–102. Print.

Waters, Daniel J., ed. "Urgent Action Needed to Preserve Scholarly Electronic Journals." *Digital Library Federation.* Digital Library Federation, 15 October 2005; updated 12 July 2006. Web. 4 October 2009.

Weisman, Adam Paul. "Reading Multiculturalism in the United States and Canada: The Anthological vs. the Cognitive." *University of Toronto Quarterly* 69.3 (2000): 689–715. Print.

White, James Boyd. *Justice as Translation: An Essay in Cultural and Legal Criticism.* Chicago: University of Chicago Press, 1990. Print.

Whittington, Les, and Bruce Campion-Smith. "Tories cut $1B despite surplus." *The Toronto Star* 26 September 2006: A1. Print.

Whitton, Bob. "SSHRC funding hinges on communication." *Daily Bulletin,* University of Waterloo 14 January 1999. Web. 5 May 2010.

"Wikipedia Founder Discourages Academic Use of His Creation." *The Chronicle of Higher Education* 12 June 2006. Web. 4 October 2009.

Williams, Jeffrey. "Edward Said's Romance of the Amateur Intellectual." *The Review of Education/Pedagogy/Cultural Studies* 17.4 (1995): 397–410. Print.

Williams, Raymond. *Keywords: A Vocabulary of Culture and Society.* London: Fontana/ Croom Helm, 1976. Print.

———. "The Future of Cultural Studies." *The Politics of Modernism: Against the New Conformists.* London: Verso, 1989. Print.

World Bank. *Culture Counts: Financing, Resources, and the Economics of Culture in Sustainable Development.* Washington, DC: World Bank, 1999. Print.

Wright, Douglas T. "Industry and the University: How We See Each Other." Abu-Laban 126–33.

Young, Judy. "No Longer 'Apart'? Multicultural Policy and Canadian Literature." *Canadian Ethnic Studies* 33 (2001): 88–110. Print.

Yudíce, George. *The Expediency of Culture: Uses of Culture in the Global Era*. Durham: Duke University Press, 2003. Print.

CONTRIBUTORS

SUSAN BROWN, of the University of Guelph and also of the University of Alberta, works on Victorian women's writing, feminist literary history, and digital humanities research methods. She co-founded, with Patricia Clements and Isobel Grundy, and now directs the collaborative Orlando Project, whose textbase, *Orlando: Women's Writing in the British Isles from the Beginnings to the Present*, appeared online in 2006 from Cambridge University Press.

DIANA BRYDON is Canada Research Chair in Globalization and Cultural Studies at the University of Manitoba and Director of the Research Centre for Globalization and Cultural Studies. Recent publications include *Renegotiating Community: Interdisciplinary Perspectives, Global Contexts*, co-edited with W.D. Coleman (UBC Press, 2008), and a special issue of *Studies in Canadian Literature*, "Poetics and Public Culture in Canada," co-edited with Manina Jones, Jessica Schagerl, and Kristin Warder (32.2, 2007). She is currently investigating global imaginaries and Canadian culture and participating in an interdisciplinary, international team project on "building global democracy."

DANIEL COLEMAN is a Canada Research Chair in the Department of English and Cultural Studies at McMaster University. He has published *Masculine Migrations: Reading the Postcolonial Male in "New Canadian" Narratives* (University of Toronto Press, 1998), *The Scent of Eucalyptus: A Missionary Childhood in Ethiopia* (Goose Lane Editions, 2003), and has co-edited seven scholarly volumes on various issues including early Canadian culture, Caribbean Canadian writing, masculinities, post-coloniality, and race for the University of Alberta Press, *The Journal of West Indian Literature, Essays on Canadian Writing, Mattoid, Jouvert, Masculinities,* and *Textual Studies in Canada. White Civility: The Literary Project of English Canada* (University of Toronto Press, 2006) won the Raymond Klibansky Prize for the best book in the humanities in Canada in 2007. His most recent book, *In Bed With the Word: Reading, Spirituality, and Cultural Politics,* was published by the University of Alberta Press in spring 2009.

PAUL DANYLUK was a SSHRC-funded Doctoral Fellow at TransCanada Insitute, and a PHD student in the School of English and Theatre Studies, University of Guelph, from 2006 to 2009. His research focussed on how performance poetries—sound poetry, dub poetry, and literary hip hop— share a lineage as critical "supplements" to Canadian poetry in particular and Canadian culture in general. He left the PHD program in 2009 to pursue other interests. Paul has a Bachelor of Arts in English and Creative Writing from York University and a Master of Arts in English from Simon Fraser University.

KIT DOBSON is an Assistant Professor of Canadian literature at Mount Royal University in Calgary. In addition to his contributions to academic and literary journals in Canada and beyond, his first book, *Transnational Canadas: Anglo-Canadian Literature and Globalization,* was published by Wilfrid Laurier University Press in 2009.

L.M. FINDLAY is an award-winning teacher, Professor of English and Director of the Humanities Research Unit at the University of Saskatchewan. He has served as President of the Association of Canadian College and University Teachers of English, as Vice-President

(External Communications) of the CFHSS, as Senior Policy Analyst for the Universities Branch of the Saskatchewan Department of Post-secondary Education and Skills Training, and is beginning his second term on the Academic Freedom and Tenure committee of CAUT. A Fellow of the Royal Society of Canada, he was the Northrop Frye Professor of Literary Theory at the University of Toronto for 2000–2001. Widely published in nineteenth-century comparative studies, literary theory, and the nature and role of universities and the humanities in Canada, his more recent work includes a co-edited collection, *Pursuing Academic Freedom: 'Free and Fearless'?* (Purich Press, 2001), and such essays as the several times–reprinted "Always Indigenize! The Radical Humanities in the Postcolonial Canadian University" (*Ariel*), "Memory's Hegelian Estate: 'Race,' Class, Treaty, and the Canadas of Alexander Morris (1826–1889)" (*ECW*), and "Spectres of Canada: Image, Text, Aura, Nation" (*UTQ*). His revised translation and edition of *The Communist Manifesto* for Broadview Press appeared in 2004, and his book *Oral Culture for Book Historians* is forthcoming from University of Toronto Press. He is currently at work on a polemic in the style of George Grant called *Dissent for a Nation* and on an intellectual biography entitled *The Cunning of the White Man and the Honour of the Crown: Alexander Morris and the Making of Treaty.*

SMARO KAMBOURELI is Professor and Canada Research Chair in Critical Studies in Canadian Literature at the University of Guelph and Director of the TransCanada Institute. Prior to her appointment at Guelph, she taught at the University of Victoria where she served as Graduate Director in the Department of English and CSPT, and as the First Associate Dean, Research, in the Humanities. Her publications include *in the second person* (1985), *On the Edge of Genre: The Contemporary Canadian Long Poem* (University of Toronto Press, 1991), and *Scandalous Bodies: Diasporic Literature in English Canada* (Oxford University Press, 2000; Wilfrid Laurier University Press, 2008), which won the Gabrielle Roy Prize for English Canadian Criticism. On the board of the non-profit NeWest Press (Edmonton) since 1981, she is the founder and general editor of The Writer as Critic series, and she has just founded and serves as the general editor of the TransCanada Series (Wilfrid Laurier University Press). She is the editor of *Making a Difference: Canadian Multicultural Literature* (Oxford University Press, 1996) and its revised edition, *Making a Difference: Canadian Multicultural Literatures in English* (Oxford University Press, 2006), and of *Canadian Literature at the Crossroads of Language and Culture* by Barbara Godard (NeWest, 2008). She has also co-edited, with Shirley Neuman, *A Mazing Space: Writing Canadian Women Writing* (NeWest Press, 1986); with Roy Miki, *Trans.Can.Lit.: Resituating the Study of Canadian Literature* (Wilfrid Laurier University Press, 2007); and with Heike Härting, "Discourses of Security, Peacekeeping Narratives, and the Cultural Imagination in Canada," Special issue, *University of Toronto Quarterly.*

ASHOK MATHUR holds a Canada Research Chair in Cultural and Artistic Inquiry at Thompson Rivers University, Kamloops, British Columbia. He works in the fields of artistic research, post-colonial studies and education, and cultural studies. He is the Director of the Centre for Innovation in Culture and the Arts in Canada, a creative think tank that supports artists in various stages of their projects. His most recent project is an interdisciplinary novel and installation entitled *A Little Distillery in Nowgong* (Arsenal Pulp Press, 2009), an investigation of Parsi history and familial generations through fiction and art.

DONNA PALMATEER PENNEE is a Professor of Canadian literature and Dean of Arts and Humanities at The University of Western Ontario. A graduate of McGill University and The School of Criticism and Theory (Dartmouth College), she is co-editor of *New Contexts of Canadian Criticism* (Broadview Press, 1997), the author of two monographs on Timothy Findley, articles on Margaret Laurence, Sheila Watson, and Adele Wiseman; cultural nationalism, post-colonialism, and state policy under globalization; pedagogy and curriculum; and the limits of white liberal feminism. An award-winning teacher, she has served as Vice-President, Equity Issues, for the CFHSS (2004–2008), and promotes accountability for equity in post-secondary education.

JESSICA SCHAGERL was a SSHRC post-doctoral fellow in the Department of English and Cultural Studies at McMaster University. She is currently completing a book-length study, *International Adventures in Wartime: the Selected Letters of Julia Grace Wales, 1915–1917*. Her research interests include Canadian literary and cultural studies, post-colonial studies, peace studies, and globalization.

MELISSA STEPHENS is a PHD Candidate in the Department of English and Film Studies at the University of Alberta. Her research explores how critical responses to U.S. cultural and economic imperialism trouble post–World War II conceptions of human rights, literacy, and globalization. Her current project uses black feminist analyses of migration, labour, and development to examine literary and filmic representations of Caribbean-U.S. relations and to suggest how documentary culture industries influence the politics and pedagogies of activism.

MARJORIE STONE is Professor of English and Gender Studies, Dalhousie University. Her publications include *Elizabeth Barrett Browning* (1995); *Literary Couplings: Writing Couples, Collaborators, and the Construction of Authorship*, co-edited with Judith Thompson (2006); and essays and articles on the Brownings, Tennyson, Dickens, Gaskell, Christina Rossetti, Toni Morrison, feminist ethics, global sex trafficking, cultural citizenship, and other subjects. She served as President of the Association of Canadian College and Teachers of English (1996–1998); as Dalhousie's first Assistant Dean, Research, for Arts and Social Sciences (1999–2002); and as a Director of the Atlantic Metropolis Centre (2004–2007), one of five Canadian centres operating under the Metropolis Project (<http://www.canada.metropolis.net>).

RITA WONG is the author of two books of poetry, *monkeypuzzle* (Press Gang, 1998) and *forage* (Nightwood Editions, 2007). A book-length collaborative poem, *sybil unrest*, co-written with Larissa Lai, was published with Line Books (2008). Wong received the Asian Canadian Writers Workshop Emerging Writer Award in 1997 and the Dorothy Livesay Poetry Prize in 2008. Her work investigates the relationships between decolonization, social justice, ecology, and contemporary poetics. An Associate Professor in Critical + Cultural Studies at the Emily Carr University of Art + Design, she has developed a humanities course focussed on water, a project for which she received a fellowship from the Center for Contemplative Mind in Society.

INDEX

choice of methodology in, 218–22

and dissemination of information, 215–18

funding of, 223–26

future of, 203

humanities mistrust of, 204–08, 209

and new literacies, 210–12

positive aspects for humanities, 208, 209–10, 228

tools for, 213–15

usability and design of, 222–23, 230n10

Di Leo, Jeffrey, 101–02

Dinello, Daniel, 207

discovery

E. Boyer on, XXIII

research as, 28

at universities, XVI, 36n12

discovery-for-application, XVII–XVIII, XIX, 28

diversity training, 129

Donoghue, Frank, XIV, 259n7

Drucker, Joanna, 219

Drucker, Peter F., 18, 19

Druick, Don, 182

Duguid, Paul, 209

education, 74, 247. *See also* students; universities

electronic publishing, 216, 224

Emily Carr University of Art + Design (ECU), 116–18, 122, 123

employment equity

outline of research project on, 115–16

positive moves by art schools, 123–24

recommendations on, 118–20, 122–23, 125–26, 129

testimony of colonization, 116–18

exchange programs, 122–23

extraordinary rendition, 42–43, 44–46, 47–48

Fanon, Frantz, 253

Farred, Grant, 234

Fatona, Andrea, 130

federal-provincial jurisdiction, 16–17

Feenberg, Andrew, 209

Fernandez, Sharon, 121–22

Findlay, Isobel, 13

Findlay, L.M., 250

First Nations. *See* Aboriginal people

Foucault, Michel, 43

Frank, Sophie, 128, 131n5

Franklin, Cynthia G., 189, 200

Fulford, Robert, 224

Fulton, Margaret E., 19, 25–26, 175, 176

Fung, Richard, 125

Gaffield, Chad, 1–2, 3–4, 23–24, 35n3, 49, 101

Gallop, Jane, 201n8

Garrett, Jeffrey, 217, 218

Geiger, Jeffrey, 247

gender, 195–97

Gilroy, Paul, 252

Giroux, Henry A., 101, 242

globalization, 24, 45, 53, 236, 249, 250

Google, 214, 217

graduate students

and collaboration, 33, 39n27, 227

and critical writing, 191–92

and curricula, 119–20

as junior research partners, 95–96, 98–102

mentoring, 102–10

pressure on, 67

Graff, Gerald, 107

Gramsci, Antonio, 254, 261n17

Grey, Stephen, 45

Grossberg, Michael, 216

Grundy, Isobel, 220

Hall, Margaret, 247–48

Haque, Eva, 150–51

Haraway, Donna, 208

Harper government

and funding business-oriented research, 187–89

knowledge
   as commodity, 10, 78
   as power, 15
   production, 199, 237, 264
   value of, 77–78, 237
knowledge economy, 18–20, 27
knowledge industries, 5, 10, 28, 38n21
knowledge management, 38n23
"The Knowledge Project", 96–97, 138

Lang, Candace, 190–91
language, 41, 43, 45–46
Lanham, Richard, 228
"Large-Scale Research Projects and the
      Humanities," 133–34
Law Commission of Canada (LCC)
      background of, 260n12
      effect of cuts to, 248–50, 260n13
      funding cuts to, 26, 245–46
      mandate, 245
      research reports of, 247–48, 258
      work of, 238
learning deficit, 70–71
Le Bouthillier, Yves, 246, 248
Leslie, Larry L., XV, XVI
Leyerle, John, 24–25
Li, David Leiwei, 12–13
libraries, 212–13
literary study, 255
Liu, Alan, 217
Lodge, Peter, 205
Lott, Eric, 236
Lowry, Glen, 172
Luan, Jing, 29

MacKinnon, Barry, 179
Major Collaborative Research Initiatives
      (MCRIS), 96, 257–58
managerialism, XIV–XV, XVIII–XIX
Marable, Manning, 43
marginalized/minoritized subjects, 30,
      116, 119, 121, 122
Martel, Yann, 146
Maruca, Lisa, 97

Marxism, 86, 89–90
Massey Report, 14–16, 63, 73
McCarty, Willard, 219, 222
McGann, Jerome, 216, 224
McLuhan, Marshall, 12
McNeil, Maureen, 234, 244
media, mainstream, 242. *See also* digital
      media
memory
      cultural, 18
      institutional, 110
      politics of, 17–18, 48–49
      and testimonial scholarship, 185, 190
mentors/mentoring
      changing relationship with research,
         266–67
      definition, 102–04
      involving junior colleagues, 107–10
      process of, 104–07
Metropolis Project
      background of, 26, 135–37
      competition protocols for, 139–43
      connection to Multiculturalism
         Project, 144, 151
      forums of exchange in, 153–54
      importance of, 134–35
      omission of word "culture" in,
         148–50, 158n10
      research priorities of, 137–39
Michael, Donald A., 175–76
Miki, Roy, 147–48, 178–79
militarization, 45, 55
"mind the gap" phrase, 204–05, 229n1
Ministry of Industry, 3, 137
Miyoshi, Masao, 12
Modernism, 28, 48, 78, 170
Modood, Tariq, 153
monographs, scholarly, 227, 231n11
Mooers, Colin, 151
Mosco, Vincent, 208
Moulthrop, Stuart, 211
multiculturalism
      and colonization, 116
      critiques for and against, 150–53